What teens and others
are saying about

7 The HABITS of Highly Effective TEENAGERS

"Unlike my book on the 7 Habits, this book, by my son Sean, speaks directly to teens in an entertaining and visually appealing style (and, Sean, I never thought you listened to a word I said). As prejudiced as this may sound, this is a remarkable book, a must-read!"

> —DR. STEPHEN R. COVEY (1932–2012), Sean Covey's dad, author of the #1 *New York Times* bestseller *The 7 Habits of Highly Effective People* and cofounder and former vice chairman of Franklin Covey Co.

" 'Like father, like son' may be a cliché, but Sean has proved it to be true. Sean is as effective as his father in providing directions to teens so that their lives become meaningful. Sean's *7 Habits* is a book every teenager should read and emulate."

> —ARUN GANDHI, president of Gandhi Worldwide Education Institute

"I have long been a fan of Stephen Covey and his book *The 7 Habits of Highly Effective People*. In fact, I liked his principles so much that we teach them to our players in the off-season as leadership principles. When I saw Sean's book *The 7 Habits of Highly Effective Teens*, I was excited to have another weapon to take our players and culture to a higher level. Whether you are a teen or not, you should read this book!"

> —ANSON DORRANCE, coach of the University of North Carolina women's soccer team, twenty-two-time national collegiate champions

"Sean's can-do examples remind me of how important it is to make the most of what I have. I play a lot of sports, though I'm not a big kid. This book helped me realize that I have to rely on my speed and my smarts if I want to reach my goals."

> —BRENT KUIK, age 15

"Growing up isn't easy, but with the help of Sean Covey's book, young adults can learn to navigate through this awkward time and come out on the other side as a highly effective adult. *The 7 Habits of Highly*

Effective Teens empowers young adults by reminding them that it is perfectly normal to make mistakes, but luckily, if and when teenagers get off course, this book will help them navigate the treacherous waters of adolescence. Through the literary experiences shared in this book, hopefully teenagers can learn to love themselves and ultimately discover the effective adult waiting underneath the surface. As a teacher, I like how this book is not only a how-to for young adults but also a jumping-off point for teachers, who are struggling to connect with their students, by giving them the tools to shape a world that they can be proud of!"

—ERIN GRUWELL, founder of Freedom Writers Foundation, author of the #1 *New York Times* bestseller *The Freedom Writers Diary*, and inspiration for the 2007 film *Freedom Writers*

"I highly recommend the simple, straightforward advice provided in *The 7 Habits of Highly Effective Teens* to teenagers, young adults, and their parents. You'll hear new perspectives on how to improve your relationships and leadership skills that will positively impact your life, resulting in greater happiness. You will see that is easier than you may have thought to start making these changes today. And more than that—you will be able to do it and be successful at anything you choose to do. I have personally read it and practiced the timeless principles with my daughters."

—DIANA THOMAS, U.S. vice president of training, learning, and development, McDonald's Corporation

"This is an easy-to-understand book full of interesting stories. I really related to Sean's personal story about the fear of performing in front of people since I am violinist. I'm sure teenagers around the globe will be able to relate as well."

—EMILY INOUYE, age 14

"Fifteen years ago Sean Covey wrote a powerful book that taught teens that they had the ability to choose their behavior but not the consequences. The decisions that teens make could change their lives forever! Every young person should read *The 7 Habits of Highly Effective Teens*. It's a must-read for all my students!"

—SALOME THOMAS-EL, award-winning educator and author of *The Immortality of Influence* and *I Choose to Stay*

"One of the most defining parts of my career was the habits I built for myself as a teen. And that's why this book is so important. The younger you are when you set your direction and goals and learn the tools that help you get there, the better off you will be. This book defines what it means to succeed and is a must-read for every young adult. I only wish someone had shown it to me during those most formative years of my life. I recommend it to anyone!"

—CHELSIE HIGHTOWER, professional ballroom dancer on *Dancing With the Stars* and *So You Think You Can Dance*

"Sean's book helps teenagers to become climbers rather than campers, to live with a goal in mind, and to confront obstacles with a no-barriers mind-set. He urges young people to 'make your life extraordinary' and provides a pathway which will get them there. In a world with so many distractions and temptations, the guidelines he provides are invaluable to a purposeful and successful life."

—ERIK WEIIENMAYER, blind adventurer, speaker, author, and filmmaker

"If you are a teen, or know someone who will be, have them read this book. It will help them establish a pattern for dealing with change, disappointment, and even success. It is truly a powerful, life-changing book."

—DEREK HOUGH, Emmy Award–winning choreographer

"The inspiring examples from real-life problems that teenagers like myself deal with every day, and their experiences and situations, have helped me make lifesaving decisions. I highly recommend this book to any teenager."

—JEREMY SOMMER, age 19

"*The 7 Habits of Highly Effective Teens* has made it easier than ever before for teens to navigate through life! If you want to live a life of contribution, set and achieve extraordinary goals, and stay focused and organized, practice every habit in Sean's book. It will help you become who you want to be."

—JULIE MORGENSTERN, author of *Organizing from the Inside Out for Teens*

"This book serves as a great sword in the battle for our young people's minds. It deserves to be more than just read but lived in everyday life. What a great explanation of human values, ethics, and overall how to live a successfully fulfilled life."

—DRAKE WHITE, country music artist, songwriter

"*The 7 Habits of Highly Effective Teens* is a valuable guide to navigate through adolescent struggles and uncertainty. I wish someone had given me Sean Covey's book during my teenage years. This book is a vital guide to encourage teens through the game of life. Whether it is advice on achieving their own goals, to discovering the right peers, to connecting more with their parents, this book has it all and is a recipe for teenage success and a solid foundation for the future. My children will be given *The 7 Habits of Highly Effective Teens* as soon as they enter their adolescent years!"

—DOMINIQUE MOCEANU, U.S. Olympic gold medalist in women's gymnastics and author of the *New York Times* bestselling *Off Balance*

"I would highly recommend Sean Covey's book *The 7 Habits of Highly Effective Teens* because it teaches whoever reads it how to set goals, get organized, prioritize, make good decisions, and most of all to help build good character. Take it from me—they are all the things that will help them achieve success in their lives. Sean does a great job with the book."

—JIMMER FREDETTE, Naismith and Wooden awards winner, NBA player

"Teens face many challenging issues. And, it's great that a 7 Habits book is now available to help direct teens toward positive living. Through my foundation's programing, we recognize the power of dreams and stress the importance of executing a detailed plan to propel you toward your goals."

—MICHAEL PHELPS, winner of twenty-two Olympic medals and founder of the Michael Phelps Foundation

"I wish I'd had this book when I was a teen."

—SHANNON HALE, author of the Newbery Honor–winning *Princess Academy* and *The Goose Girl*

"Life is such a precious and beautiful thing that so many people take for granted. Even at a very young age, my son was able to leave a tremendous legacy and influence the lives of so many people forever. In his short life, he experienced and overcame great difficulty and did so with an extraordinary positive spirit. He exhibited so many of the habits taught in *The 7 Habits of Highly Effective Teens*. Had my son had the chance to grow up, I know this book would have been a great guide and given him the tools he needed to navigate his way through life. If you are lucky enough to grow up, make mistakes, and learn from them, having someone like Sean guide you with this book is truly a gift."

—MAYA THOMPSON, founder of the Ronan Thompson Foundation

"*The 7 Habits of Highly Effective Teens* gives you new insight into the meaning of being powerfully successful. It teaches the importance of setting goals and sticking to them in order to achieve your dreams."

—PICABO STREET, National Ski Hall of Famer, Olympic gold medalist, and former member of the U.S. ski team

"What? Sean Covey wrote a book? You've got to be kidding!!"

—Sean's high school English teacher

"*The 7 Habits of Highly Effective Teens* is a touchdown! The sooner you develop good, strong habits, the more effective your life will be. This book will help you do just that."

—STEVE YOUNG, NFL Hall of Famer and Super Bowl MVP

"I used one of the stories from your book in a speech I gave at leadership camp and it helped me to be elected governor! Thanks, Sean Covey!!!"

—LEISY OSWALD, age 16

"The best way to 'make it happen' in your life is to make the right choices as a teen. *The 7 Habits of Highly Effective Teens* lets teens see themselves as the principal force in their lives, regardless of their background or current walk of life."

—STEDMAN GRAHAM, chairman and CEO of S. Graham & Associates, founder of Athletes Against Drugs, author of *New York Times* bestseller *You Can Make it Happen* and *Identity: Your Passport to Success*

"For a professional athlete, winning basketball games is important— but winning at the game of life is even more important. *The 7 Habits of Highly Effective Teens* provides a game plan for teens to become team players with their teammates in life, their families and friends. It presents strategies for becoming a better all-around person and elevating individual skills."

—SHERYL SWOOPES, head coach of Loyola University women's basketball team, four-time WNBA champion, three-time MVP, NCAA champion, and three-time Olympic gold medalist

"Today's teens are the future leaders of our families, communities, and nation. *The 7 Habits of Highly Effective Teens* teaches them the value of hard work, setting and achieving goals, and taking responsibility and initiative, all of which are characteristics of effective leaders."

—MICHAEL O. LEAVITT, former U.S. Secretary of Health and Human Services

"I have been juggling family, school activities, friends, and after-school responsibilities. When I read *The 7 Habits of Highly Effective Teens* it helped me become a more organized person. I used a lot of the cartoons to help me remember stories and examples."

—JOY DENEWELLIS, age 18

"Stephen Covey must be rightfully proud of his son Sean, who absorbed his father's lessons well. Those who wish to avoid the temptations and devastation of drugs, including alcohol, would be wise to implement *The 7 Habits of Highly Effective Teens*. Written for teenagers, this book is an indispensable tool, helping young people make the right choices, while growing up in the chaos of today. I wish there had been a book like this for those of us who grew up in the sixties."

—CANDACE LIGHTNER, president of We Save Lives and founder of Mothers Against Drunk Driving

**Other Books from
Franklin Covey Co.**

The 7 Habits of Happy Kids

The 4 Disciplines of Execution

The Speed of Trust

The 7 Habits of Highly Effective People

*The 6 Most Important Decisions You'll Ever Make:
A Guide for Teens*

Principle-Centered Leadership

First Things First

The Leader in Me

The 3rd Alternative

The 8th Habit

The Wisdom and Teachings of Stephen R. Covey

Let's Get Real or Let's Not Play

Great Work, Great Career

Smart Trust

The 7 Habits of Highly Effective Families

Life Matters

What Matters Most

The 10 Natural Laws of Successful Time and Life Management

The Power Principle

The 7 HABITS of Highly Effective TEENAGERS

The Ultimate Teenage Success Guide

Sean Covey

SIMON & SCHUSTER

London · New York · Sydney · Toronto · New Delhi

A CBS COMPANY

To Mom

FOR ALL THE LOVE, LULLABIES,

AND LATE-NIGHT TALKS

First published in Great Britain by Simon & Schuster UK Ltd, 1999
This trade paperback edition published by Simon & Schuster UK Ltd, 2014
A CBS COMPANY

Designed and illustrated by Raeber Graphics Inc.

1 3 5 7 9 10 8 6 4 2

Simon & Schuster UK Ltd
1st Floor
222 Gray's Inn Road
London WC1X 8HB

www.simonandschuster.co.uk

Simon & Schuster Australia, Sydney
Simon & Schuster India, New Delhi

A CIP catalogue record for this book is available from the British Library

ISBN: 978-1-47113-686-3
B format Export ISBN: 978-1-47113-687-0
Ebook ISBN: 978-0-85720-647-3

Printed and bound by CPI Group (UK) Ltd, Croydon, CR0 4YY

What's Inside

What's Inside

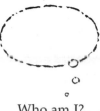

Who am I?

I am your constant companion. I am
your greatest helper or heaviest burden.
I will push you onward or drag you down
to failure. I am completely at your command.
Half the things you do you might just as
well turn over to me and I will be able to do
them quickly and correctly.

I am easily managed—you must merely
be firm with me. Show me exactly how you
want something done and after a few
lessons I will do it automatically. I am the
servant of all great individuals and, alas, of
all failures, as well. Those who are great, I
have made great. Those who are failures,
I have made failures.

I am not a machine, though I work
with all the precision of a machine plus
the intelligence of a human. You may run
me for a profit or run me for ruin—it
makes no difference to me.

Take me, train me, be firm with me,
and I will place the world at your feet. Be
easy with me and I will destroy you.

Who am I?

I am
Habit.

INTRODUCTION

The world has totally changed since I wrote the first version of this book. Back then, there was no Facebook or Twitter. There were no smartphones. There was no DIRECTV or Netflix. How boring!

Even with all these changes, a few things haven't changed. Choice hasn't changed. We are still free to choose what we do with our lives. The importance of relationships hasn't changed. Relationships are still the thing that matters most. And principles—such as responsibility, vision, teamwork, service, and renewal—haven't changed. They still rule.

That is why the 7 Habits will never go out of style, because they are based on timeless principles that endure. In fact, as the world gets crazier, the 7 Habits will only become more essential. There will always be a need to be proactive and take initiative. There will always be a need to seek first to understand another person before seeking to be understood. The 7 Habits aren't going anywhere.

Over the past many years I have received thousands of emails and letters from teen readers all around the globe, sharing their problems and successes. Upon reading these I picked up on three recurring themes.

First, everyone has problems with relationships—with friends, boyfriends and girlfriends, moms and dads, aunts and uncles, you name it. So if you have relationship problems, you're not alone. Welcome to the club.

Second, virtually every teen who wrote me wants to change and get better. They want to stop doing drugs or start doing better in school or lose weight or break out of the depression they are in or whatever. If you're like them, you want to get better, too.

Third, the 7 Habits really do work. Remarkably well! Among other things, they help you triumph over setbacks, build friendships, make smarter choices about dating and sex, do better in school, take charge of your life, build self-worth, and, believe it or not, even get along with your parents,.

A teenage girl wrote me about how learning Habit 1, Be Proactive, turned her life around:

> In the past six months, I've been through a lot. The love of my life broke my heart and refused to talk to me. From there he started up a friendship with my best friend. My parents went back and forth on divorce decisions. My brother got into drugs. My life just started falling apart. Then my mom bought this 7 Habits book and it really changed my way of

thinking. The part that stuck out was when the book said that no one can ever make you mad and/or ruin your day unless you let them. I always based my whole day on if one certain person talked to me or if something happened or whatnot. Now I don't care. When something bad happens, I smile through it anyway. And when HE doesn't say hi to me, I say hi to someone hotter and make my own day. It's so much easier to make your own day than to let someone else do it. All my friends have noticed a difference. I actually smile and am happy for once.

I know you have to deal with a lot of hard things in life. You have bad hair days. People say mean things. Parents get divorced. People you love pass away. Accidents happen. In the larger world, you have to cope with terrorism, wars, AIDS, cancer, global competition, cyberbullying, drugs, pornography, and trans fats.

All that said, I believe that if you could choose any time period in which to live during the world's existence, you couldn't find a better time than now. Truly, today is the best time in history to be born! It's a far better life than what the Egyptians or Romans or Aztecs or Ming Dynasty people ever experienced. Think about it. There is more freedom, information, wealth, and opportunity available today and to more people than ever before.

Consider information and technology. Through the Internet, the world is at your fingertips. You have hundreds of television channels and radio stations. If you want to learn about Greek mythology, you don't have to go to a library or find an expert, like your parents did when they were your age, you Google it! If you want to learn how to play the guitar, make a cheesecake, or even fly a helicopter (not that I'm suggesting that), search YouTube and there you have it!

With your smartphone you can check out the seven-day weather forecast for Jakarta or take high-definition photos of your dog or view a map of every single street in the civilized world. Imagine that! And it's not slowing down. Moore's Law says that the microchip's computing power doubles every eighteen months. I can't wait for my hover car!

The speed of change is accelerating as well. For instance, India and China are impacting everything. Companies like Amazon and Facebook spring up almost overnight and become global powerhouses.

Opportunities are everywhere. Who would have guessed that a twenty-eight-year-old programmer named Pierre Omidyar would become an almost overnight billionaire by writing code for a company he called eBay that brings buyers and sellers together on the Internet?

Yep, even with the challenges of our day, it is a great time to be alive. There is so much good we can do. There are so many people we can help. As one wise leader put it, "This is a magnificent time to live. It is a time when our influence can be tenfold what it might be in more tranquil times."

As well, I hope you'll never forget what Uncle Ben told Spider-Man. "With great power comes great responsibility." No, you're not Spider-Man or Katniss Everdeen. But you do have great freedom and opportunity, more than any generation that has ever lived, and with that comes great responsibility.

So enjoy this new edition of *The 7 Habits of Highly Effective Teens*, updated for the Internet age. You'll love the new language, stories, and anecdotes spread throughout the book. I wish you all my best as you build a future so bright you'll have to wear shades.

—Sean Covey

PART I

The Set-up

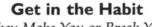

Get in the Habit
They Make You or Break You

Paradigms and Principles
What You See Is What You Get

Get in the Habit

THEY MAKE YOU OR BREAK YOU

Welcome! My name is Sean and I wrote this book. I don't know how you got it. Maybe your mom gave it to you to shape you up. Or maybe you bought it with your own money because the title caught your eye. Regardless of how it landed in your hands, I'm really glad it did. Now you just need to read it.

A lot of teens read books, but I wasn't one of them. (I did read several book summaries, however.) So if you're like I was, you may be ready to shelve this book. But before you do that, hear me out. If you promise to read on, I'll promise to make it an adventure. In fact, to keep it fun, I've stuffed it with cartoons, clever ideas, great quotes, and powerful stories about real teens from all over the world . . . along with a few other surprises. So, with that in mind: will you give it a try?

Okay? Okay!

Let's dive in, then. This book is based on another book that my dad, Stephen R. Covey, wrote several years ago entitled *The 7 Habits of Highly Effective People.* Surprisingly, that book has become one of the best-selling books of all time. He owes a lot of the credit for its success to me and my brothers and sisters, however. You see, we

> We first make
> our habits,
> then our habits
> make us.
>
> ENGLISH POET

Kids
in the
sixties
▶

Kids
today
◀

were his guinea pigs. He tried out all of his psycho experiments on us, and that's why my brothers and sisters have major emotional problems (just kidding, siblings). Luckily, I escaped uninjured.

So why did I write this book? I wrote it because life for teens is no playground. It's a jungle out there. And if I've done my job right, this book can be like a compass to help you navigate through it. Unlike my dad's book, which was written for old people (and can get really boring at times), this book was written especially for teens and is always interesting.

Although I'm a retired teenager, I still remember what it was like to be one. I could've sworn I was riding an emotional roller coaster most of the time. Looking back, I'm actually amazed that I survived. Barely. I'll never forget the time in seventh grade when I fell in love with a girl named Nicole. I told my friend Clar to tell her that I liked her (I was too scared to speak directly to girls so I used messengers). Clar completed his mission and returned and reported.

"Hey, Sean, I told Nicole that you liked her."

"What'd she say!?" I asked impatiently.

"She said, 'Ohh, Sean? He's fat!'" Clar laughed.

I was devastated. I felt like hiding in my room and never coming out again. I vowed to hate girls for life. Luckily my hormones prevailed and I began liking girls again.

I've interviewed a lot of teens in the making of this book. I suspect that some of the struggles they shared with me will be familiar to you too:

"There's too much to do and not enough time. I've got school, homework, job, friends, parties, and family on top of everything else. I'm totally stressed out. Help!"

"How can I feel good about myself when I don't match up? Everywhere I look I am reminded that someone else is smarter, or prettier, or more popular. I can't help but think, 'If I only had her hair, her clothes, her personality, her boyfriend, then I'd be happy.'"

"If I could only get my parents off my back I might be able to live my life. It seems they're constantly nagging, and I can't ever seem to satisfy them."

"I know I'm not living the way I should. I'm into everything—drugs, drinking, sex, you name it. But when I'm with my friends, I give in and just do what everyone else is doing."

"I've started another diet. I think it's my fifth one this year. I really do want to change, but I just don't have the discipline to stick with it. Each time I start a new diet I have hope. But it's usually only a short time before I blow it. And then I feel awful."

"I'm not doing too well in school right now. If I don't get my grades up I'll never get into college."

"I'm moody and get depressed often and I don't know what to do about it."

"I feel as if my life is out of control."

These problems are real, and you can't turn off real life. I won't pretend you can. Instead, I'll give you a set of tools to help you deal with real life. What are they? The 7 Habits of Highly Effective Teens or, said another way, the seven characteristics that happy and successful teens all over the world have in common.

By now, you're probably wondering what these habits are so I might as well end the suspense. Here they are, followed by a brief explanation:

Habit 1: **Be Proactive**
Take responsibility for your life.

Habit 2: **Begin with the End in Mind**
Define your mission and goals in life.

Habit 3: **Put First Things First**
Prioritize, and do the most important things first.

Habit 4: **Think Win-Win**
Have an everyone-can-win attitude.

Habit 5: **Seek First to Understand, Then to Be Understood**
Listen to people sincerely.

Habit 6: **Synergize**
Work together to achieve more.

Habit 7: **Sharpen the Saw**
Renew yourself regularly.

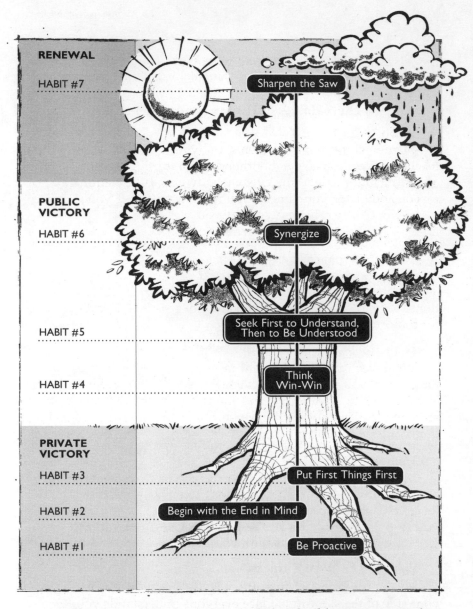

RENEWAL

HABIT #7

Sharpen the Saw

PUBLIC
VICTORY

HABIT #6

Synergize

HABIT #5

Seek First to Understand,
Then to Be Understood

HABIT #4

Think
Win-Win

PRIVATE
VICTORY

HABIT #3

Put First Things First

HABIT #2

Begin with the End in Mind

HABIT #1

Be Proactive

As the above diagram shows, the habits build upon one another. Habits 1, 2, and 3 deal with self-mastery. We call it the "private victory." Habits 4, 5, and 6 deal with relationships and teamwork. We call it the "public victory." You've got to get your personal act together before you can be a good team player. That's why the private victory comes before the public victory. The last habit, Habit 7, is the habit of renewal. It feeds all of the other six habits.

The habits seem pretty simple, don't they? But just wait till you see how powerful they can be! One great way to understand what the 7 Habits are is to understand what they are *not*. So here are the opposites, or:

The 7 Habits of Highly Defective Teens

Habit 1: *React*

Blame all of your problems on your parents, your stupid teachers, your lousy neighborhood, your boy- or girlfriend, the government, or something or somebody else. Be a victim. Take no responsibility for your life. If you're hungry, eat. If you're bored, make trouble. If someone yells at you, yell back. If you feel like doing something you know is wrong, go for it.

Habit 2: *Begin with No End in Mind*

Don't have a plan. Avoid goals at all costs. And never think about tomorrow. Why worry about the consequences of your actions? Live for the moment. Sleep around, get wasted, and party on, for tomorrow you die.

Habit 3: *Put First Things Last*

Whatever is most important in your life, don't do it until you have spent sufficient time watching videos of cute animals on YouTube, texting endlessly, and lounging around. Always put off studying until tomorrow. Make sure that fun things come before important things.

Habit 4: *Think Win-Lose*

See life as a vicious competition. If you want to be at the top of the popularity list, you'd better knock someone else off first. Don't let anyone else succeed at anything because, remember, if they win, you lose. If it looks like you're going to lose, however, make sure you drag that sucker down with you.

Habit 5: *Seek First to Talk, Then Pretend to Listen*

You were born with a mouth, so use it. Talk a *lot*. Always express your side of the story first. Once everyone understands your views, pretend to listen to theirs by nodding and saying "uh-huh" while daydreaming about what's for lunch. Or, if you really want their opinion, give it to them.

Habit 6: *Don't Cooperate*

Let's face it, other people are weird because they're different from you. So why try to get along with them? Teamwork's for the dogs. Since you always have the best ideas, you're better off doing everything by yourself. Be your own island.

Habit 7: *Wear Yourself Out*

Be so busy with life that you never take time to renew or improve yourself. Never study. Don't learn anything new. Avoid exercise like the plague. And, for heaven's sake, stay away from good books, nature, or anything else that may inspire you.

As you can see, the habits listed above are recipes for disaster. Yet many of us indulge in them . . . regularly (me included). And, given this, it's no wonder that life can really stink at times.

● WHAT EXACTLY ARE HABITS?

Habits are things we do repeatedly. But most of the time we're hardly aware that we even have them. They're on autopilot.

Some habits are good, such as:
- Exercising regularly
- Planning ahead
- Showing respect for others

Some are bad, including:
- Thinking negatively
- Feeling inferior
- Blaming others

And some don't really matter, like:
- Taking showers before bed instead of in the morning
- Putting hot sauce on every meal
- Listening to music while you exercise

Depending on what they are, our habits will either make us or break us. We become what we repeatedly do. As writer Samuel Smiles put it:

> *Sow a thought, and you reap an act;*
> *Sow an act, and you reap a habit;*
> *Sow a habit, and you reap a character;*
> *Sow a character, and you reap a destiny.*

Luckily, you are stronger than your habits. You can change them. For example, try folding your arms. Now fold them in the opposite way. Feels pretty strange, right? But if you folded them in the opposite way for thirty days in a row, it wouldn't feel so strange. You wouldn't even have to think about it. You'd get in the habit.

At any time you can look yourself in the mirror and say, "Hey, I don't like that about myself," and you can exchange a bad habit for a better one. It may not always be easy, but it's always possible.

Maybe not every idea in this book will work for you. But you don't have to be perfect to see results, either. Just living some of the habits some of the time can help you experience changes in your life you never thought possible.

The 7 Habits can help you:

- Get control of your life
- Improve your relationships with your friends
- Make smarter decisions
- Get along with your parents
- Overcome addictions and self-destructive habits
- Define your values and what matters most to you
- Get more done in less time
- Increase your self-confidence
- Be happy
- Find balance between school, work, friends, dating, and everything else

One final point. It's your book, so use it. Get out a pen or highlighter and mark it up. Don't be afraid to underline, circle, or bookmark your favorite ideas. Take notes in the margins. Scribble. Reread the stories that inspire you and memorize the quotes that give you hope. Try doing the "baby steps" at the end of each chapter, which were designed to help you start living the habits immediately. You'll get a lot more out of the book if you do.

You may also want to check out the hotlines and websites listed at the back of the book for additional help or information.

If you're the kind of reader who likes to skip around looking for cartoons and tidbits, that's fine. But at some point you ought to read the book from start to finish, because the 7 Habits are sequential. Each chapter builds on the last. Habit 1 comes before Habit 2 (and so on) for a reason.

So what do you say? Make my day and read this book!

COMING ATTRACTIONS

Up next, we'll take a look at ten of the dumbest statements ever made. You don't want to miss them. So read on!

Paradigms and Principles

WHAT YOU SEE IS WHAT YOU GET

The following is a list of statements made many years ago by experts in their fields. At the time they were said they sounded intelligent. With the passing of time, they sound idiotic.

Top 10 All-Time Stupid Quotes:

(10) "There is no reason for any individual to have a computer in their home."
KENNETH OLSEN, PRESIDENT AND FOUNDER OF DIGITAL EQUIPMENT CORPORATION, IN 1977

(9) "Airplanes are interesting toys but of no military value."
MARSHAL FERDINAND FOCH, FRENCH MILITARY STRATEGIST AND FUTURE WORLD WAR I COMMANDER, IN 1911

(8) "[Man will never reach the moon] regardless of all future scientific advances."
DR. LEE DE FOREST, INVENTOR OF THE AUDION TUBE AND FATHER OF RADIO, ON FEBRUARY 25, 1967

(7) "[Television] won't be able to hold on to any market it captures after the first six months. People will soon get tired of staring at a plywood box every night."
DARRYL F. ZANUCK, HEAD OF 20TH CENTURY—FOX, IN 1946

Better keep yourself clean and bright; you are the window through which you see the whole world.
GEORGE BERNARD SHAW ENGLISH PLAYWRIGHT

(6) "We don't like their sound. Groups of guitars are on the way out."
DECCA RECORDS REJECTING THE BEATLES, IN 1962

(5) "For the majority of people, the use of tobacco has a beneficial effect."
DR. IAN G. MACDONALD, LOS ANGELES SURGEON, AS QUOTED IN *NEWSWEEK*, NOVEMBER 18, 1969

(4) "This 'telephone' has too many shortcomings to be seriously considered as a means of communication. The device is inherently of no value to us."
WESTERN UNION INTERNAL MEMO, IN 1876

(3) "The earth is the center of the universe."
PTOLEMY, THE GREAT EGYPTIAN ASTRONOMER, IN THE SECOND CENTURY

(2) "Nothing of importance happened today."
WRITTEN BY KING GEORGE III OF ENGLAND ON JULY 4, 1776

(1) "Two years from now, spam will be solved."
BILL GATES, WORLD ECONOMIC FORUM, 2004

Having read these, let me share with you another list of statements made by real teens just like you. You've heard them before, and they are just as ridiculous as the list above.

"No one in my family has ever gone to college. I'd be crazy to think I could make it."

"It's no use. My stepdad and I will never get along. We're just too different."

"Being smart is a 'white' thing."

"My teacher's out to get me."

"She's so pretty—I bet she's a diva."

"You can't get ahead in life unless you know the right people."

"Me? Skinny? Are you kidding? My whole family is full of fat people."

"It's impossible to get a good job around here 'cause nobody wants to hire a teen."

So What's a Paradigm? What do these two lists of statements have in common? First, they're all *perceptions* about the way things are, not facts. Second, these perceptions are all inaccurate or incomplete—even though the people who said them are convinced they're true.

Another word for perceptions is *paradigms* [pair-a-dimes]. A paradigm is the way you see something, it's your point of view, frame of reference, or belief. Sometimes our paradigms are way off the mark, and, as a result, they create limitations. For instance, you may be convinced that you don't have what it takes to get into college. But, remember, Ptolemy was just as convinced that the earth was the center of the universe.

And think about the teen who believes she can't get along with her stepdad. If that is her paradigm, is she likely to ever get along with him? Probably not, because that belief will hold her back from really trying.

Paradigms are like glasses. When you have incomplete paradigms about yourself or life in general, it's like wearing glasses with the wrong prescription. That lens affects how you see everything else. As a result, what you see is what you get. If you believe you're dumb, that very belief will make you dumb. Or, if you believe your little sister is dumb, you'll look for evidence to support your belief, find it, and she'll remain dumb in your eyes. On the other hand, if you believe you're smart, that belief will cast a rosy hue on everything you do.

A teen named Kristi once shared with me how much she loved the beauty of the mountains. One day she went to visit her eye doctor and, to her surprise, discovered that her sight was much worse than she had thought. After putting in her new contacts, she was astonished at how well she could see. As she put it, "I realized that the mountains and trees and even the signs on the side of the road have more detail than I had ever imagined. It was the strangest thing. I didn't know how bad my eyes were until I experienced how good they could be." That's often the way it is. We don't know how much we're missing because we have messed-up paradigms.

We have paradigms about ourselves, about other people, and about life in general. Let's take a look at each.

• PARADIGMS OF SELF

Stop right now and consider this question: Are your paradigms of yourself helping or hindering you?

When my wife, Rebecca, was a junior at Madison High School in Idaho, a sign-up sheet for the Miss Madison pageant was passed around in class. Rebecca, along with many other girls, signed up. Linda, who sat next to Rebecca, passed without signing.

"Sign up, Linda," insisted Rebecca.

"Oh, no. I couldn't do that."

"Come on. It will be fun."

"No, really. I'm not the type."

"Sure you are. I think you'd be great!" chimed Rebecca.

Rebecca and others continued to encourage Linda until she finally signed.

Rebecca didn't think anything of the situation at the time. However, seven years later, she received a letter from Linda describing the inner struggle she had gone through that day and thanking Rebecca for being the spark that helped her change her life. Linda related how she suffered from a poor self-image in high school and was shocked that Rebecca would consider her a candidate for a talent pageant. She had finally agreed to sign up just to get Rebecca and the others off her back.

Linda said she was so uncomfortable about being in the pageant that she contacted the pageant director the following day and demanded her name be removed from the list. But, like Rebecca, the director insisted that Linda participate.

Reluctantly, she agreed.

But that was all it took. Linda noted that although she hadn't won a single title or award, she had overcome an even bigger obstacle: her low perception of herself. The following year Linda became a student body officer, and, as Rebecca relates, developed a vivacious and outgoing personality.

Linda experienced what's called a "paradigm shift." By daring to participate in an event that demanded the best in her, Linda began to see herself in a new light. In her letter, Linda thanked Rebecca from deep within for, in essence, taking off her warped glasses, shattering them against the floor, and insisting she try on a new pair.

Just as negative self-paradigms can put limitations on us, positive self-paradigms can bring out the best in us, as the following story about the son of King Louis XVI of France illustrates:

King Louis had been taken from his throne and imprisoned. His young son, the prince, was taken by those who dethroned the king. They thought that inasmuch as the king's son was heir to the throne, if they could destroy him morally, he would never realize the great and grand destiny that life had bestowed upon him.

They took him to a community far away, and there they exposed the lad to every filthy and vile thing that life could offer. They exposed him to foods the richness of which would quickly make him a slave to appetite. They used vile language around him constantly. They exposed him to lewd and lusting women. They exposed him to dishonor and distrust. He was surrounded twenty-four hours a day by everything that could drag the soul of a man as low as one could slip. For over six months he had this treatment—but not once did the young lad buckle under pressure. Finally, after intensive temptation, they questioned him. Why had he not submitted himself to these things—why had he not partaken? These things would provide pleasure, satisfy his lusts, and were desirable; they were all his. The boy said, "I cannot do what you ask for I was born to be a king."

Prince Louis held that paradigm of himself so tightly that nothing could shake him. In like manner, if you walk through life wearing glasses that say "I can do it" or "I matter," that belief will put a positive spin on everything else.

At this point you may be wondering, "If my paradigm of myself is all contorted, what can I do to fix it?" One way is to spend time with someone who already believes in you and builds you up. My mother was such a person to me. When I was growing up, my mom always believed in me, especially when I doubted myself. She was always saying stuff like "Sean, of course you should run for class president," and "Ask her out. I'm sure she would just die to go out with you." Whenever I needed to be affirmed I'd talk to my mom and she'd clean any negativity from my glasses.

Ask any successful person and most will tell you that they had a person who believed in them . . . a teacher, a friend, a parent, a guardian, a sibling, a grandparent. It only takes one person, and it doesn't really matter who it is. Don't be afraid to lean on this person and to get nourished by them. Go to them for advice. See yourself the way they see you. Oh, what a difference a new pair of glasses can make! As someone once said, "If you could envision the type of person God intended you to be, you would rise up and never be the same again."

At times, you may not have anyone to lean on—and you may need to go solo. If this is the case with you, pay special attention to the next chapter, which will give you some handy tools to help build your self-image.

● PARADIGMS OF OTHERS

We have paradigms not only about ourselves, but also about other people. And they can be way out of whack, too. Seeing things from a different point of view can help us understand why other people act the way they do.

Becky told me about her paradigm shift:

As a junior in high school, I had a friend named Kim. She was essentially a nice person, but as the year progressed, it became more and more difficult to get along with her. She was easily offended and often felt left out. She was moody and difficult to be around. It got to the point where my friends and I started calling her less and less. Eventually we stopped inviting her to things.

I was gone for a good part of the summer after that year, and when I returned I was talking to a good friend of mine, catching up on all the news. She was telling me about all the gossip, the different romances, who was dating who, and so on, when suddenly she said, "Oh! Did I tell you about Kim? She's been having a hard time lately because her parents are going through a really messy divorce. She's taking it really hard."

When I heard this, my whole perspective changed. Rather than being annoyed by Kim's behavior, I felt terrible about my own. I felt I had deserted her in her time of need. Just by knowing that one little bit of information, my whole attitude toward her changed. It was really an eye-opening experience.

And to think that all it took to change Becky's paradigm was a smidgen of new information. We too often judge people without having all the facts.

Monica had a similar experience:

I used to live in California, where I had a lot of good friends. I didn't care about anybody new because I already had my friends and I thought that new people should deal with it in their own way. Then, when I moved, I was the new kid and wished that someone would care about me and make me part of their group of friends. I see things in a very different way now. I know what it feels like to not have any friends.

Seeing things from another point of view can make all the difference in our attitude toward others. I'll bet Monica will never treat new kids on the block the same way again.

FRANK & ERNEST ® by Bob Thaves

The following anecdote from *Reader's Digest* (contributed by Dan P. Greyling) is a classic example of a paradigm shift:

A friend of mine, returning to South Africa from a long stay in Europe, found herself with some time to spare at London's Heathrow Airport. Buying a cup of coffee and a small package of cookies, she staggered, laden with luggage, to an unoccupied table. She was reading the morning paper when she became aware of someone rustling at her table. From behind her paper, she was flabbergasted to see a neatly dressed young man helping himself to her cookies. She did not want to make a scene, so she leaned across and took a cookie herself. A minute or so passed. More rustling. He was helping himself to another cookie.

By the time they were down to the last cookie in the package, she was very angry but still could not bring herself to say anything. Then the young man broke the cookie in two, pushed half across to her, ate the other half and left.

Some time later, when the public-address system called for her to present her ticket, she was still fuming. Imagine her embarrassment when she opened her handbag and was confronted by her package of cookies. She had been eating his.

Consider this lady's feelings toward the neatly dressed young man before the turn of events: "What a rude, presumptive young man."

Imagine her feelings after: "How embarrassing!? How kind of him to share his last cookie with me!"

So what's the point? It's simply this: often our paradigms are incomplete, inaccurate, or kinda messed up. We shouldn't be so quick to judge, label, or form rigid opinions of others—or of ourselves, for that matter. From a limited point of view, it's hard to see the whole picture or have all the facts.

In addition, we should open our minds and hearts to new information, ideas, and points of view. We should be willing to change our paradigms when it becomes clear that they're wrong. Is it obvious that if you want to make big changes in your life, change your lens. Everything else will follow.

When you really think about it, you'll realize that most of your problems (with relationships, self-image, attitude) are the result of a messed-up paradigm or two. For instance, if you have a poor relationship with, say, your dad, it's likely that both of you have a warped paradigm of each other. You may think he's being harsh, or putting too much pressure on you; he may see you as being a spoiled, ungrateful brat. In reality, both of your paradigms are probably incomplete and are holding you back from real communication with each other.

As you'll see, this book will challenge many of your paradigms and, hopefully, will help you create more accurate and complete ones. So get ready.

• PARADIGMS OF LIFE

We don't just have paradigms about ourselves and others, we also have paradigms about the world in general. You can usually tell what your paradigm is by asking yourself a few questions: "What is the driving force of my life?" "What do I spend my time thinking about?" "Who or what are my obsessions?" Whatever's most important to you will become your paradigm, your glasses, or, as I like to call it, your life-center. Some of the more popular life-centers for teens include Friends, Stuff, Boyfriend/Girlfriend, School, Parents, Sports/Hobbies, Heroes, Enemies, Self, and Work. Of course they each have their good points, but they are all incomplete in one way or another, and, as I'm about to show you, they'll mess you up if you center your life on them. Luckily, there is one center that you can always count on. We'll save it for last.

Friend-Centered

There's nothing better than belonging to a great group of friends and nothing worse than feeling like an outcast. Friends are important but should never become your center. Why? Well, occasionally they're fickle. Now and then they're fake. Sometimes they talk behind your back or develop new friendships and forget yours. They have mood swings. They move.

In addition, if you base your identity on being accepted, being popular, or having the most friends on Facebook, you may find yourself compromising your standards or changing them every weekend to accommodate your friends.

SORRY, GUYS, WE CAN'T DO **EVERYTHING** TOGETHER!

Believe it or not, the day will come when friends will not be the biggest thing in your life. In high school I had an amazing group of friends. We did everything together—swam in irrigation canals, gorged at all-you-can-eat buffets, snowmobiled all through the night, dated one another's girlfriends . . . you name it. I loved these guys. I figured we'd be close forever.

Since high school graduation, though, I've been shocked by how seldom we see one another. Now, years later, we live far apart, and new relationships, jobs, and family take up our time. As a teen, I never could have fathomed this.

Make as many friends as you can, but don't build your life on them. It's an unstable foundation. People will change, you will change.

Stuff-Centered

Sometimes we see the world through the lens of possessions or "stuff." We live in a material world that teaches us that "He who dies with the most toys wins." We feel as if we're supposed to have the fastest car, the nicest clothes, the latest smartphone, the best hairstyle, and the many other *things* that apparently bring happiness. Possessions also come in the form of titles and accomplishments, such as—head cheerleader, star of the play, valedictorian, student body officer, editor in chief, or MVP.

There is nothing wrong with achieving success and enjoying our stuff, but *things* should never become the center of our lives. In the end, they have no lasting value. Our confidence needs to come from *within*, not from without. From the *quality of our hearts*, not the *quantity of things* we own. After all, he who dies with the most toys . . . still dies.

I knew a girl who had the most beautiful and expensive wardrobe I'd ever seen. She never wore the same outfit twice. After getting to know her better, I started to notice that she had a bad case of "elevator eyes." It seemed that whenever she talked with another girl, she'd eye her from head to foot to see if her outfit was as nice as her own, which usually gave her a superiority complex. Her self-confidence depended on owning *stuff*. It didn't come from her own personality, smarts, or kindness. It was a real turnoff to me.

I read a saying once that says it better than I can: "If who I am is what I have and what I have is lost, then who am I?"

Boyfriend/Girlfriend-Centered

This may be the easiest trap of all to fall into. I mean, who *hasn't* been focused on a crush or a boyfriend or girlfriend at one point?

Let's pretend Brady centers his life on his girlfriend, Tasha. Now, watch the instability it creates in Brady.

TASHA'S ACTIONS	BRADY'S REACTIONS
Makes a thoughtless comment:	*"My day is ruined."*
Talks to Brady's best friend:	*"Are they flirting? They're both betraying me."*
"I think we should date other people:"	*"My life is over. You never loved me."*

The ironic thing is that the more you center your life on someone, the less attractive you become to that person. How's that? Well, first of all, if you're centered on someone, you're no longer hard to get. Second, it's irritating when someone builds their *entire* emotional life around you. Since their security comes from you and not from within themselves, they always need to have those sickening "where do we stand" talks (shudder).

If who I am
is what I have
and what I have is
lost, then
who am I?

ANONYMOUS

When I began dating my wife, one of the things that attracted me most was that she didn't center her life on me. I'll never forget the time she turned me down (with a smile and no apology) for a very important date. I loved it! She was her own person and had her own inner strength. Her moods were independent of mine.

Believe me, you'll be a better boyfriend or girlfriend if you're not totally obsessed with your partner. This goes for *getting* a boyfriend or girlfriend, too. If you make your crush the center of your life, it can sometimes come off as desperate or needy. Independence is far more attractive than dependence.

Besides, centering your life on another doesn't show that you love them, only that you're dependent on them. You can usually tell when a couple becomes centered on each other because they are forever breaking up and getting back together. Although their relationship has gone to pot, their emotional lives and identities are so intertwined that they can't let go of each other.

Have as many girlfriends or boyfriends as you'd like, just don't make them your center, because, although there are exceptions, teenage romantic relationships are usually about as stable as a yo-yo.

School-Centered

Among teens, centering one's life on school is more common than you might think. Lisa, from Canada, regrets being school-centered for so long:

I have been so ambitious and so school-centered that I haven't enjoyed my youth. It has not only been unhealthy for myself—but it's been selfish, because all I cared about was me and my achievements.

As a seventh grader I was already working as hard as a college student. I wanted to be a brain surgeon, just because it was the hardest thing I could think of. I would get up at six every morning all through school and not go to bed before 2 A.M. in order to achieve.

I felt teachers and peers expected it of me. They would always be surprised if I didn't get perfect grades. My parents tried to loosen me up, but my own expectations were as great as that of teachers and peers.

I realize now that I could have accomplished what I wanted without trying so hard, and I could have had a good time doing it.

Our education is vital to our future and should be a top priority. But we must be careful not to let ACT or SAT scores, GPA's, and AP classes take over our lives. School-centered teens often become so obsessed with getting good grades that they forget that the real purpose of school is to learn. You can do extremely well in school and still maintain a healthy balance in life.

Thank goodness our worth isn't measured by our GPA.

Parent-Centered

Your parents can be your greatest source of love and guidance and you should respect and honor them, but living to please them above everything else can become a real nightmare. (Don't tell your parents I said that or they might take away your book . . . just kiddin'.) Read what happened to this young girl from Louisiana:

I worked so hard all semester. I just knew that my parents would be pleased—six A's and one B+. But all I could see in their eyes was disappointment. All they wanted to know was why the B+ wasn't an A. It was all I could do not to cry. What did they want from me?

That was my sophomore year of high school, and I spent the next two years trying to make my parents proud of me. I played basketball and I hoped that they would be proud—they never came to see me play. I made the honor roll every semester—but after a while straight A's were just expected. I was going to go to college to be a teacher, but there was no money in that, and my parents felt that I would be better off studying something else—so I did.

Every decision I made was prefaced with the questions—What would Mom and Dad want me to do? Would they be proud? Would they love me? But no matter what I did, it was never good enough. I had based my whole life on the goals and aspirations my parents thought were good, and it didn't make me happy. I felt out of control. I felt worthless, useless, and unimportant.

Eventually I realized that my parents' approval wasn't coming, and if I didn't get my act together, I would destroy myself. I needed to find a center that was timeless, unchanging, and real—a center that couldn't shout, disapprove, or criticize. So I started to live my own life, by the principles that I thought would bring me happiness—like honesty (with myself and my parents), faith in a happier life, hope for the future, and belief in my own goodness. In the beginning I sort of had to pretend that I was strong, but, over a period of time, I became strong.

UMMM... I NEED TO GO TO WORK NOW, HONEY.

Finally I struck out on my own and had a falling out with my folks, but it made them see me for who I was, and they loved me. They apologized for all the pressure they put on me and expressed their love. I was eighteen years old before I ever remember my dad saying "I love you," but they were the sweetest words I have ever heard, and well worth the wait. I still care about what my parents think, and I am still influenced by their opinions, but, ultimately, I have become responsible for my life and my actions, and I try to please myself before anybody else.

Other Possible Centers

The list of possible centers could go on and on. Being *sports-* or *hobbies-centered* is a big one. How many times have we seen a sports-centered jock build his identity around being a great athlete only to suffer a career-ending injury? It happens all the time. And the poor kid is left to rebuild his life from scratch. The same goes for any hobbies and interests—dance, debate, drama, music, or clubs.

And what about being *hero-centered*? If you build your life around a rock star, famous athlete, entrepreneur, or powerful politician, what happens if they die, do something really stupid, or end up in jail? Who will you look up to then?

Sometimes we can even become *enemy-centered*, and build our lives around hating a group, a person, or an idea. There are countless websites dedicated to hating particular topics or celebrities. What a waste of time! Why not put that energy toward something that makes you happy?

Becoming *work-centered* is a sickness that usually afflicts older people but can also reach teens. Workaholism is usually driven by a compulsive need to have more stuff, like money, cars, status, or recognition, which can never fully satisfy—because there's always a new model of iPhone coming out that will put your old one to shame!

Another common center is being *self-centered*, or thinking the world revolves around you and your problems. This often results in being so worried about your own condition that you're oblivious to the walking wounded all around you.

As you can see, all these and many more life-centers do not provide the stability that you and I need in life. I'm not saying we shouldn't strive to become excellent in something like dance or debate, or strive to develop rich relationships with our friends and parents. We should. But there's a fine line between having a passion for something and basing your entire existence on it. And that's the line we shouldn't cross.

Principle-Centered—*The Real Thing*

In case you were starting to wonder, there is a center that actually works. What is it? (Drumroll, please.) It's being *principle-centered*. We are all familiar with the effects of gravity. Throw a ball up and it comes down. It's a natural law or principle. Just as there are principles that rule the physical world, there are principles that rule the human world. Principles aren't religious. They aren't based on nationality or race. They aren't mine or yours. They aren't up for discussion. They apply equally to everyone, male or female, rich or poor, famous or obscure. They can't be bought or sold. If you live by them, you will excel. If you break them, you will fail (hey, that sorta' rhymes). It's that simple.

Here are a few examples: Honesty is a principle. Service is a principle. Love is a principle. Hard work is a principle. Respect, gratitude, moderation, fairness, integrity, loyalty, and responsibility are principles. There are dozens and dozens more. They are not hard to identify. Just as a compass always points to true north, your heart will recognize true principles.

For example, think about the principle of hard work. You may be able to scrape by using shortcuts and faking it for a while, but eventually it'll catch up to you.

I remember one time being invited to play in a golf tournament with my college football coach. He was a great golfer. Everyone, including my coach, expected that I'd be a fine golfer as well. After all, I was a college athlete and all college athletes should be great golfers. Right? Wrong. You see, I stunk at golf. I'd only played a few times in my life, and I didn't even know how to hold a club properly. I was nervous about everyone finding out how bad I was at golf. Especially my coach. So I was hoping that I could fool him and everyone else into thinking I was good. On the very first hole there was a small crowd gathered around. I was first up to tee off. Why me? As I stepped up to hit the ball, I prayed for a miracle.

Swooooosssssshhhhh. It worked! A miracle! I couldn't believe it! I had hit a long shot, straight down the middle of the fairway.

I turned around and smiled to the crowd and acted as if I always hit like that. "Thank you. Thank you very much."

I had them all fooled. But I was only fooling myself because there were 17½ more holes to go. In fact, it took only about five more shots for everyone around me, including my coach, to realize that I was a complete golf sham. It wasn't long until the coach was trying to show me how to swing the club. I'd been exposed. Ouch!

You can't fake playing golf, tuning a guitar, or speaking Arabic if you haven't paid the price to get good. There's no way around it. Hard work is a principle. As the NBA great Larry Bird put it, "If you don't do your homework, you won't make your free throws."

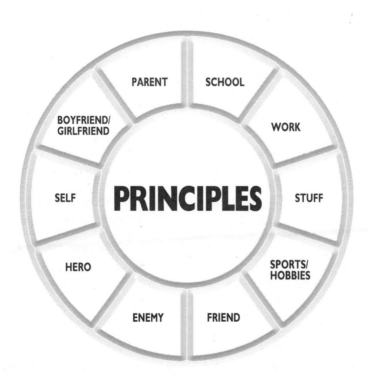

Principles Never Fail

It takes faith to live by principles, especially when you see people close to you get ahead in life by lying, cheating, indulging, manipulating, and serving only themselves. What you don't see, however, is that breaking principles *always* catches up to them in the end.

Take the principle of honesty. If you're a big liar, you may be able to get by for a while, even for a few years. But you'd be hard-pressed to find a liar who achieved success over the *long haul*. As Cecil B. DeMille observed about his classic movie *The Ten Command-*

ments, "It is impossible for us to break the law. We can only break ourselves against the law."

Unlike all the other centers we've looked at, principles will never fail you. They'll never gossip behind your back. They don't move away. They don't suffer career-ending injuries. They don't play favorites based on skin color, gender, wealth, or appearance. A principle-centered life is simply the most stable, immovable, unshakable foundation you can build upon, and we all need one of those.

To grasp why principles always work, just imagine living a life based on their opposites—a life of dishonesty, laziness, indulgence, ingratitude, selfishness, and hate. I can't imagine any good things coming out of that. Can you?

> It is impossible for us to break the law. We can only break ourselves against the law.
>
> CECIL B. DEMILLE,
> FILM DIRECTOR

Ironically, living a principle-centered life is the key to excelling in all the other centers. If you live the principles of service, respect, and love, for instance, you're likely to pick up more friends and be a more stable boyfriend or girlfriend. Putting principles first is also the key to becoming a person of character.

Decide today to make principles your core life-center, or paradigm. In whatever situation you find yourself, ask, "What's the principle in play here?" For every problem, search for the principle that will help you solve it.

If you're feeling worn out and beaten up by life, perhaps you should try the principle of *balance.*

If you find no one trusts you, the principle of *honesty* might just be the cure you need.

In the story *Loyalty to a Brother* by Walter MacPeek, *loyalty* was the principle in play:

> *One of two brothers fighting in the same company in France fell by a German bullet. The one who escaped asked permission of his officer to go and bring his brother in.*
>
> *"He is probably dead," said the officer, "and there is no use in your risking your life to bring in his body."*
>
> *But after further pleading the officer consented. Just as the soldier reached the lines with his brother on his shoulders, the wounded man died.*
>
> *"There, you see," said the officer, "you risked your life for nothing."*
>
> *"No," replied Tom. "I did what he expected of me, and I have my reward. When I crept up to him and took him in my arms, he said, 'Tom, I knew you would come—I just felt you would come.'"*

In the upcoming chapters, you'll discover that each of the 7 Habits is based upon a basic principle or two. And that's where they get their power from.

The long and short of it is *principles rule.*

★ COMING ATTRACTIONS

Up next, we'll talk about how to get rich, in a way you probably never thought of. So carry on!

A Word About Baby Steps One of my family's favorite movies is on old classic called *What About Bob?* starring Bill Murray. It is the story of a dysfunctional, phobia-laden, immature, pea-brained leech named Bob who never, ever goes away. He attaches himself to Dr. Marvin, a renowned psychiatrist, who wants nothing more than to get rid of Bob and finally gives him a book he wrote called *Baby Steps.* He tells Bob that the best way to solve his problems is not to bite off too much at once but to just take "baby steps" to reach his goals. Bob is delighted! He no longer has to worry about how to get all the way home from Dr. Marvin's office, a big task for Bob. Instead, Bob only has to baby step his way out of the office, and then baby step his way onto the elevator, and so on.

So I'll give you some baby steps at the end of each chapter, starting with this one—small, easy steps that you can do immediately to help you apply what you just read. Though small, these steps can become powerful tools in helping you achieve your larger goals. So, come along with Bob (he really becomes very likable after you accept the fact that you can't shake him) and take some baby steps.

1 The next time you look in the mirror say something positive to yourself.

2 Show appreciation for someone's point of view today. Say something like "Hey, that's a cool idea."

3 Think of a limiting paradigm you might have of yourself, such as "I'll never be outgoing." Now, do something today that totally contradicts that paradigm.

4 Think of a loved one or close friend who has been acting out of character lately. Consider what might be causing them to act that way.

5 When you have nothing to do, what is it that occupies your thoughts? Remember, whatever is most important to you will become your paradigm or life-center.

What occupies my time and energy?..

....

6 The Golden Rule rules! Begin today to treat others as you would want them to treat you. Don't be impatient, complain about what's for dinner, or bad-mouth someone, unless you want the same treatment.

7 Sometime soon, find a quiet place where you can be alone. Think about what matters most to you.

8 Listen carefully to the lyrics of the music you listen to most frequently. Consider if they are in harmony with the principles you believe in.

9 When you do your chores at home or work tonight, try out the principle of hard work. Go the extra mile and do more than is expected.

10 The next time you're in a tough situation and don't know what to do, ask yourself, "What principle should I apply (i.e., honesty, love, loyalty, hard work, patience)?" Follow that principle and don't look back.

PART II

The Private Victory

The Personal Bank Account
Starting with the Man in the Mirror

Habit 1—Be Proactive
I Am the Force

Habit 2—Begin with the End in Mind
Control Your Own Destiny or Someone Else Will

Habit 3—Put First Things First
Will and Won't Power

The Personal Bank Account

STARTING WITH THE MAN IN THE MIRROR

Before you'll ever win in the public arenas of life, you must first win the private battles within yourself. All change begins with you. I'll never forget how I learned this lesson.

"What's wrong with you? You're disappointing me. Where's the Sean I once knew in high school?" Coach glared at me. "Do you even *want* to be out there?"

I was shocked. "Yes, of course."

"Oh, gimme a break. You're just going through the motions and your heart's not in it. You better get your act together or the younger quarterbacks will pass you up and you'll be a benchwarmer."

It was my sophomore year at Brigham Young University (BYU) during preseason football camp. Several colleges recruited me straight out of high school, but I chose BYU because they had a tradition of producing all-American quarterbacks like Jim McMahon and Steve Young, both of whom went on to the pros and led their teams to Super Bowl victories. Although I was the third-string quarterback at the time, I planned on being the next all-American!

> I'm starting with the man in the mirror
> I'm asking him to change his ways
> And no message could have been any clearer
> If you wanna make the world a better place
> Take a look at yourself, and then make a change.
>
> "MAN IN THE MIRROR"
> BY SIEDAH GARRETT
> AND GLEN BALLARD

When Coach told me that I was "stinkin' up the field," it came as a cold, hard slap in the face. The thing that really bugged me, though, was that he was right. Even though I was spending long hours practicing, I wasn't truly committed. I was holding back, and I knew it.

I had a hard decision to make—I had to either quit football or triple my commitment. Over the next several weeks, I waged a war inside my head and came face-to-face with many fears and self-doubts. Did I have what it took to be the starting quarterback? Could I handle the pressure? Was I big enough? It soon became clear to me that I was scared, scared of competing, scared of being in the limelight, scared of trying and perhaps failing. And all these fears were holding me back from giving it my all.

There's a great quote by Arnold Bennett that describes what I finally decided to do about my dilemma. He wrote, "The real tragedy is the tragedy of the man who never in his life braces himself for his one supreme effort—he never stretches to his full capacity, never stands up to his full stature."

Having never enjoyed tragedy, I decided to brace myself for one supreme effort. So I committed to give it my all. I decided to stop holding back and to start laying it all on the line. I didn't know if I would ever get a chance to be first string, but if I didn't, at least I was going to strike out swinging.

The real tragedy is the tragedy of the man who never in his life braces himself for his one supreme effort—he never stretches to his full capacity, never stands up to his full stature.

ARNOLD BENNETT

No one heard me say, "I commit." There was no applause. It was simply a private battle that I fought and won inside my own mind over a period of several weeks.

Once I committed myself, everything changed. I began taking chances and making big improvements on the field. My heart was in it now. I knew it, and the coaches saw that.

As the season began and the games rolled by one by one, I sat on the bench. Although frustrated, I kept working hard and kept improving.

Midseason featured the big game of the year. We were to play nationally ranked Air Force on ESPN, in front of 65,000 fans. A week before the game, Coach called me into his office and told me that I would be the starting quarterback. Gulp! Needless to say, that was the longest week of my life.

Game day finally arrived. At kickoff my mouth was so dry I

could barely talk. But after a few minutes I settled down and led our team to victory. I was even named the ESPN Player of the Game. Afterward, lots of people congratulated me on the victory and my performance. That felt good. But they didn't really understand.

They didn't know the full story. They thought that victory had taken place on the field that day in the public eye. I knew it happened months before in the privacy of my own head, when I decided to face my fears, to stop holding back, and to brace myself for one supreme effort. Beating Air Force was a much easier challenge than overcoming myself. Private victories always come before public victories. As the saying goes, "We have met the enemy and he is us."

• INSIDE OUT

We crawl before we walk. We learn addition before algebra. We must fix ourselves before we can fix others. If you want to make a change in your life, the place to begin is with yourself, not with your parents, your teacher, or your girlfriend or boyfriend. All change begins with Y-O-U. Think about it. It's inside out. Not outside in. I am reminded of the writings of an Anglican bishop:

> *When I was young and free and my imagination had no limits, I dreamed of changing the world;*
>
> *As I grew older and wiser I realized the world would not change.*
>
> *And I decided to shorten my sights somewhat and change only my country. But it too seemed immovable.*
>
> *As I entered my twilight years, in one last desperate attempt, I sought to change only my family, those closest to me, but alas they would have none of it.*
>
> *And now here I lie on my death bed and realize (perhaps for the first time) that if only I'd changed myself first, then by example I may have influenced my family and with their encouragement and support I may have bettered my country, and who knows I may have changed the world.*

This is what this book is all about. Changing from the inside out, starting with the man or woman in the mirror. This chapter ("The Personal Bank Account") and the ones that follow on Habits 1, 2, and 3 deal with *you* and your character, or the private victory. The next four chapters, "The Relationship Bank Account," and Habits 4, 5, and 6, deal with *relationships,* or the public victory.

Before diving into Habit 1, let's take a look at how you can immediately begin to build your self-confidence and achieve a private victory.

The Personal Bank Account

How you feel about yourself is like a bank account. Let's call it your *personal bank account* (PBA). Just like a checking or savings account at a bank, you can make deposits into and take withdrawals from your PBA by the things you think, say, and do. For example, when I stick to a commitment I've made to myself, I feel in control. It's a deposit. *Cha-ching.* On the other hand, when I break a promise to myself, I feel disappointed and make a withdrawal.

So let me ask you. How is your PBA? How much trust and confidence do you have in yourself? Are you loaded or bankrupt? The symptoms listed below might help you evaluate where you stand.

Possible Symptoms of a Low PBA
- You cave in to peer pressure easily.
- You wrestle with feelings of worthlessness and inferiority.
- You're overly concerned about what others think of you.
- You act arrogant to help hide your insecurities.
- You self-destruct by getting heavily into drugs, pornography, vandalism, or gangs.
- You get jealous easily, especially when someone close to you succeeds.

Possible Symptoms of a Healthy PBA
- You stand up for yourself and resist peer pressure.
- You're not overly concerned about being popular.
- You see life as a generally positive experience.
- You trust yourself.
- You are goal driven.
- You are happy for the successes of others.

If your personal bank account is low, don't get discouraged. It doesn't have to be permanent. Just start making small, humble deposits today—deposits worth $1, $5, or $10. You'll feel your confidence growing. Small deposits over a long period of time is the way to a healthy and rich PBA.

With the help of various teen groups, I've compiled a list of six key deposits that can help you build your PBA. And, just like Newton's Law of Motion, with every deposit, there is an equal and opposite withdrawal.

PBA DEPOSITS	PBA WITHDRAWALS
Keep promises to yourself	Break personal promises
Do small acts of kindness	Keep to yourself
Be gentle with yourself	Beat yourself up
Be honest	Lie
Renew yourself	Wear yourself out
Magnify your talents	Bury your talents

- ## KEEP PROMISES TO YOURSELF

Have you ever had flakey friends? They say they'll text you back and they don't. They promise to hang out on the weekend and they forget. After a while, you stop trusting them. Their commitments mean nothing. The same thing happens when you continually make and break self-promises, such as "I'm going to study right when I get home," when next thing you know you're Facebook chatting with friends. After a while of flaking out on yourself, you don't trust yourself, either.

We should treat the commitments we make to ourselves as seriously as those we make to the most important people in our lives. If you're feeling out of control in life, focus on the single thing you can control—you. Make a promise to yourself and keep it. Start with small $5 commitments that you know you can complete, like not drinking soda pop today. After you've built up some self-trust, you can then go for the more difficult $100 deposits—like deciding to break up with an abusive boyfriend or girlfriend or making up your mind to overcome an addiction.

- ## DO SMALL ACTS OF KINDNESS

I remember reading a statement by a psychiatrist who said that if you're feeling depressed, the best thing to do is to do something for someone else. Why? Because it gets you focused outward, not inward. It's hard to be depressed while helping someone else. Ironically, a by-product of serving others is feeling wonderful yourself.

I remember sitting in an airport one day, waiting for my flight. I was excited because I'd been upgraded to first-class. And in first class the flight attendants are nicer, the food is edible, and there's room to stretch your legs so they're not curled up like a pretzel. In fact, I had the best seat on the entire plane. Seat 1A. Before boarding, I noticed a young lady who had several carry-on bags and was holding a crying baby. Having just finished reading a book on doing random acts of kindness, I heard my conscience speak to me, "You scumbag. Let her have your ticket." I fought these promptings for a while but eventually caved in:

"Excuse me, but you look like you could use this first-class ticket more than me. I know how hard it can be flying with kids. Why don't you let me trade you tickets?"

"Are you sure?"

"Oh yeah. I really don't mind. I'm just going to be working the whole time, anyway."

"Well, thank you. That's very kind of you," she said, as we swapped tickets.

As we boarded the plane, I was surprised at how good it made me feel to watch her sit down in seat 1A. In fact, under the circumstances, sitting way back near the bathrooms didn't seem that bad at all. At one point during the flight I was so curious to see how she was doing that I got up out of my seat, walked to the first-class section, and peeked in through the curtain that separates first class from coach. There she was with her baby, both asleep in big and comfortable seat 1A. And I felt like a million bucks. *Cha-ching.* I've got to keep doing this kind of thing.

This sweet story shared by a teen named Tawni is another example of the joy of service:

There is a girl in our neighborhood who lives in a duplex with her parents, and they don't have a lot of money. For the past three years, when I grew out of my clothes, me and my mom took them over to her. I'd say something like "I thought you might like these," or "I'd like to see you wearing this."

When she wore something I gave her, I'd think it was really cool. She would say, "Thank you so much for the new shirt." I'd reply, "That color looks really good on you!" I tried to be sensitive so that I didn't make her feel bad, or give her the impression that I thought she was poor. It makes me feel good, knowing that I'm helping her have a better life.

Go out of your way to invite the kid who sits alone in class out with you and your friends. Write an email or thank-you note to someone who has made a difference in your life, like a friend, a teacher, or a coach. The next time you're at a tollbooth, pay for the car behind you. Giving gives life not only to others but also to yourself. I love these lines from *The Man Nobody Knows* by Bruce Barton, which illustrate this point so well:

> *There are two seas in Palestine. One is fresh, and fish are in it. Splashes of green adorn its banks. Trees spread their branches over it and stretch out their thirsty roots to sip of its healing waters.*
>
> *The River Jordan makes this sea with sparkling water from the hills. So it laughs in the sunshine. And men build their houses near to it, and birds their nests; and every kind of life is happier because it is there.*
>
> *The River Jordan flows on south into another sea.*
>
> *Here is no splash of fish, no fluttering leaf, no song of birds, no children's laughter. Travelers choose another route, unless on urgent business. The air hangs heavy above its water, and neither man nor beast nor fowl will drink.*
>
> *What makes this mighty difference in these neighbor seas? Not the River Jordan. It empties the same good water into both. Not the soil in which they lie; not in the country round about.*
>
> *This is the difference. The Sea of Galilee receives but does not keep the Jordan. For every drop that flows into it another drop flows out. The giving and receiving go on in equal measure.*
>
> *The other sea is shrewder, hoarding its income jealously. It will not be tempted into any generous impulse. Every drop it gets, it keeps.*
>
> *The Sea of Galilee gives and lives. This other sea gives nothing. It is named the Dead.*
>
> *There are two kinds of people in this world. There are two seas in Palestine.*

• BE GENTLE WITH YOURSELF

Being gentle means many things. It means not expecting yourself to be perfect by tomorrow morning. If you're a late bloomer, as many of us are, be patient and allow yourself enough time to grow.

It means learning to laugh at the stupid things you do. I have a friend Chuck who's extraordinary when it comes to laughing at himself and never taking life too seriously. I've always been amazed at how his upbeat attitude attracts people to him, almost magnetically.

Being gentle also means forgiving yourself when you mess up. And who hasn't done that? We should learn from our mistakes, but we shouldn't beat ourselves up over them. The past is just that, past. Consider what went wrong and why. Learn, and make amends if you need to. Then drop it and move on. Throw that voodoo doll out with the trash.

"One of the keys to happiness," says Rita Mae Brown, "is a bad memory."

A ship at sea for many years picks up thousands of barnacles that attach themselves to the bottom of the ship and eventually weigh it down, becoming a threat to its safety. The easiest way to get rid of them is for the ship to harbor in a freshwater port, free of salt water. Here, the barnacles loosen on their own and fall off. The ship is then able to return to sea, relieved of its burden.

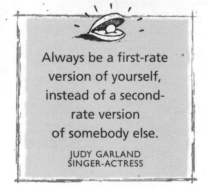

Always be a first-rate version of yourself, instead of a second-rate version of somebody else.

JUDY GARLAND
SINGER-ACTRESS

Are you carrying around barnacles in the form of mistakes, regrets, and pain from the past? Perhaps you need to allow yourself to soak in fresh water for a while. Hit the refresh button. Letting go of a burden and giving yourself a second chance may just be the deposit you need right now.

As Bruno Mars sings, "Life's too short to have regrets. . . . Only have one life to live, so you better make the best of it."

- ## BE HONEST

I Googled the word *honest* the other day and these are a few of the related words I found: upstanding, incorruptible, moral, principled, truth-loving, steadfast, true, real, right, good, straight-shooting, genuine. Not a bad set of words to be associated with, don't you think?

Honesty comes in many forms. First there's self-honesty. When people look at you, do they see the genuine article or do you appear through smoke and mirrors? I find that if I'm ever fake and try to be something I'm not, I feel unsure of myself and make a PBA withdrawal. I love how singer Judy Garland put it, "Always be a first-rate version of yourself, instead of a second-rate version of somebody else."

Then there's honesty in our actions. If you've been dishonest in the past, and I think we all have, try being honest, and notice how whole it makes you feel. It's a relief not to hide who you are, or to have to cover up your actions. This goes for your Internet persona, too. Just because people can't see you directly doesn't mean you can lie—after all, *you'll* know you're not telling the truth. Remember, you can't do wrong and feel right. This story by Jeff is a good example of that:

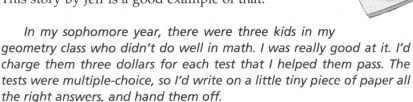

In my sophomore year, there were three kids in my geometry class who didn't do well in math. I was really good at it. I'd charge them three dollars for each test that I helped them pass. The tests were multiple-choice, so I'd write on a little tiny piece of paper all the right answers, and hand them off.

At first I felt like I was making money, kind of a nice job. I wasn't thinking about how it could hurt all of us. After a while I realized I shouldn't do that anymore, because they weren't learning anything, and it would only get harder down the road. Cheating certainly wasn't helping me.

It takes courage to be honest when people all around you seem to be getting away with cheating on tests, lying to their parents, and stealing from work. But, remember, every act of honesty is a deposit into your PBA and will build strength. As the saying goes, "My strength is as the strength of ten because my heart is pure." Honesty is always the best policy, even when it may not be popular.

● RENEW YOURSELF

You've gotta take time for yourself, to renew and to relax. If you don't you'll get burned-out and lose your zest for life.

It seems like half the planet has seen the movie *Avatar*, the highest grossing film of all time. Why was it so successful? Besides groundbreaking special effects and great filmmaking, I believe the story hits home because we all need to practice what it's preaching.

The story takes place in the year 2154 on Pandora, a forested moon in the Alpha Centauri star system, and revolves around the character of Jake Sully, a former Marine, now paralyzed, confined to a wheelchair, trapped and unfulfilled. Being able to mentally live through his "avatar"—a 10-foot tall replica of the planet's blue natives, he at first feels alive because he can run and enjoy a working body, even if only in his mind. But it quickly becomes much more than that. Meeting the natives, Jake falls in love with Neytiri, a female Na'vi native. The more time he spends with Neytiri and her people, the more he comes to see the beauty and peace and power of their world—a world Jake's loud, natural-resource-thirsty humans have come to pillage and plunder.

The message for us here is about rejuvenation, about unplugging, about taking time to listen to the natural world around us. It's about putting yourself in a self-imposed *time-out* once in a while.

Now you don't have to become a 10-foot-tall semi-human blue dude in order to find peace, but like Jake Sully, finding your own place to escape to, your own sanctuary of some kind, is essential. Go sit somewhere and ponder the clouds. Find a tree stump and listen to the wind or birds or maybe even the beating of your own heart. If you don't have access to a big cool glowing Tree of Souls like Jake,

maybe you can find a rooftop, a park bench, some piece of grass somewhere, just a place to be alone. Now all this might sound a bit hokey, but trust me, humans today live in a constant storm of stuff and we all need to take a deep breath and unplug occasionally, just to renew our spirits.

Theodore, from Canada, had his hideout:

Whenever I'd get too stressed out, or when I wasn't getting along with my parents, I'd just go into the basement. There I had a hockey stick, a ball, and a bare concrete wall on which I could take out my frustrations. I'd just shoot the ball for half an hour and go back upstairs refreshed. It did wonders for my hockey game, but it was even better for my family relationships.

Arian told me about his refuge. Whenever he got too stressed out, he would slip into his high school's large auditorium through a back door. All alone in the quiet, dark, and spacious auditorium, he could get away from all the hustle and bustle, have a good cry, or just relax.

Allison found a garden all her own:

My dad died in an industrial accident at work when I was little. I really don't know the details because I've always been afraid to ask my mother very many questions about it. Maybe it's because I've created this perfect picture of him in my mind that I don't want to change. To me he's this perfect human being who would protect me if he were here. He's with me all the time in my thoughts, and I imagine how he would act and help me if he was here.

When I really need him I go to the top of the slide at the local grade school playground. I have this silly feeling that if I can go to the highest place I will be able to feel him. So I climb up to the top of the slide and just lie there. I talk to him in my thoughts and I can feel him talking to my mind. I want him to touch me, but of course know that he cannot. I go there every time something really is bothering me and I just share my burdens with him.

Besides finding a place of refuge, there are so many other ways to renew yourself and build your PBA. Exercise can do it, like going for a walk, running, dancing, or kickboxing. Some teens have suggested watching old movies, talking to friends who crack you up, or recording music and making videos on your computer. Others have found that writing in their journals helps them cope.

Habit 7, Sharpen the Saw, is all about taking time to renew your body, heart, mind, and soul. We'll talk more about it when we get there. So hold your horses.

• MAGNIFY YOUR TALENTS

Finding and then developing a talent, hobby, or passion can be one of the single greatest deposits you can make into your PBA.

Why is it that when we think of talents we think in terms of the "traditional" high-profile talents, such as the athlete, dancer, or award-winning scholar? The truth is, talents come in a variety of packages. Don't think small. You may have a knack for reading, writing, or speaking. You may have a gift for rhythm, being hilarious, remembering details, or being accepting of others. You may have organizational, musical, or leadership skills. It doesn't matter where your talent may lie, whether it's chess, drama, or skateboarding, when you do something you like doing and have a talent for—it's exhilarating. It's a form of self-expression. And as this girl attests, it builds esteem.

You might die laughing when I tell you that I have a real talent and love for weeds. And I'm not talking about the kind you smoke but weeds and flowers that grow everywhere. I realized that I always noticed them, while others just wanted them cut down.

So I started picking them and pressing them—and eventually making beautiful pictures and postcards and art objects with them. I have been able to cheer many a sad soul with one of these personalized cards. I'm often asked to do arrangements of flowers for others and to share my knowledge of preserving pressed plants. It's given me so much joy and confidence—just knowing I have the special gift and appreciation for something most people ignore. But it even goes beyond that—it's taught me that if there's so much to just simple weeds, how much more is there to almost everything else in life? It's made me look deeper. It makes me an explorer.

My brother-in-law Bryce told me how developing a talent helped build his self-confidence and find a career in which he could make a difference. His story is set in the Teton mountain range that stretches high above the plains of Idaho and Wyoming. The Grand Teton, the tallest of the Teton peaks, juts 13,776 feet above sea level.

As a young boy, Bryce had the picture-perfect baseball swing. Until his tragic accident. While playing with a BB gun one day, Bryce accidentally shot himself in the eye. Fearing that surgery might permanently impair his vision, the doctors left the BB in his eye.

Months later, when Bryce returned to baseball, he began striking out each time at bat. He had lost his depth perception and much of his vision in one eye and could no longer judge the ball. Said Bryce, "I was an all-star player the year before and now I couldn't hit the ball. I was convinced that I would never be able to do anything again. It was a big blow to my confidence."

Bryce's two older brothers were good at so many things, and he wondered what he could do now, given his new handicap. Since he lived near the Tetons he decided to give climbing a try. So he dropped by the local Army store and bought nylon rope, carabiners, chalks, pitons, and other climbing necessities. He checked out climbing books and studied how to tie knots, hook up a harness, and rappel. His first real climbing experience was rappelling off his friend's chimney. Soon he began climbing some of the smaller peaks surrounding the Grand Teton.

Bryce soon realized that he had a knack for it. Unlike many of his climbing partners, his body was strong and lightweight and seemed to be perfectly built for rock climbing.

After training for several months, Bryce finally climbed the Grand Teton all by himself. It took him two days. Reaching this goal gave him a massive confidence boost.

He'd drive to the Tetons, run up to the base of the climb, do the climb, and run back down. Bryce got faster and stronger every time. Bryce's friend Kim noticed how seriously he took climbing, and told him, "Hey, you ought to go after the record on the Grand Teton."

Kim told Bryce all about it. A climbing ranger named Jock Glidden had set a record on the Grand by running to the top and back in four hours and eleven minutes. *That's absolutely impossible*, thought Bryce. *I'd like to meet this guy someday.* But as Bryce continued to do these types of runs, his times became faster and Kim kept saying, "You have to go after the record. I know you can do it."

On one occasion, Bryce finally met Jock, the superhuman with the insurmountable record. Bryce and Kim were sitting in Jock's tent when Kim, a well-known climber himself, said to Jock, "This guy here is thinking about going after your record." Jock gazed at Bryce's 125-pound frame and laughed aloud, as if to say, "Get a clue, you little runt." Bryce felt devastated but quickly gathered himself. And Kim kept affirming him: "You can do it. I know you can do it."

Early one morning, carrying a small orange backpack and a light jacket, Bryce ran to the top of the Grand and back in three hours, forty-seven minutes, and four seconds. He stopped only twice: once to take rocks out of his shoes and once to sign the register at the summit to prove he had been there. He felt utterly amazing. He'd not only broken the record, he'd shattered it!

A few years later, Bryce received a surprise call from Kim. "Bryce, have you heard? Your record has just been broken." Of course, he added, "You need to get it back. I know you can do it!" A man named Creighton King, who had recently won the heralded Pike's Peak Marathon in Colorado, dashed to the top and back in three hours, thirty minutes, and nine seconds.

Two years after his last assault on the mountain, and ten days after his record had been broken, Bryce stood in the Lupine Meadows parking lot at the base of the Grand Teton in brand-new running shoes, ready and eager to break King's record. With him were friends, family, Kim, and a crew from the local television station to film his run.

As before, he knew the hardest part of the climb would be the mental aspect. He obviously did *not* want to become one of the two or three who die each year while attempting to scale the Grand.

Sportswriter Russell Weeks describes running the Grand as follows: "From the parking lot you face a run of about nine or ten miles up switchback trails, through a canyon, up two glacial moraines, two saddles, a gap between two peaks, and a 700-foot climb up the west wall of the Grand to the top. The rise and fall in altitude from Lupine Meadows to the top and back is about 15,000 feet. Leigh Ortenburger's *Climber's Guide to the Teton Range* lists the last 700 feet alone as a three-hour climb."

Bryce took off running. As he ascended up, up, up the mountain, his heart pounded and his legs burned. Concentration was intense. Scaling the last 700 feet in twelve minutes, he reached the summit in one hour and fifty-three minutes and placed his verification card under a rock. He knew that if he were to break King's record he would have to do it coming down. The descent became so steep at times that he was taking ten- to fifteen-foot strides. He passed some friends who later told him his face had turned purple from oxygen depletion. Another climbing party apparently knew he was going for the record because, as he passed, they yelled, "Go! Go!"

Amid cheers, Bryce returned to Lupine Meadows with bleeding knees, thrashed tennis shoes, and one horrific headache, three hours, six minutes, and twenty-five seconds after he had left. He had done the impossible!

Word spread fast and Bryce became known as the fastest climber in the West. "It gave me an identity," said Bryce. "Everyone wants to be known for something, and so did I. My ability to climb gave me something to work for and was a great source of  self-esteem. It was my way of expressing myself."

Today, Bryce is founder and president of a very successful company that makes high-performance backpacks for climbers and mountain runners. Most important, Bryce has found a way to make a living doing what he loves to do. It's what he's good at, and he's used this talent to bless his life and the lives of many others.

Oh, by the way, the record still stands. (Now, don't get any wild ideas.) And Bryce still has that BB in his eye.

So, my friends, if you need a shot of confidence, start making some deposits into your PBA starting today. You'll feel the results instantly. And, remember, you don't have to climb a mountain to make a deposit. There are, oh I don't know, a billion and one safer ways.

★★★

COMING ATTRACTIONS

Up ahead we'll talk about the many ways in which you and your dog are different. Read on and you'll see what I mean!

Keep Promises to Yourself

1 Get up when your alarm goes off. Don't hit the snooze button or turn the alarm off and go back to sleep.

2 Identify one easy task that needs to be done today, like practicing the piano, putting in a batch of laundry, or finishing a book for an English assignment. Decide when you will do it. Then keep your word and do it.

Do Random Acts of Service

3 Sometime today, do a kind deed anonymously, like taking out the trash, fixing your mom's laptop, or making someone's bed.

4 Organize a "positive social media attack." Get your friends to attack someone via social media with kind words and compliments.

Magnify Your Talents

5 List a talent you would like to develop this year. Write down specific steps to get there.

Talent I want to develop this year: ....

How do I get there: ....

....

....

....

6 Make a list of the talents you most admire in other people.

Person: Talents I admire:

Be Gentle with Yourself

7 Think about an area of life you feel inferior in. Now breathe deeply and remind yourself, "It's not the end of the world."

8 Go an entire day without negative self-talk. Each time you catch yourself putting yourself down, you have to replace it with three positive thoughts about yourself. Try it.

Renew Yourself

9 Decide on a fun activity that will lift your spirits and do it today. For example, turn up the music and dance.

10 Feeling lethargic? Get up right now and go for a fast walk around the block.

Be Honest

11 The next time someone asks you about what you're up to, or what you're feeling, share the complete story. Don't leave out information meant to mislead or deceive.

12 For one day, try not to exaggerate or embellish! Good luck!

HABIT ①

Be Proactive

I Am the Force

Growing up in my home was at times a big pain. Why? Because my dad always made me take responsibility for everything in my life.

Whenever I said something like "Dad, my girlfriend makes me so mad," without fail Dad would come back with: "Now come on, Sean, no one can make you mad unless you let them. It's your choice. You choose to be mad."

> People are just about as happy as they make up their mind to be.
>
> ABRAHAM LINCOLN
> U.S. PRESIDENT

Or if I said, "My new biology teacher is the worst. I'm never going to learn a thing," Dad would say, "Why don't you go to your teacher and give him some suggestions? Change teachers. Find a tutor if you have to. If you don't learn biology, Sean, it's your own fault, not your teacher's."

He never let me off the hook. He was always challenging me, making sure that I never blamed someone else for the way I acted. Luckily my mom let me blame other people and things for my problems or I might have turned out psycho.

I often screamed back, "You're wrong, Dad! I didn't choose to be mad. She MADE, MADE, *MADE* me mad. Just get off my back and leave me alone."

You see, Dad's idea that you are responsible for your life was hard medicine for me to swallow as a teenager. But, with hindsight, I see the wisdom in what he was doing. He wanted me to learn that there are two types of people in this world—the proactive and the reactive—those who take responsibility for their lives and those who blame; those who make it happen and those who get happened to.

Habit 1, Be Proactive, is the key to unlocking all the other habits and that's why it comes first. Habit 1 says "*I* am the force. I am the captain of my life. I can choose my attitude. I'm responsible for my own happiness or unhappiness. I am in the driver's seat of my destiny, not just a passenger."

Being proactive is the first step toward achieving the private victory. Can you imagine doing algebra before learning addition and subtraction? Not gonna happen. The same goes for the 7 Habits. You can't do Habits 2, 3, 4, 5, 6, and 7 before doing Habit 1. That's because until you feel you are in charge of your own life, nothing else is really possible, now, is it? Hmmmm . . .

Proactive or Reactive ... the Choice Is Yours

Each day you and I get about 100 chances to choose whether to be proactive or reactive. In any given day, the weather is bad, you get a mean text, you can't find a job, your sister steals your hoodie, you lose an election at school, your friend talks behind your back, someone graffities your locker, your parents don't let you take the car (for no reason), you get a parking ticket, and you flunk a test. So what're you going to do about it? Are you in the habit of reacting to these kinds of everyday things, or are you proactive? The choice is yours. It really is. You don't have to respond the way everyone else does, or the way people think you should.

How many times have you been driving down the road when suddenly somebody cuts in front of you, making you hit the brakes? What do you do? Scream at them? Swear? Flip them the bird? Let it ruin your day? Or do you just let it go? Laugh about it. Move on.

The choice is yours.

Reactive people make choices based on impulse. They are like a can of soda pop. When life shakes them up a bit, the pressure builds and they suddenly explode.

Reactive ▼

▲ Proactive

"Hey, you stupid jerk! Get out of my lane!"

Proactive people make choices based on values. They *think* before they act. They recognize they can't control everything that happens to them, but they can control *what they do about it.* Unlike reactive people who are full of carbonation, proactive people are like water. Shake them up all you want, take off the lid, and nothing. No fizzing, no bubbling, no pressure. They stay calm, cool, and in control.

"I'm not going to let that guy get me upset and ruin my day."

The best way to understand the proactive mind-set is to compare proactive and reactive responses to situations that happen all the time.

Scene One

You see pictures on Facebook of your best friend at a party the night she said she was too busy to hang out with you. She doesn't know you saw the photos. Just five minutes ago, this same friend was sweet-talking you right to your face. You feel hurt and betrayed.

Reactive choices

- Chew her out. Shove past her as you storm off.
- Go into a deep depression because you feel so bad about her leaving you out.
- Decide that she's a two-faced liar and give her the silent treatment.
- Go out of your way to exclude her. After all, she did it to you.

Proactive choices

- Forgive her and give her a second chance.
- Confront her and share how you feel that she lied to you.
- Realize that she has weaknesses just like you and that occasionally you don't include her in things without really meaning any harm.

Scene Two

You've been working at your retail job for a while now and have been completely committed and dependable. Recently, a new employee joined the crew and he gets the coveted Saturday afternoon shift—the shift you were hoping for.

Reactive choices

- Spend half your waking hours complaining to everyone and their dog about how unfair this decision was.
- Scrutinize the new employee and find his every weakness.
- Text your boss messages asking why he doesn't like you.
- Begin to slack off while working your shift.

Proactive choices

- Talk with your supervisor about why the new employee got the better shift, or if you and he can alternate.
- Continue to be a hard-working employee so you get the next promotion.
- Learn what you can do to improve your performance.
- If you determine you are in a dead-end job, begin looking for a new one.

• LISTEN TO YOUR LANGUAGE

You can usually tell the difference between proactive and reactive people by the language they use. Reactive language usually sounds like this:

"That's me. That's just the way I am." What they're really saying is, *I'm not responsible for the way I act. I can't change. I was predetermined to be this way.*

"If my chem teacher wasn't such a jerk, things would be different." What they're really saying is, *School is the cause of all my problems, not me.*

"Thanks a lot. You just ruined my day." What they're really saying is, *I'm not in control of my own moods. You are.*

"If only I went to a different school, had better friends, had cooler parents, had a boyfriend . . . then I'd be happy." What they're really saying is, *I'm not in control of my own happiness, "things" are. I must have things to be happy.*

Notice that reactive language takes power away from you and gives it to something or someone else. As my friend John Bytheway explains in his book *What I Wish I'd Known in High School*, when you're reactive it's like giving someone else the remote control to your life and saying, "Here, change my mood anytime you wish." Proactive language, on the other hand, puts the remote control back into your own hands. You're free to choose which channel you want to be on.

REACTIVE LANGUAGE	PROACTIVE LANGUAGE
I'll try	*I'll do it*
That's just the way I am	*I can do better than that*
There's nothing I can do	*Let's look at all our options*
I have to	*I choose to*
I can't	*There's gotta be a way*
You ruined my day	*I'm not going to let your bad mood rub off on me*

• THE VICTIMITIS VIRUS

Some people suffer from a contagious virus I call "victimitis." Perhaps you've seen it. People infected with victimitis believe that everyone has it in for them and that the world owes them something . . . which isn't the case at all. I like the way author Mark Twain put it: "Don't go around saying the world owes you a living. The world owes you nothing. It was here first."

I played college football with a guy who had a bad case of victimitis. His comments drove me crazy:

"I would be starting, but the coaches have something against me."

"I was about to intercept the ball, but somebody cut me off."

"I would have got a better 40-yard-dash time, but my shoes came loose."

"Yeah, right," I always felt like saying. "And I'd be President if my dad weren't bald." To me, it was obvious why he never played. In his mind, the problem was always "out there." He never considered that perhaps *his* attitude was the problem.

Adreana, an honor student from Chicago, grew up in a home where feeling victimized caused a lot of tension:

I'm black and proud of it. Color has not stood in my way and I learn so much from white and black teachers and counselors alike. But in my own home it's a different thing. My mother, who dominates the family, is fifty years old, came from the South, and still acts as though slavery was just abolished. She sees my doing good in school as a threat, as if I am joining the "white folks." She still uses language like "the man is keeping us from doing this and that. He is keeping us boxed up and won't let us do anything."

I always rebut with "No man is keeping you from doing anything, only yourself, because you keep thinking the way you think." Even my boyfriend falls into the white-man-is-holding-me-back attitude. When he was recently trying to purchase a car and the sale didn't go through, he remarked with frustration, "The white man doesn't want us to get anything." I almost lost it and confronted him with how silly that kind of thinking was. But it only resulted in him feeling that I was taking the side of the white man.

I remain convinced that the only person who can hold you back is yourself.

Besides feeling like victims, reactive people:
- Are easily offended
- Blame others
- Get angry and say things they later regret

- Criticize and complain
- Wait for things to happen to them
- Change only when they have to

• IT PAYS TO BE PROACTIVE

Proactive people are a different breed. Proactive people:
- Can brush things off without getting offended
- Take responsibility for their choices
- Think before they act
- Bounce back when something bad happens
- Always find a way to move forward
- Focus on things they can do something about, and don't worry about things they can't

I remember starting a new job and working with a guy named Randy. I don't know what his problem was, but for some reason he didn't like me—and he wanted me to know it. He'd say rude things to me daily. I mean, like, *all the time*. Once I returned from vacation and a friend told me, "Boy, Sean, if you only knew what Randy has been saying about you. You'd better watch your back."

Having a nemesis is a drag. There were times I wanted to pound the guy, but I somehow managed to keep my cool and ignore him. Whenever he insulted me, I made it a personal challenge to treat him well in return. I had faith that things would work out in the end if I acted this way.

In a matter of a few months things began to change. Randy could see that I wasn't going to play his game and began to lighten up. He even told me one time, "I've tried to offend you, but you won't take offense." After being at the company for about a year, we became friends and gained respect for each other. Had I reacted to his attacks, which was my gut instinct, I'm certain we wouldn't be friends today. (I'm also certain that at least one of us would've wound up missing a few teeth.) Often all it takes is one person to create a friendship.

Mary Beth discovered for herself the benefits of being proactive:

I'd taken a class at school where we'd talked about proactivity, and I'd wondered about how to really apply it. One day as I was checking groceries for a guy, he suddenly told me that the groceries I had just rung up weren't his. My first reaction was to say, "You idiot," then put the bar down between the other customer's groceries. "Why didn't you stop me sooner?" So I have to delete it all and call to get the changes approved by a supervisor while he just stands there and thinks it's funny. Meanwhile the air is rising and I'm getting real irritated. To top it off he then has the nerve to question the price I charged him for the broccoli.

To my horror, I discovered that he was right. I had put the wrong code numbers in the register for the broccoli. Now I was extra irritated and so tempted to lash out at him to cover for my own mistake. But then this idea popped into my mind: "Be Proactive."

So I said, "You're right, sir. It's completely my fault. I'll correct the pricing. It will just take a couple of seconds." I also remembered that being proactive doesn't mean you're a doormat, so I reminded him nicely that to avoid this kind of thing in the future he would need to always put the bar down that separates orders.

It felt so good. I had apologized, but I had also said what I wanted to say. It was such a simple little thing, but it gave me such inner conversion and confidence in this habit.

At this point you're probably ready to shoot me and say, "Now come on, Sean. It's not that easy." I won't argue with you. Being reactive is way, way easier. It's easy to lose your cool. That doesn't take any control. And it's easy to whine and complain. Without question, though, being proactive is the higher road and one that will take you much farther in the not-so-long run.

But, remember, you don't have to be perfect. In reality, you and I aren't either completely proactive or reactive but probably somewhere in between. The key then is to get in the habit of being proactive so you can run on autopilot and not even have to think about it. If you're choosing to be proactive 20 out of 100 times on average each day, try doing it 30 out of 100 times. Then 40. Never underestimate the huge difference small changes can make.

● WE CAN CONTROL ONLY ONE THING

The fact is, we can't control everything that happens to us. We can't control where our ancestors came from, who will win the Superbowl, how much tuition will be next fall, or how others might treat us. But there is one thing we *can* control: *how we respond to what happens to us.* And that is what counts! This is why we need to stop worrying about things we can't control and start worrying about things we *can.*

Picture two circles. The inner circle is our circle of control. It includes things we have control over—ourselves, our attitudes, our choices, our response to whatever happens to us. Surrounding the circle of control is the circle of no control. It includes the thousands of things we can't do anything about.

Now, what will happen if we spend our time and energy worrying about things we can't control, like a rude comment, a past mistake, or the fact that it's raining on a good hair day? You guessed It! We'll feel even more out of control, as if we were victims. For instance, if your sister annoys you and you're always complaining about her weaknesses (something you have control over), that won't do anything to fix the problem. It'll only cause you to blame your problems on her and lose power yourself. Ignore the rude comment, avoid making the mistake next time, and get an umbrella for the rain. You are the star of your own life. Focus on what you can influence.

Renatha told me a story that illustrates this point. A week before her upcoming volleyball game, she learned that the mother of a player on the opposing team had made fun of Renatha's volleyball skills. Instead of ignoring the comments, Renatha became angry and spent the rest of the week stewing. When the game arrived, her only goal was to prove to this woman that she was a good player. To make a long story short, Renatha played poorly, spent much of her time on the bench, and her team lost the game. She was so focused on something she couldn't control (a stranger's opinion of her) that she lost control of the only thing she could control, herself.

Proactive people, on the other hand, focus elsewhere . . . on the things they *can* control. By doing so they experience inner peace and are primed for whatever comes their way. They learn to live with the many things they can't do anything about, even to smile and laugh about them. They may not like them, but they know it's no use worrying.

• TURNING SETBACKS INTO TRIUMPHS

Life often deals us a bad hand but it's up to you to think to yourself: "I've got this. I can get through it." By the way, think of how boring you'd be if nothing challenging ever happened to you—you'd never learn, and then you'd never change! Every setback is an opportunity for us to turn it into a triumph, as this account by Brad Lemley from *Parade* magazine illustrates:

"It's not what happens to you in life, it's what you do about it," says W. Mitchell, a self-made millionaire, a sought-after speaker, a former mayor, a river rafter, and skydiver. And he accomplished all this after his accidents.

If you saw Mitchell you'd find this hard to believe. You see, this guy's face is a patchwork of multicolored skin grafts, the fingers of both his hands are either missing or mere stubs, and his paralyzed legs lie thin and useless under his slacks. Mitchell says sometimes people try to guess how he was injured. A car wreck? Vietnam? The real story is more astounding than one could ever imagine. On June 19, 1971, he was on top of the world—young, healthy, and popular. The day before, he had bought a beautiful new motorcycle. That morning, he soloed in an airplane for the first time.

"That afternoon, I got on that motorcycle to ride to work," he recalls, "and at an intersection, a laundry truck and I collided. The bike went down, crushed my elbow and fractured my pelvis, and the gas can popped open on the motorcycle. The gas poured out, the heat of the engine ignited it, and I got burned over 65 percent of my body." Fortunately, a quick-thinking man in a nearby car lot doused Mitchell with a fire extinguisher and saved his life.

Even so, Mitchell's face had been burned off, his fingers were black, charred, and twisted, his legs were nothing but raw, red flesh. It was common for first-time visitors to look at him and faint. He was unconscious for two weeks, and then he awakened.

Over four months, he had 13 transfusions, 16 skin-graft operations, and several other surgeries. Four years later, after spending months in rehabilitation and years learning to adapt to his new handicaps, the unthinkable happened. Mitchell was involved in a freak airplane crash, and was paralyzed from the waist down. "When I tell people there were two separate accidents," he says, "they can hardly stand it."

After his paralyzing plane crash accident, Mitchell recalls meeting a nineteen-year-old patient in the hospital's gymnasium. "This guy had also been paralyzed. He had been a mountain climber, a skier, an active outdoors person, and he was convinced his life was over. Finally, I went over to this guy and said, 'You know something? Before all this happened to me, there were 10,000 things I could do. Now there are 9,000. I could spend the rest of my life dwelling on the 1,000 that I lost, but I choose to focus on the 9,000 that are left.'"

Mitchell says his secret is twofold. First is the love and encouragement of friends and family, and second is a personal philosophy he has gleaned from various sources. He realized he did not have to buy into society's notion that one must be handsome and healthy to be happy. "I am in charge of my own spaceship," he states emphatically. "It is my up, my down. I could choose to see this situation as a setback or a starting point."

I like how Helen Keller put it, "So much has been given to me. I have no time to ponder that which has been denied."

Although most of our setbacks won't be as severe as Mitchell's, all of us will have our fair share. You might get dumped, you may lose an election at school, you may get beaten up, you may not get accepted to the school of your choice, you may become seriously ill. I hope and believe that you will be proactive and strong in these defining moments.

I remember a major setback of my own. Two years after I had become the starting quarterback in college, I seriously injured my knee, had surgery, fell behind, and subsequently lost my position. Coach called me into his office just before the season began and told me they were handing the starting job to someone else.

I felt sick. I'd worked my whole life to get to this position. It was my senior year. This *wasn't* supposed to happen.

As a backup, I had a choice to make. I could complain, badmouth the new guy, and feel sorry for myself. Or . . . I could make the most of the situation.

Luckily, I decided to deal with it. I was no longer throwing touchdowns, but I could help in other ways. So I swallowed my pride and kept supporting the team, working hard and preparing for each game as if I were the starter. I chose to keep my chin up.

Was it easy? Not at *all*. I often felt like a failure. Sitting out every game after being the starter was humiliating. Keeping a good attitude was a constant struggle.

Was it the right choice, though? Definitely. I wore out my bum on the bench all year but I contributed to the team in other ways by supporting the new guy and helping to prepare our defense each week for the opposing team's offense. Most important, I took responsibility for my attitude. I cannot begin to tell you what a positive difference this singular decision made in my life.

● **RISING ABOVE ABUSE**

One of the most intense and difficult setbacks of all is coping with abuse. I'll never forget the morning I spent with a group of teens— mostly young women, but also some young men—who had been sexually abused as children, were victims of date rape, or were otherwise abused emotionally or physically.

Heather told me this story:

I was sexually abused at fourteen. It happened when I was at a fair. A boy from school came up to me and said, "I really need to talk to you, come with me for a few minutes." I never suspected anything because this kid was my friend and had always been really nice to me. He took me on a long walk and we ended up down at the dugouts at the high school. That was where he raped me.

He kept telling me, "If you tell anyone, no one will believe you. You wanted this to happen to you anyway." He also told me that my parents would be so ashamed of me. I kept quiet about it for two years.

Finally, I was attending a help session where people who were abused told their stories and this one girl got up and told a story similar to mine. When she said the name of the boy that abused her, I started to cry because it was the same one who had raped me. It turned out that there were six of us who were victimized by him.

Fortunately, Heather is now on the road to recovery and has found tremendous strength in being part of a teen group that is trying to help other abuse victims. By coming forward, she put a stop to more girls getting attacked by the same boy. *That* is a proactive and powerful act.

Bridgett's story, unfortunately, is very common:

At the age of five I was sexually abused by a family member. Too afraid to tell anyone I tried to bury my hurt and anger. Now that I have come to terms with what happened, I look back on my life and can see how it has affected everything. In trying to hide something terrible I ended up hiding myself. It wasn't until thirteen years later that I finally confronted my childhood nightmare.

Many people have been through the same experience as I have or something that is related. Most hide it. Why? Some are afraid for their lives. Others want to protect themselves or someone else. But whatever the reason, hiding it isn't the answer. It only leaves a cut so deep in the soul that it seems that there's no way of healing it. Confronting it is the only way to sew up that bleeding gash. Find someone to talk to, someone you feel comfortable with, someone you can trust. It is a long and difficult process, but once you come to terms with it, it's only then that you can start to live.

If you've been abused, it's *never* your fault. And the truth has to be told. Abuse thrives in secrecy. By telling another person, you immediately lighten the load you carry. Talk with a loved one or friend you can trust, go to sexual-abuse support meetings, or visit a professional therapist. If the first person you share your troubles with isn't receptive, don't give up—keep sharing until you find someone who is. Sharing your secret with another is an important step in the healing process. Take the initiative to do it. You don't need to live with this burden for one day longer. (Please refer to the abuse hotlines listed at the back of the book for help or information.)

HABIT 1

● BECOMING A CHANGE AGENT

I once asked a group of teenagers, *Who are your role models?* One girl mentioned her mother. Another kid talked about his brother. One guy was noticeably silent. I asked him whom he admired. He said quietly, "I don't have a role model." All he wanted to do was make sure he didn't turn out like the people who should have been his role models. Unfortunately, this is the case with many teens. They come from messed-up families and may not have anyone to pattern their lives after.

The scary thing is that bad habits such as abuse, alcoholism, and welfare dependency are often passed down from parents to kids, and, as a result, dysfunctional families keep repeating themselves. Sometimes these problems go back for generations. You may come from a long line of alcohol or drug abusers. You may come from a long line of dependency on welfare. Perhaps no one in your family has ever graduated from college or even high school.

The good news is that you can stop the cycle. Because you are proactive, you can stop these bad habits and circumstances from being passed on. You can become a "change agent" and pass on good habits to future generations, starting with your own kids.

A tenacious girl named Hilda shared with me how she has become her family's change agent. Education wasn't a priority in her home; there were too many other things to worry about. Says Hilda: "My mom worked in a sewing factory for very little money, and my father worked for slightly over minimum wage. I would hear them arguing over the money and how they were going to pay the rent. The highest grade my parents went to in school was the sixth grade."

Whether I fail
or succeed shall be
no man's doing
but my own.
I am the force.

ELAINE MAXWELL

As a young girl, Hilda vividly remembers her dad being unable to help her with her homework because he couldn't read English. This was hard on her, and she could see the consequences of a lack of education.

When Hilda was in junior high, her family moved from California back to Mexico. Hilda soon realized that there were limited educational options for her there, so she asked if she could move back to the States to live with her aunt. For the next several years Hilda made great sacrifices to stay in school.

"It was hard to be crowded into a room with my cousin," she says, "and have to share a bed and work to pay them rent as well as go to school, but it was worth it.

"Even though I had a kid and got married in high school, I kept going to school and working toward finishing my education. I wanted to prove to my dad that no matter what, he was wrong when he said than no one in our family could become a professional."

Hilda will soon be graduating with a university degree in finance. She wants her educational values to be passed on to her kids: "Today, every time I can, when I am not in school, I sit on the sofa and I read to my son. I am teaching him how to speak English and Spanish. I'm trying to save money for his education. One day he will need help with his homework, and I will be there to help him."

I interviewed another sixteen-year-old kid named Shane from

the Midwest who is also becoming a change agent in his family. Shane lives with his parents and two siblings in the projects, a low-income section of town. Although his parents are still together, they're constantly fighting and accusing each other of having affairs. His dad drives a truck and is never home. His mom smokes weed with his twelve-year-old sister. His older brother failed two years of high school and finally dropped out. At one point Shane had lost hope.

Just when he'd thought he'd hit rock bottom, he got involved in a character development class at school (that taught the 7 Habits), and he began to see that there were things he could do to seize control of his life and create a future for himself.

Fortunately, Shane's grandfather owned the upstairs apartment where Shane's family lived, so Shane paid him one hundred dollars a month rent, and he moved to that apartment. He now has his own sanctuary and is able to block out everything he doesn't want to be part of on the floor below. Says Shane: "Things have gotten better now. I treat myself better and I show myself respect. My family doesn't have very much respect for themselves. Although nobody in my family has ever gone to college, I have been accepted to three different universities. Everything I do now is for my future. My future is going to be different. I know I won't sit down with my twelve-year-old daughter and smoke weed."

You have the power within you to rise above whatever may have been passed down to you. You may not have the option of moving upstairs to escape from it all as Shane did, but you can figuratively move upstairs in your mind. No matter how bad your predicament is, you can become a change agent and create a new life for yourself and whatever may follow.

● GROWING YOUR PROACTIVE MUSCLES

The following poem is a great summary of what it means to take responsibility for one's life and how a person can gradually move from a reactive to a proactive frame of mind.

AUTOBIOGRAPHY IN
FIVE SHORT CHAPTERS

From *There's a Hole in My Sidewalk*
by Portia Nelson

I
I walk down the street.
There is a deep hole in the sidewalk.
I fall in.
I am lost . . . I am helpless.
It isn't my fault.
It takes forever to find a way out.

II
I walk down the same street.
There is a deep hole in the sidewalk.
I pretend I don't see it.
I fall in again.
I can't believe I am in the same place.
But, it isn't my fault.
It still takes a long time to get out.

III
I walk down the same street.
There is a deep hole in the sidewalk.
I see it is there.
I still fall in. It's a habit.
My eyes are open.
I know where I am.
It is my fault. I get out immediately.

IV
I walk down the same street.
There is a deep hole in the sidewalk.
I walk around it.

V
I walk down another street.

You, too, can take responsibility for your life and stay away from potholes by flexing your proactive muscles. It's a "breakthrough" habit that will save your you-know-what more often than you could ever imagine!

NOTHING CAN HURT "PROACTIVE MAN"!

- ### CAN-DO

Being proactive really means two things. First, you take responsibility for your life. Second, you have a "can-do" attitude. Can-do is very different from "no-can-do." Just take a peek.

CAN-DO PEOPLE	NO-CAN-DO PEOPLE
Take initiative to make it happen	Wait for something to happen to them
Think about solutions and options	Think about problems and barriers
Act	Are acted upon

If you think can-do, and you're creative and persistent, it's amazing what you can accomplish. During college, I remember being told that to fulfill my language requirement, I would "have to" take a class that I had no interest in and was meaningless to me. Instead of taking this class, however, I decided to create my own. So I put together a list of books I would read and the assignments I would do and found a teacher to sponsor me. I then went to the dean of the school and presented my case. He bought into my idea and I completed my language requirement by taking my self-built course.

American aviator Elinor Smith once said, "It has long since come to my attention that people of accomplishment rarely sat back and let things happen to them. They went out and happened to things."

It's so true. To reach your goals in life, you must seize the initiative. If you're feeling bad about not being asked out on dates, don't just sit around and sulk, do something about it. Find ways to meet people. Be friendly and try smiling a lot. Ask *them* out. They may not know how great you are.

Don't wait for that perfect job to fall in your lap, go after it. Be bold. Send out your résumé, network with people you admire, gain experience by volunteering to work for free.

If you're at a store and need assistance, don't wait for the salesperson to find you, you find them.

Some people mistake can-do for being pushy, aggressive, or obnoxious. Wrong. Can-do is courageous, persistent, and smart. Others think can-do people stretch the rules and make their own laws. Not so. Can-do thinkers are creative, enterprising, and extremely resourceful.

Pia, a friend of mine, shared the following story. It took place a long time ago, but the principle of can-do is the same:

I was a young journalist in a big city in Europe, working full-time as a reporter for United Press International. I was inexperienced and always nervous that I wouldn't be able to live up to the expectations of a tough and much older male press crew. The Beatles were coming to town, and to my amazement I was appointed to cover their stay. (My editor didn't know how big they were.) They were the hottest thing in Europe in those days. Girls fainted by the hundreds just by their presence, and here I was going to cover their press conference.

The press conference was exciting and I was elated to be there, but I realized that everyone would have the same story—I needed something more, something meaty, something that really would make front page. One by one, all the experienced reporters went back to their papers to report and the Beatles went up to their rooms. I stayed behind. I've got to figure out a way to get to these guys, I thought. And there's no time to lose.

I walked to the hotel lobby, picked up the house phone, and dialed the penthouse. I guessed they would be staying there. Their manager answered. "This is Pia Jensen from United Press International. I would like to come talk to the Beatles," I said confidently. (What did I have to lose?)

To my amazement he said, "Come on up."

Trembling and feeling like I had hit the jackpot, I entered the elevator and went up to the royal suites of the hotel. I was led into an area as big as an entire floor—and here they all sat, Ringo, Paul, John, and George. I gulped down my nervousness and inexperience and tried to act like a world-class reporter.

I spent the next two hours laughing, listening, talking, writing, and having the best time of my life. They treated me royally and gave me all the attention in the world!

My story was splashed on the front page of the leading newspaper in the country the next morning. And my more extended interviews with each of the Beatles appeared as a feature in most of the newspapers of the world within the next few days. When the Rolling Stones came to town after that—guess who they sent? Me, a young, female, inexperienced reporter. I used the same approach with them and it worked again. I soon realized what I could accomplish by being pleasantly persistent. A pattern was set in my mind, and I was convinced anything was possible. With this approach, I usually got the best story, and my news career took on a new dimension.

George Bernard Shaw, the English playwright, knew all about can-do. Listen to how he said it: "People are always blaming their circumstances for what they are. I don't believe in circumstances. The people who get on in this world are the people who get up and look for the circumstances they want, and if they can't find them, make them."

Pay attention to how Denise was able to create the circumstances she wanted:

I know it's strange for a teenager to want to work in a library, but I really wanted that job—more than I had ever wanted anything, but they weren't hiring. I would go to the library every day and read, hang out with my friends, and just get away from home—what better place to work than someplace I already hung out at? Although I didn't have a job there, I got to know the office staff, and I volunteered for special events and pretty soon I was one of the regulars. It paid off. When they finally had an opening, I was their first choice, and I found one of the best jobs I ever had.

• JUST PUSH PAUSE

So when someone is rude to you, where do you get the power to resist being rude back? For starters, just push pause. Yep, just reach up and push the pause button to your life just as you would on your remote control. (If I remember right, the pause button is found somewhere in the middle of your forehead.) Sometimes life is moving so fast that we instantly react to everything out of sheer habit. If you can learn to pause, get control, and think about how you want to respond, you'll make smarter decisions.

Yes, your childhood, your parents, your genes, and your environment *influence you* to act in certain ways, but they can't *make you* do anything. Your life is not predetermined and you are free to choose.

While your life is on pause, open up your toolbox (the one that you were born with) and use your four human tools to help you decide what to do. Animals don't have these tools and that's why you're smarter than your dog. These tools are self-awareness, conscience, imagination, and willpower. You might want to call them your power tools.

SELF-AWARENESS: *I can stand apart from myself and observe my thoughts and actions.*

CONSCIENCE: *I can listen to my inner voice to know right from wrong.*

IMAGINATION: *I can envision new possibilities.*

WILLPOWER: *I have the power to choose.*

Let's illustrate these tools by imagining a teen named Rosa and her dog, Woof, as they go for a walk:

"Here, boy. Let's go outside," says Rosa as Woof leaps up and down, wagging his tail.

It's been a rough week for Rosa. Not only has she just broken up with her boyfriend, Eric, but she and her mom are barely on speaking terms.

As she strolls down the sidewalk, Rosa begins thinking about the past week. "You know what?" she muses to herself. "Breaking up with Eric has really been tough on me. It's probably why I've been so rude to Mom and taking out all my frustrations on her."

You see what Rosa is doing? She's standing apart from herself and evaluating and measuring her actions. This process is called **self-awareness.** *It's a tool that is native to all humanoids. By using her self-awareness, Rosa is able to recognize that she's allowing her breakup with Eric to affect her relationship with her mom. This observation is the first step to changing the way she has been treating her mother.*

Meanwhile, Woof sees a cat up ahead and instinctively takes off in a frenzy after it.

Although Woof is a loyal dog, he is completely unaware of himself. He doesn't even know that he is a dog. He is incapable of standing apart from himself and saying, "You know what? Ever since Suzy (his dog friend next door) moved, I've been taking out my anger on all the neighborhood cats."

As she continues her stroll, Rosa's thoughts begin to wander. She can hardly wait for the school concert tomorrow, when she will be performing a solo. Music is her life. Rosa imagines herself singing at the concert. She sees herself dazzling the audience, then bowing to receive a rousing standing ovation from all of her friends and teachers . . . and, of course, all the cute guys.

*In this scene, Rosa is using another one of her human tools, **imagination**. It is a remarkable gift. It allows us to escape our present circumstances and create new possibilities in our heads. It gives us a chance to visualize our futures and dream up what we would like to become.*

While Rosa is imagining visions of grandeur, Woof is busily digging up the earth trying to get at a worm.

Woof's imagination is about as alive as a rock. Zilch. He can't think beyond the moment. He can't envision new possibilities. Can you imagine Woof thinking, "Someday, I'm going to have my own dream dog house with a revolving door and a large bay window"?

GARFIELD © 1981 Paws, Inc. Reprinted with permission of UNIVERSAL PRESS SYNDICATE. All rights reserved.

Suddenly, Rosa feels a vibration in her pocket. She gets a text from her new friend Taylor. "Hiii, whatcha doin'?"

"Hey! Takin' Woof for a walk" replies Rosa.

Just then she gets another message: "I heard about what happened with u & Eric. Major bummer."

Rosa is bothered by Taylor's reference to Eric. It's none of her business. Although she is tempted to be curt with Taylor, she knows Taylor is just trying to get to know her better and doesn't mean any harm. Rosa feels that being warm and friendly is the right thing to do.

"Yea, breaking up's rough. Anyway, what's up with u?"

Rosa has just used her human tool called **conscience.** *A conscience is an "inner voice" that will always teach us right from wrong. Each of us has a conscience. And it will either grow or shrink depending upon whether or not we follow its cues.*

Meanwhile, Woof is relieving himself on Mr. Newman's newly painted white picket fence.

Woof has absolutely no moral sense of right and wrong. After all, he is just a dog. And dogs will do whatever their instincts compel them to do.

Rosa's walk with Woof comes to an end. As she opens the front door to her house, she hears her mom yell from the other room, "Rosa, where've you been? I called you a dozen times."

Rosa had already made up her mind to not lose her cool with her mom, so, despite wanting to yell back "Get out of my face," she responds calmly,

"Just out for a walk with the dog, Mom . . ."

"Woof! Woof! Come back here," screams Rosa as Woof darts out the open door to chase the mailman.

While Rosa is using her fourth human tool of **willpower** *to control her anger, Woof, who has been told not to chase the mailman, is overcome by his instincts. Willpower is the power to act. It says that we have the power to choose, to control our emotions, and to overcome our habits and instincts.*

As you can see in the above example, we either use or fail to use our four human tools every day of our lives. The more we use them, the stronger they become and the more power we have to be proactive. However, if we fail to use them, we tend to *react* by instinct like a dog and not *act* by choice like a human.

• HUMAN TOOLS IN ACTION

Dermell Reed once told me how his proactive response to a family crisis changed his life forever. Dermell was raised in one of East Oakland's roughest neighborhoods, the fourth in a family of seven kids. No one in the Reed family had ever graduated from high school before, and Dermell wasn't about to be the first. He was unsure about his future. His family was struggling. His street was filled with gangs and drug dealers. Could he ever get out? While in his house, on a still summer night before his senior year, Dermell heard a series of gunshots.

"It's an everyday thing to hear gunshots, and I didn't pay it no mind," said Dermell.

Suddenly one of his friends, who'd been shot in the leg, burst through the door and began hollering that Dermell's little brother, Kevin, had just been shot and killed in a drive-by shooting.

"I was upset and I was angry and I was hurt and I lost somebody I ain't never going to see again in my life," Dermell told me. "He was only thirteen years old. And he was shot over a petty little street scuffle. I can't explain how life went after that. It was just straight downhill for the whole family."

Dermell's kneejerk reaction was to kill the murderer. It felt like the only real way he could pay back his dead brother. The police were still trying to figure out who did it, but Dermell knew. On a muggy August night, a few weeks after Kevin's death, Dermell got hold of a .38 caliber revolver and went out in the streets to get revenge on Tony "Fat Tone" Davis, the crack dealer who had killed his brother.

"It was dark. Davis and his friends couldn't see me. There he was sitting, talking, laughing, having fun, and here I am within fifty feet of him, crouched behind a car with a loaded gun. I was sitting there thinking, 'I could just pull this little trigger and kill the guy who killed my brother.'"

Big decision.

At this point, Dermell pushed pause and caught hold of himself. Using his *imagination,* he thought about his past and his future. "I thought about my life in a matter of seconds. I weighed my options. I weighed the chances of me escaping, not getting caught, the police trying to figure out who I was. I thought about the times Kevin would come watch me play football. He always told me I was going to be a pro football player. I thought about my future, about going to college. About what I wanted to make of my life."

Pausing, Dermell listened to his *conscience.* "I'm holding a gun, I'm shaking, and I think the good side of me told me to get up and go home and go to school. If I took revenge, I'd be throwing away my future. I'd be no better than the guy who shot my brother."

Using raw *willpower,* Dermell, instead of giving in to his anger and throwing away his life, got up, walked home, and vowed that he would finish college for his beloved dead brother.

Nine months later Dermell had made the honor roll and was graduating from high school. People in his school couldn't believe it. Five years later, he'd become a college football star and a college graduate, the first in his family.

Like Dermell, each of us will face an extraordinary challenge or two along the way, and we can *choose* whether to rise to those challenges or to be conquered by them.

Elaine Maxwell sums up the entire matter quite well: "Whether

I fail or succeed shall be no man's doing but my own. I am the force; I can clear any obstacle before me or I can be lost in the maze. My choice; my responsibility; win or lose, only I hold the key to my destiny."

It's kind of like the old Volkswagen commercials. "On the road of life, there are passengers and there are drivers . . . Drivers wanted!" So let me ask you, are you in the driver's seat of your life or are you merely a passenger? Are you conducting your symphony or simply being played? Are you acting like a can of soda pop or a bottle of water?

After all that's been said and done, *the choice is yours!*

COMING ATTRACTIONS

In the chapter that follows, I'll take you on a ride you'll never forget called The Great Discovery. Come along. It's a thrill a minute!

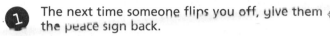

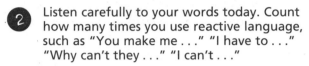

1 The next time someone flips you off, give them the peace sign back.

2 Listen carefully to your words today. Count how many times you use reactive language, such as "You make me . . ." "I have to . . ." "Why can't they . . ." "I can't . . ."

Reactive language I use most: _____

_____

_____

3 Do something today that you have wanted to do but never dared. Leave your comfort zone and go for it. Ask someone out on a date, raise your hand in class, or join a team. What's the worst thing that could happen? If you don't make it or get rejected, so what? It's better than not trying at all.

4 Leave yourself a message—in your phone or on a Post-it—that says: "I will not let _____

_____

decide how I'm going to feel." Refer to it often.

5 At the next party, don't just sit against the wall and wait for excitement to find you, you find it. Walk up and introduce yourself to someone new.

6 The next time you receive a grade that you think is unfair, don't blow it off or cry about it, make an appointment with the teacher to discuss it and then see what you can learn.

7 If you get in a fight with a parent or a friend, make amends and be the first to apologize.

HABIT **1**

BABY STEPS

8. Identify something in your circle of no control that you are always worrying about. Decide now to drop it.

   Thing that I can't control that I always worry about:

   _____

   _____

9. If someone sends you a mean or rude text, push the pause button. Do not respond when you're angry. Do not push send. Cool down first. Then decide how best to handle it.

10. Use your tool of self-awareness right now by asking yourself, "What is my most unhealthy habit?" Make up your mind to do something about it.

    Most unhealthy habit: _____

    _____

    What I'm going to do about it: _____

    _____

    _____

    _____

HABIT 2

Begin with the End in Mind

**Control
Your Own
Destiny**
OR SOMEONE
ELSE WILL

"**Would** you tell me please which way I ought to walk from here?"

"That depends a good deal on where you want to get to," said the Cat.

"I don't much care where–" said Alice.

"Then it doesn't matter which way to walk," said the Cat.

FROM *ALICE'S ADVENTURES IN WONDERLAND*

It's a rainy day and you're stuck indoors. You and a friend decide to put on some music and do a jigsaw puzzle, for old times' sake. You pour out all 1,000 pieces, spreading them out across a large table. You check out the lid to the box to see what you're putting together. But there's no picture! It's blank! How will you guys ever be able to finish the puzzle without knowing what it looks like? If you only had a one-second glimpse of what it's supposed to be. That's all you'd need. What a difference it would make! Without it, you have no clue where to even start.

Now think about your own life and your 1,000 pieces (at least 1,000!). Do you have an end in mind? Do you have a clear picture, even an idea, of who you want to be one year from now? Five years from now? Or do you feel lost?

Habit 2, Begin with the End in Mind, means developing a clear picture of where you want to go with your life. It means deciding what your values are and setting goals. Habit 1 says you are the driver of your life, not the passenger. Habit 2 says, since you're the driver, decide where to go and draw a map of how to get there.

"Ummm, hold up," you might be thinking. "I'm too young to have an end in mind. I don't know what I want to be when I grow up, and frankly right now I don't care." If it makes you feel any better, I'm grown up and I still don't know what I want to be. By saying begin with the end in mind, I'm not talking about deciding every little detail of your future, like choosing your career or deciding whom you'll marry. I'm simply talking about thinking beyond today and deciding what direction you want to take so that each step you take is always in the right direction.

Begin with the End in Mind— What It Means

You may not realize it, but you do it all the time. Begin with the end in mind, that is. You draw up a blueprint before you build a house. You read a recipe before you bake a cake. You create an outline before you write a paper (at least I hope you do). It's part of life.

Let's have a begin-with-the-end-in-mind experience right now using your tool of imagination. Find a place where you can be alone without interruption.

There. Now, clear your mind of everything. Don't think about texting your friend; forget about that zit on your forehead. Just focus with me for a second; breathe deeply, and open your brain wide.

In your mind's eye, visualize someone walking toward you about half a block away. At first you can't see who it is. As this person gets closer and closer, you suddenly realize, believe it or not, it's *you*. But it's not you today, it's you as you'd *like to be* one year from now.

Now think deeply.

What have you done with your life over the past year?

How do you feel inside?

What do you look like?

Has your personality grown? (Remember, this is you as you would *like to be* one year from now.)

You can float back to reality now. If you were a good sport and actually tried this experiment, you probably got in touch with your deeper self. You got a feel for what's important to you and what you'd like to accomplish this next year. That's what beginning with the end in mind is all about. And it doesn't even hurt.

As Jim discovered, beginning with the end in mind is a powerful way to help turn your dreams into realities:

When I feel frustrated or get depressed, I've found something that really helps me. I go someplace where I can be alone, and then I close my eyes and visualize mentally where I want to be and where I wanna go when I am older. I try to see the whole picture of my dream life—and then I automatically begin to think about what it's going to take to get there, what I need to change. This technique started when I was a ninth grader, and today I'm on my way to making some of those visualizations become a reality.

In fact, thinking beyond today can be really exciting and, as this high school senior attests, can help you take charge of your life:

HABIT 2

I've never planned a thing in my life. I just do things as they pop up. The thought that one should have an end in mind never, ever entered my mind. It's been so exciting to learn, because I suddenly find myself thinking beyond the now. I'm now not only planning my education but also thinking about how I want to raise my kids, how I want to teach my family, and what kind of home life we should have. I'm taking charge of me—and not blowing in the wind anymore!

Why's it so important to have an end in mind? I'll give you two good reasons. The first is that you're at a critical crossroads in life, and the paths you choose now can affect you forever. The second is that if you don't decide your own future, someone else'll do it for you.

● THE CROSSROADS OF LIFE

Let's take a look at the first important reason. So here you are. You're young. You're free. You have your whole life before you. You're standing at the crossroads of life and you have to choose which paths to take:

Do you want to go to college? Graduate school?
Do you want to travel? Learn another language?
Should you try out for a team?
What type of friends do you want to have?
Will you cut class again?
Do you want to date? What kind of person?
Will you have sex before marriage?
Will you drink, smoke, do drugs?
What values will you choose?
What kind of relationships do you want with your family?
What will your attitude toward life be?
What will you stand for?
How will you contribute to your community?

The paths you choose today can shape you forever. It's both frightening and exciting that we have to make so many vital decisions during the seven years of teenagehood, when we're so young and full of hormones, but such is life.

What About Friends?

Take your choice of friends as an example. Have you ever noticed what a powerful influence they can have on your attitude, reputation, and direction? The need to be accepted and be part of a group is powerful. But too often we choose our friends based on whoever will accept us. And that's not always good. For example, to be accepted by the kids who do drugs, all you have to do is do drugs yourself.

The wrong group can lead you down all kinds of paths you really don't want to be on. And retracing your steps can be a long, hard journey. Sometimes it's actually better to just hang out alone, to be honest.

If you're having trouble making good friends, remember that your friends don't always have to be your age. I once spoke to a guy who only had a few friends at school, but he did have a grandpa who listened to him, made him laugh, and was a great friend. It filled the "popularity" void he had in his life.

It can feel empowering to connect with people over the Internet or through apps, especially when you're struggling to connect with people in person. Ben's story goes like this:

> Last fall I got pretty into online gaming, and it was a really good way to connect with people who were into the same kind of stuff as me, stuff that other people called "nerdy." I didn't know that many people at my new school, but I had this really amazing supportive community online.
>
> There were chat threads that all the users commented on, and there were some really interesting people on it. It felt safe to finally talk with people who didn't make fun of me for being into games, and I thought about meeting a group of them in person. Then I remembered hearing news stories about cyberstalkers and online harassment, and that kinda freaked me out. I just realized that I had to be smart—I mean, all these people I was talking to seemed cool, not dangerous, but I just knew I shouldn't share personal info with them or meet them—because really, I didn't know who they were! So I told them I didn't feel comfortable meeting and most of them agreed that was cool, so we just left it as an online friendship. Only once did someone really creep me out—one user asked me for my address and photo, but before I even started stressing about it, I realized I could be in control of the situation. I blocked them and never heard from them again. Actually, having this community online has made me more confident, and I've been making more friends at my new school.

You can't be too careful about sharing personal info online, and Ben seems to have got it down. Even if you video chat with someone or follow them on Instagram and they seem nice or attractive—there's no way of knowing that they're not a total psycho in person.

What about sending explicit texts or sexting photos of yourself—

even to someone you already know and trust? It might seem funny at the time, but who knows what the person you're sending them to will do down the road. What if you and your boy- or girlfriend break up and they wind up sharing your texts or photos to hurt you? Ouch! It seems like once a week some celebrity or politician is getting in trouble for that sort of thing. If you keep your end in mind and avoid these kinds of situations, there's way less risk of having someone take advantage of you.

The long and short of it is, just be wise when choosing friends and partners. Be selective about the people you trust, because so much of your future hangs on whom you hang out with.

What About Sex?

And what about sex? Talk about an important decision. If you wait until the "heat of the moment" to choose which path to take, it's too late. Decide now. The path you choose affects your health, the way you feel about yourself, how fast you grow up, your reputation, whom you'll date and perhaps marry, and so much more. Think this decision through . . . carefully. One way to do this is to imagine the kind of person you hope to end up with. How do you hope your future mate is leading his or her life right now?

In a recent poll, going to movies was ranked as the favorite pastime of teens. I love movies, too, so I'm right there with you. But I'd be careful about the values they promote. Most movies lie, especially when it comes to issues like sex. They glamorize sleeping around and having one-night stands without addressing the potential risks and consequences. The movies don't show you the life-altering reality of contracting a Sexually Transmitted Infection (STI) or a disease like AIDS. They rarely address what it's like to become pregnant and to have to deal with everything that brings with it. They don't tell you what it's like living on minimum wage because you had to drop out of high school (and the father of the child is long gone and sends no money), or what it's like spending your weekends changing diapers and caring for a baby instead of cheering on your volleyball team, going to dances, and just being a kid.

We are free to choose our paths, but we can't choose the consequences that come with them. Have you ever gone water sliding? You can choose which slide you want to go down, but once you're sliding, you can't very well stop. You must live with the consequences . . . to the end. A teenage girl from Illinois shared this story:

I had one bad year—my freshman year—when I did everything from drinking, drugs, older guys, bad crowds, etc., mostly because I was frus-

trated and unhappy. It just lasted a year, but I'm still paying for those past mistakes. No one forgets and it's hard to have to deal with a past you aren't too proud of. I feel as though it will haunt me forever. All kinds of people still come up to my boyfriend and say, "I hear your girlfriend drinks, and smokes, and is easy." And things like that. But the worst is probably the fact that every time I have a problem of any kind, I immediately think, "Maybe if I hadn't done that, everything would be okay."

What About School?

What you do about your schooling can also shape your future in a major way. Krista's experience shows how much beginning with the end in mind in your educational pursuits pays off:

As a junior in high school, I decided to take an Advanced Placement (AP) U.S. history class. At the end of the year, I'd have a chance to take a national exam to qualify for college credit.

It was difficult to keep up, but I was determined to do well in the class and pass the exam. With this goal in mind, it was easy to put in my full effort.

One assignment was particularly time consuming. The instructor asked each student to watch a documentary on the Civil War and write a paper on each segment. The series lasted ten days and each segment was two hours long. As an active high school student, it was difficult to find the time, but I did. I submitted the report and discovered I was one of only a handful of students who watched the series.

The day of the exam finally arrived. The students were nervous and the air was thick. The test administrator announced, "Begin." I took a deep breath and broke the seal on the first section—multiple-choice. With each question, I gained confidence. I KNEW the answers! I completed the section several minutes before I heard, I finished "Pencils down."

Next we would each write an essay. I nervously opened the seal of the essay book and scanned the questions quickly. I answered a question related to the Civil War using references from my reading as well as the documentary. I felt calm and confident as I completed the exam.

Several weeks later I received my score in the mail—I had passed!

● WHO'S IN THE LEAD?

Besides being at the crossroads of the most important decisions you'll ever make, the other reason to visualize your future is because if you don't, someone else will do it for you. As Jack Welch, former teen and current business executive, put it, "Control your own destiny or someone else will."

"Who will?" you may ask.

Could be anyone—friends, parents, the media. Do you want your friends to tell you what you stand for? You may have fine parents, but do you want them to draw up the blueprint for your life? Their interests may be far different from yours. And how about the media? Do you want to adopt the values portrayed in video games or gossip blogs or on TV?

By now you might be thinking, "I'm gonna chill and worry about the future when it comes. I like to live in the moment and go with the flow." I agree with the *live in the moment* part. We should enjoy the moment and not have our heads too far in the clouds. But I disagree with the *go with the flow* part. If you decide to just go with the flow, you'll end up where the flow goes, and sometimes it's headed straight downhill into a pile of sludge. You'll end up doing what everyone else is doing, which may not be *your* end in mind at all. "The road to anywhere is really a life to nowhere," the saying goes. You need to decide what direction feels right to you. It's really never too early.

Without an end in mind of our own, we often wind up following anyone who's willing to lead, even into things that won't get us far. It reminds me of an experience I once had at a 10K road race. Some other runners and I were waiting for the race to start, but no one knew where the starting line was. Then a few runners began walking down the road as if they knew. Everyone, including me, began following. We just assumed they knew where they were going. After walking for about a mile, we all suddenly realized, that like a herd of dumb sheep, we were following some dingus who had no idea where he was going. It turned out that the starting line was back right where we had begun.

Never assume that the herd must know where they are going because they usually don't.

A Personal Mission Statement So if it's so important to have an end in mind, how do you do it? The best way I've found is to write a personal mission statement. A personal mission statement is like a personal credo or motto that states what your life is about. It is like the blueprint to your life. Countries have constitutions, which function just like a mission statement. And most companies, like Apple and Pepsi, have mission statements. But I think they work best with people.

So why not write your own personal mission statement? Many teens have. They come in all types and varieties. Some are as long as a whole Bible passage and some are as short as a 140-character Tweet. Some are poems and some are rap lyrics. Some teens use their favorite quote as a mission statement. Others use a picture or a photograph.

Let me share a few teenage mission statements with you.

This first one was contributed by a teen named Beth Haire:

First and foremost, I will remain faithful always to my God.

I will not underestimate the power of family unity.

I will not neglect a true friend, but I will set aside time for myself as well.

I will cross my bridges as I come to them (divide and conquer).

I will begin all challenges with optimism, rather than doubt.

I will always maintain a positive self-image and high self-esteem, knowing that all my intentions begin with self-evaluation.

June's mission statement comes from a quote from her favorite musician, Taylor Swift:

"To me, Fearless is not the absence of fear. It's not being completely unafraid. To me, Fearless is having fears. Fearless is having doubts. Lots of them. To me, Fearless is living in spite of those things that scare you to death."

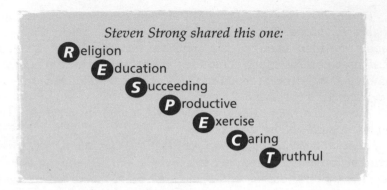

Steven Strong shared this one:

Religion
  Education
    Succeeding
      Productive
        Exercise
          Caring
            Truthful

I met a teen named Adam Sosne from North Carolina who was familiar with the 7 Habits and was "on fire" about his future plans. Not surprisingly, he had a mission statement, which he volunteered:

MISSION STATEMENT

- Have confidence in your-self and everyone else around you.
- Be kind, courteous, and respectful to all people.
- Set reachable goals.
- Never lose sight of these goals.
- Never take the simple things in life for granted.
- Appreciate other people's differences and see their differences as a great advantage.

- Ask questions.
- Strive each day to reach interdependence.
- Remember that before you can change some-one else, you must first change yourself.
- Speak with your actions, not with your words.
- Make the time to help those less fortunate than yourself or those who are having a bad day.
- Read the 7 Habits every day.

Read this mission statement every day.

So what can writing a mission statement do for you? Tons. The most important thing it will do is open your eyes to what's really important to you and help you make decisions accordingly. A twelfth grader shared how writing a mission statement made such a difference in her life:

During my junior year I couldn't concentrate on anything because I had a boyfriend. I wanted to do everything for him to make him happy, and then, naturally, the subject of sex came up—and I wasn't at all prepared for it, and it became a nagging constant thing on my mind. I felt like I wasn't ready and that I didn't want to have sex—but everyone else kept saying, "Just do it."

Then I participated in a character development class at school where they taught me to write a mission statement. I started to write and kept on writing and writing, and kept adding things to it. It gave me direction and a focus and I felt like I had a plan and a reason for doing what I was doing. It really helped me to stick to my standards and not do something I wasn't ready for.

A personal mission statement is like a tree with deep roots. It's stable and it's not going anywhere, but it's also alive and continually growing.

Standing like a tree with deep roots helps you survive all of the storms of life that beat you up. As you've probably noticed already, life is anything but stable. Think about it. People are fickle. Your boyfriend loves you one minute and then dumps you the next. You're someone's best friend one day, and they're talking behind your back the next.

Think about all of the events you can't control. You family has to move. Your mom loses her job. The country is at war. A family member dies.

Fads come and go. Skinny jeans are popular one year and out the next. Vampires are the thing. Vampires are overrated.

While everything about you changes, a personal mission statement can be your deep-rooted tree that never moves. You can deal with change if you have an immovable trunk to hang on to.

• UNCOVERING YOUR TALENTS

An important part of developing a personal mission statement is discovering what you're good at. One thing I know for sure is that everyone has a talent, a gift, something they are good at. Some talents, like having the singing voice of an angel, attract a lot of attention. But there are many other talents, maybe not as attention grabbing but every bit as important if not more—things like being a good listener, making people laugh, forgiving, drawing, or just being nice.

Another truth is that we all blossom at different times. So if you're a late bloomer, relax. It may take you a bit longer to uncover your talents.

After carving a beautiful sculpture, Michelangelo was asked how he was able to do it. He replied by saying that the sculpture was already in the block of granite from the very beginning; he just had to chisel off everything else around it.

Likewise, Victor Frankl, a revered Jewish-Austrian psychiatrist who survived the death camps of Nazi Germany, taught that we don't *invent* our talents in life but rather we *detect* them. In other words, you are already born with your talents, you just need to uncover them.

I'll never forget my experience with finding a talent I never thought I had. To fulfill Mr. Williams's creative writing assignment for freshman English, I excitedly turned in my first high school paper, entitled "The Old Man and the Fish." It was the same story my father had often told me at bedtime while I was growing up. I just assumed he had made it up. He didn't bother telling me he had stolen the plot directly from Ernest Hemingway's award-winning novel *The Old Man and the Sea.* I was shocked when my paper was returned with the remarks, "Sounds a bit trite. Like Hemingway's *Old Man and the Sea.*" "Who's this guy Hemingway?" I thought. "And how come he copied my dad?" That was my poor start to four years of rather boring high school English classes, which were about as exciting to me as a clump of dirt.

It wasn't until college, when I took a short story class from an amazing professor, that I began to detect my passion for writing. If you can believe it, I even majored in English. Mr. Williams would've freaked.

The Great Discovery The Great Discovery* is a fun activity designed to help you get in touch with your deeper self as you prepare to write a mission statement. As you walk through it, answer the questions honestly. You can write your answers in the book or you can just think them through. When you're finished, I think you'll have a way better idea of what inspires you, what you enjoy doing, whom you admire, and where you want to take your life.

---

* For additional worksheets of The Great Discovery, please call 1-800-952-6839.

THE
GREAT
DISCOVERY!

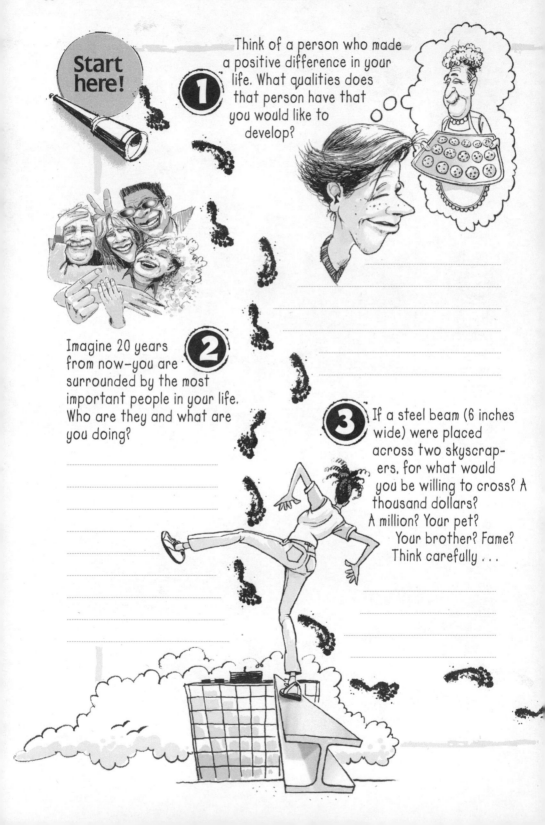

Start here!

1 Think of a person who made a positive difference in your life. What qualities does that person have that you would like to develop?

2 Imagine 20 years from now—you are surrounded by the most important people in your life. Who are they and what are you doing?

3 If a steel beam (6 inches wide) were placed across two skyscrapers, for what would you be willing to cross? A thousand dollars? A million? Your pet? Your brother? Fame? Think carefully . . .

6 Describe a time when you were deeply inspired.

....

....

....

....

....

5 List 10 things you love to do. It could seriously be anything—Web design, dance, freestyle rapping, Pinterest browsing, eating ethnic foods, daydreaming . . . anything you absolutely love to do!

1 ....

2 ....

3 ....

4 ....

5 ....

6 ....

7 ....

8 ....

9 ....

10 ....

4 If you could spend one day in a great library studying anything you wanted, what would it be?

....

....

....

7 Five years from now, a major news site is going to doing a feature piece on you and they want to interview three people you're close to. Who are they and what would you want them to say about you?

....

....

....

8 Think of something that represents you . . . a flower, a song, an animal . . . Why does it represent you?

....

....

....

....

....

9 If you could spend an hour with any person who ever lived, who would that be? Why that person? What would you ask them?

....

....

....

....

The Local Informant

Family & friends declare: "Gr-r-eat guy!"

E=MC²

HEY, LOOK WHAT I FOUND. IT'S **ME**!

Good with numbers
Good with words
Creative thinking
Athletics
Making things happen
Sensing needs   Speaking
Mechanical   Writing
Artistic   Dancing
Working well with people   Listening
Memorizing things   Singing
Decision making   Humor
Building things   Sharing
Accepting others   Music
Predicting what will happen   Trivia

10 Everyone has one or more talents. Which of the ones above are you good at? Or write down some not listed.

ALMOST THERE !

Getting Started on Your Mission Statement (N)ow that you've taken the time to walk through The Great Discovery, you've got a good jump-start on developing a mission statement. Below, I've listed four easy methods to help you get started writing your own mission statement. You may want to try one of them or combine all four of them in any way you see fit. These are just suggestions, so feel free to find your own method.

Method #1: The Quote Collection. Collect a few of your very favorite quotes. The sum of these quotes then becomes your mission statement. For some, great quotes are very inspiring. They put your feelings into words.

Method #2: The Brain Dump. Speed write about your mission for ten minutes. Don't worry about what's coming out. Don't edit what you're writing. Just keep writing and don't stop writing. Get all of your ideas down on paper. If you get stuck, reflect upon your answers to The Great Discovery. That should get your imagination in gear. When your brain has been sufficiently purged, take another twenty minutes to edit, arrange, and make sense of your brain dump.

The result is that in just thirty minutes, you'll have a rough draft of your own mission statement, that you've created yourself. Then over the next several weeks, you can edit it, add to it, or do whatever else you need to make it inspire you.

Method #3: The Retreat. Plan a large chunk of time, like an entire afternoon, and go to a place you adore where you can be alone and turn off your phone. Think deeply about your life and what you want to make of it. Review your answers to The Great Discovery. Look to the mission statement examples in this book for ideas. Take your time and construct your own mission statement using any method you see fit.

Method #4: The Big Lazy. If you're really lazy, use the U.S. Army's recruiting slogan "Army Strong" as your personal mission statement. (Hey, I'm only joking.)

A big mistake people make when writing a mission statement is that they spend so much time thinking about making it perfect they never get started. You're much better off writing an imperfect rough draft and then improving it over time, learning as you go.

Another mistake is trying to make your mission statements look like everyone else's. That doesn't work. Mission statements come in many forms—a poem, a song, a quote, a picture, many words, a single word, a collage of images on Tumblr. There is no single right way to do it! You're not writing it for anyone else but you. You're not writing it for your English teacher and it's not going to be graded by anyone. It is *your* secret document. So make it sing! The most important question to ask yourself is, "Does it inspire me?" If you can answer yes, you did it right.

Once you have it written, put it in a place where you can easily access it, in your phone, or on your mirror for example. Then, refer to it often, or, even better, memorize it.

Here are two more examples of teen mission statements, each very different in style and length:

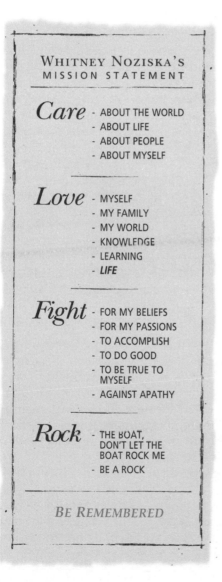

WHITNEY NOZISKA'S
MISSION STATEMENT

Care - ABOUT THE WORLD
- ABOUT LIFE
- ABOUT PEOPLE
- ABOUT MYSELF

Love - MYSELF
- MY FAMILY
- MY WORLD
- KNOWLEDGE
- LEARNING
- *LIFE*

Fight - FOR MY BELIEFS
- FOR MY PASSIONS
- TO ACCOMPLISH
- TO DO GOOD
- TO BE TRUE TO MYSELF
- AGAINST APATHY

Rock - THE BOAT, DON'T LET THE BOAT ROCK ME
- BE A ROCK

BE REMEMBERED

This one was written by Katie Hall. It is short, but to her it means everything:

— MY —
MISSION
STATEMENT

**NOTHING
LESS.**

HABIT 2

- ## THREE WATCH-OUTS

As you strive to begin with the end in mind and develop a personal mission statement, watch out for dangerous roadblocks!

Watch-Out #1: Negative Labels. Have you ever felt labeled by others in a negative way? By your family, teachers, or friends?

"You guys from the east side are all the same. Always gettin' into trouble."

"You're the laziest bro I know. Why don't you get off your butt and do something for a change?"

"There goes Lizzie. I hear she's such a pothead."

I'm sure your school has its own labels. In my school we had the Cowboys, the Nerds, the Airheads, the Pretty Boys, the Partyers, the Preppies, the "It" Girls, the Burn-outs, the Jocks, the D-Wingers (you had to be there), and many other groups. I was labeled in the Jock category. The term "Jock" meant that you played sports, were totally stuck on yourself, and had a brain the size of a peanut.

Labels are an ugly form of prejudice. Break down the word *prejudice* and what do you get? Ta-da! Pre-judge. When you label someone you're pre-judging them; that means making conclusions about someone without knowing them. I don't know about you, but I can't stand it when I'm unfairly judged by someone who doesn't know a thing about me.

You and I are much too complex to be neatly shelved into a category like clothing in a department store, as if there were only a handful of different types of people in the world instead of billions of unique individuals.

If you've been falsely labeled, you can live with it. The real danger comes when you start to believe the labels yourself, because labels are just like paradigms. For instance, if you've been labeled as being lazy, and you begin to believe it yourself, it will become a self-fulfilling belief. You'll act out the label. Just remember, you are not your labels. Don't let other people's pre-judgments limit you.

Watch-Out #2: "It's All Over" Syndrome. Another thing to watch out for is when you've made a mistake or three and feel so bad about what you've done that you say to yourself, "It's all over. I've blown it. Who cares what happens now?" At this point you'll often begin to self-destruct and let it all hang out.

Let me just say this. It's never over. It seems that many teens go through a time where they lose it and experiment and do a whole bunch of things they aren't proud of . . . almost as if they are testing the boundaries of life. If you've made mistakes: Congratulations, you're normal! Every teenager has. Every adult has. Just get your head screwed on straight as quickly as you can and you'll be fine. Promise.

> So often, in our quest
> to be more popular
> and to be part
> of the "in-group,"
> we lose sight of
> things that are far
> more important . . .

Watch-Out #3: Wrong Wall. Have you ever worked really hard to get something you wanted only to feel totally unsatisfied when you get it? So often, in our quest to be more popular and to be part of the "in-group," we lose sight of things that are far more important, like self-respect, real friendships, and peace of mind. We're often so busy climbing the ladder of success that we never take time to see if our ladder is leaning against the right wall. Having no end in mind is a problem. But having an end in mind that leads us in the wrong direction can be an even bigger problem.

I once played football with a guy who was an insanely good athlete. He had everything going for him, including being the team captain and having the ultimate ripped body. Each game he'd excite fans with heroic efforts and spectacular athletic feats. Fans praised his name, young boys worshipped him, and women adored him. He had it all.

Or so it appeared.

You see, even though he was shining on the field, he wasn't doing right off the field. And he knew it. And so did I, because I'd grown up with the guy. As his fame increased, I watched him turn away from his principles and lose his direction. He gained the high fives of the crowd but compromised something else far more meaningful, his character. It doesn't really matter how fast you're going or how good you're lookin' if you're headed in the wrong direction.

How can you tell if your ladder is leaning against the right wall? Stop, take a moment right now and ask yourself: "Is the life I'm living leading me in the right direction?" Be brutally honest as you pause and listen to your conscience, that inner voice. What is it telling you?

Our lives don't always require 180-degree shifts in direction. More often, we need only small shifts. But small changes can make huge destination differences. Imagine this: If you wanted to fly from New York to Tel Aviv, Israel, but made a one degree change north, you would end up in Moscow, Russia, instead of Tel Aviv.

- ## GO FOR THE GOAL

Once you have your mission in place you will want to set goals. Goals are specific and can help you break down your mission into bite-sized pieces. If your personal mission was to eat a whole pizza, your goal would be how to do it, a slice at a time.

Sometimes when we hear the word *goals* we go on a guilt trip. It reminds us of what we should be doing and what we haven't done yet. But forget about any mistakes you may have made in the past. Follow the advice of George Bernard Shaw, who said: "When I was a young man I observed that nine out of ten things I did were failures. I didn't want to be a failure, so I did ten times more work."

Here are five keys to goal setting.

KEY NO. 1: *Count the Cost*

How many times do we set goals when we are in the mood but then later find we don't have the strength to follow through? Why does this happen? It's because we haven't counted the cost.

Let's pretend you set a goal to get better grades in school this year. That's great. But now, before you begin, count the cost. What will it require? For instance, you will have to spend more time doing math and grammar and less time trolling the Internet. You will have to stay up late some nights. Finding more time for schoolwork might mean watching less TV or staying in on a Friday once in a while.

Now, having counted the cost, consider the benefits. What could good grades bring you? A feeling of accomplishment? A scholarship to college? A good job? Now ask yourself, "Am I willing to make the sacrifice?" If not, then don't do it. Don't make commitments to yourself you know you're going to break because you'll take withdrawals from your PBA.

A better way is to make the goal more bite-sized. Instead of setting a goal to get better grades in all your classes, you might set a goal to get better grades in just two classes. Then, next semester, take another bite. Counting the cost will always add a touch of needed realism to your goals.

KEY NO. 2: *Write It Out*

It's been said, "A goal not written is only a wish." There are no ifs and buts about it, a written goal carries ten times the power.

A young woman named Tammy told me how writing down her goals helped her eventually choose the right person to marry. Tammy had been in an emotionally abusive relationship with a guy named Tom for several years and felt trapped. They were codependent and she was miserable. A visit from a trusted friend one day finally gave her the inner spark she needed to make a change. This is an excerpt from Tammy's journal when she was eighteen:

Just yesterday I found enough strength and strong will to leave Tom and the environment I was a part of for the past 2½ years. I needed to make a 180-degree change in order to find inner strength enough to succeed. I drew up a mental picture of where I wanted to be in five years and how I wanted to feel. I had a vision of being my own person, of having the strength to make good decisions for my life and most of all being with someone in a good, healthy relationship. I came up with a list of qualities I wanted in a relationship, and I think I'll write them down now for future reference.

Qualities for a Relationship/Future Spouse:

1. *Respect*
2. *Unconditional love*
3. *Honesty*
4. *Loyalty*
5. *Will support me in my pursuits/goals in life*
6. *Righteous (spiritual nature)*
7. *Fun/good sense of humor*
8. *Makes me laugh every day*
9. *Will make me feel whole—not torn apart*
10. *Good father/good with children*
11. *Good listener*
12. *Will make time for me and will want the best for me in life*

Now that I have this list documented I have someplace to turn to get a glimpse of what the future can hold. It gives me hope when I read it, and it reminds me of a better way to live life.

HABIT 2

Tammy later met and married a great guy who measured up to her standards. Happy endings do happen. Don't settle for less.

As Tammy discovered, there is something magical about writing down your goals. Writing forces you to be specific, which is very important in goal setting. As actress Lily Tomlin has said, "I always wanted to be somebody. But I should have been more specific."

KEY NO. 3: *Just Do It!*

I once read a story about Cortés and his expedition to Mexico. With over five hundred men and eleven ships, Cortés sailed from Cuba to the coast of the Yucatán in 1519. On the mainland he did something no other expedition leader had thought of: He burned his ships. By cutting off all means of retreat, Cortés committed his entire force and himself to the cause. It was conquest or bust.

"To every thing there is a season," says the Bible. A time to say, "I'll try," and a time to say, "I will." A time to make excuses, and a time to burn your ships. Of course, there are times when trying our best is all we can do. But I also believe there is a time for doing. Would you lend $2,000 to a business partner who said, "I'll try to return it"? Would you get married if your partner, when asked to take you as their lawfully wedded husband or wife, said, "I'll try"? Am I making sense?

I once heard a story about a captain and a lieutenant:

"Lieutenant, would you please deliver this letter for me."

"I'll do my best, sir."

"No, I don't want you to do your best. I want you to deliver this letter."

"I'll do it or I'll die, sir."

"You misunderstand, lieutenant. I don't want you to die. I want you to deliver this letter."

Finally the lieutenant caught on and said clearly, "I will do it, sir."

Once we are fully committed to doing a task, our power to complete it will increase. "If you do the thing," said Ralph Waldo Emerson, "you will have the power." Each time I have committed myself to a goal, I seem to dig up gold mines of willpower, skill, and creativity I never thought I possessed. Those who are committed always find a way.

The following passage by writer W. H. Murray is one of my all-time favorites. It describes what happens inside when we say "I will."

Until one is committed, there is hesitancy, the chance to draw back, always ineffectiveness. There is one elementary truth, the ignorance of which kills countless ideas and splendid plans, that the moment one definitely commits oneself then providence moves too. All sorts of things begin to occur which would never otherwise have occurred, and a whole stream of events issues from the decision, raising in one's favor all manner of unforeseen incidents and material assistance which no man could have dreamt would have come his way. I have learned a deep respect for one of Goethe's couplets:

Whatever you can do or dream you can begin it.
Boldness has genius, power, and magic in it.

In the words of Yoda, the great Jedi Master: "Do or do not. There is no try."

KEY NO. 4: *Use Momentous Moments*

 Certain moments in life contain momentum and power. The key is to harness these moments for goal setting.

Things with starts and finishes or beginnings and ends carry momentum. For example, a new year represents a start. Breaking up, on the other hand, represents an end. I remember how sick I felt after breaking up with my girlfriend after two years of dating. But I also remember the excitement of realizing that now I could meet cool, new girls.

The following is a list of moments that can provide momentum for you as you set out to make new goals:

- A new school year
- A life-changing experience
- Breaking up
- A new job
- A new relationship
- A second chance
- Birth
- Death
- An anniversary
- A triumph

- A setback
- An invention
- Moving to a new city
- A new season
- Graduation
- Marriage
- Divorce
- A new home
- A new hairstyle
- A new day

Often, tough experiences can carry momentum. Are you familiar with the myth of the phoenix bird? After every lifespan of 500 to 600 years, the beautiful phoenix would burn itself at the stake.

Out of the ashes, it would later arise, reborn. In like manner, we can regenerate ourselves out of the ashes of a bad experience. Setbacks and tragedies can often serve as a springboard for change. They motivate you, and make you stronger.

Learn to harness the power of key moments, to set goals and make commitments when you are in the mood to do it. Be assured, as well, that the mood to do it will pass. Sticking with it when you don't feel like it is the true test of your character. As someone once put it:

Character is the discipline to follow through with resolutions long after the spirit in which they were made has passed.

KEY NO. 5: *Rope Up*

My brother-in-law, the mountain climber, once escorted me and a friend up the 13,776-foot Grand Teton. It was terrifying! As we ascended, the mountain turned vertical. At that point, we "roped up," or tied ourselves together with ropes to aid us in climbing and to save our lives if one of us fell. On two occasions that rope kept me from taking thousand-foot falls to my death. Believe me, I loved that rope as I've never loved a rope before. By assisting each other and relying on the ropes, we finally reached the summit safely.

You'll accomplish much more in life if you'll rope up and borrow strength from others. Let's suppose you set a goal to get in great shape. Now think. How could you rope up? Well, maybe you could find a friend who has the same-sized goal as you, and the two of you could work out together and be each other's cheerleaders. Or maybe you could tell your parents about your goal and get their support. Or maybe you could join an online community with others who are trying to get into shape. Get creative. Rope up with friends, brothers, sisters, boy or girlfriends, parents, counselors, grandparents, pastors, or whomever else you can. The more ropes you have out, the greater your chances for success.

● GOALS IN ACTION

When I was a sophomore in high school, I weighed 180 pounds. My brother David, a freshman, weighed a whopping 95 pounds. We were only one year apart, yet I was twice his size. But David had a mountain of a spirit and did incredible things to get to where he wanted to go. This is his story:

I will never forget when I tried out for the freshman football team at Provo High. At five feet two inches and weighing only 90 pounds, I was even smaller than the stereotypical 98-pound weakling. I couldn't find any football equipment to fit me; it was all too big. I was issued the smallest helmet they had but still had to tape three ear pads together on each side of it to make it fit my head. I looked like a mosquito with a balloon on its head.

I used to dread football practice, especially when we had to crack heads with the sophomores. We used to line up facing each other about ten yards apart with the freshmen on one side and the sophomores on the opposite side. When coach blew the whistle, you were supposed to hit your opponent until the whistle blew again.

I used to count the players in my line to see when my turn would come up, and then count the players in the sophomore line to see who would have the privilege of teaching me how to fly. It seemed that I always ended up getting the biggest, meanest sophomore as my opponent. "I'm dead meat," was my constant thought. I would line up, wait for the whistle, and in a moment find myself flying backwards and upwards through the air.

That winter I tried out for the wrestling team. I wrestled in the 98-pound division. Even though I weighed in with all my clothes on after eating a big meal, I still couldn't tip the scales at 98 pounds. In fact I was the only guy on the team who didn't have to lose weight to wrestle. My brothers thought I would be a good wrestler because, unlike football, wrestling allowed me to compete with guys about my own weight. But to make a long story short, I got pinned almost every match.

In the spring I tried out for track. But as luck would have it, I was one of the slowest guys on the team. Little wonder—you should have seen my pencil-thin legs.

One day after track workouts I just couldn't stand it anymore. "That's it," I said to myself. "I am sick of this." That night, in the privacy of my room, I wrote down some goals I wanted to achieve during high school. To be successful in my athletics, I knew I had to get bigger and stronger, so I set goals in these areas first. By my senior year I set a goal to be six feet tall, to weigh 180 pounds, and to bench-press 250 pounds. In football, I set a goal to be the starting wide receiver on the varsity football team. And in track I set a goal to be an all-state sprinter. I also envisioned myself being captain on both the football team and the track team.

HABIT 2

A lot of nice dreams, wouldn't you say? At that moment, however, I was staring reality in the face. All 90 pounds of it. But I stuck with my plan from my freshman until my senior year.

Let me illustrate. As part of my weight-gaining process, I made a rule that my stomach would never be empty. So I ate constantly. Breakfast, lunch, and dinner were merely three meals in an eight-meal day. I made a secret agreement with Cary, the starting varsity linebacker for Provo High, who stood six feet three inches tall and weighed 235 pounds. He promised me that if I helped him with his Algebra II homework, he would allow me to eat lunch with him every day for weight gain and protection purposes.

I was determined to eat the same amount he ate, so each day at lunch I bought two lunches, three milks, and four rolls. We must have been a hilarious sight together! I was also taking my Gain Weight Fast protein powder along with my lunch. I would mix the sickening powder in each of my milks and nearly barfed each time I drank it.

During my sophomore year I began working out with my good friend Eddie who was also yearning to get big. He added another requirement to my food list: ten full teaspoons of straight peanut butter and three glasses of milk each night before bed. Each week we were required to gain two pounds. If we didn't "make weight" on the official weigh-in day, we were required to eat or drink water until we did.

My mom read an article that said if a young kid slept ten hours a night in a completely dark room and drank two to three extra glasses of milk a day, he could grow one to two inches more than he normally would. I believed this and followed it rigidly. After all, I needed to reach my goal of six feet, and my dad's height of five feet ten inches wasn't going to help me. "Dad," I said, "I want the darkest room in the house." I got it. Then I put towels under the door crack and over the window. No light was going to shine on me!

Next I set a sleeping timetable: I went to bed around 8:45 P.M. and got up around 7:15 A.M. This ensured me 10½ hours of sleep. Finally, I drank all the milk I could.

I also began lifting weights, running, and catching the football. Each day I would work out at least two hours. When Eddie and I lifted at the weight room, we would check out the XL shirts in hopes that one day we would fill them. At first I could only bench-press 75 pounds, slightly more than the bar.

As the months passed I began to see results. Small results. Slow results. But results. By the time I was a sophomore I was five feet five inches and about 120 pounds. I had grown three inches and gained 30 pounds. And I was much stronger.

Some days I felt like a lone man against the whole world. I espe-

cially hated it when people would ask me, "How come you're so skinny? Why don't you just eat more?" I felt like saying back, "You idiot. Do you have any idea of the price I've been paying?"

By my junior year I was five feet eight inches and 145 pounds. I continued with my weight-gain program, the running, the lifting, and the skill development. In my track workouts, I made it a goal never to loaf, not even for one sprint. And I never missed a practice, even when I was sick. Then suddenly the sacrifice really started paying off. I got real big, real fast. In fact I grew so fast that I have stretch marks across my chest, as if I was mauled by a bear.

As I approached my senior year at Provo High, I had reached my goal of becoming six feet tall and fell only five pounds short of my goal of 180 pounds. I became a starting wide receiver on the varsity football team and was also elected as a team captain.

My senior year in track was even more rewarding. Again I was selected as a team captain, became the fastest sprinter on the team, and one of the fastest sprinters in the state.

At the end of the year, weighing 180 pounds and bench-pressing 255 pounds, I was awarded "Best Body" by the senior girls of the high school, the award that I loved most of all.

I did it! I really did it! I accomplished most of the goals I had set that night in my room years ago. Truly, as Napoleon Hill wrote, "Whatever the mind of man can conceive and believe, the hand of man can achieve."

• TURNING WEAKNESSES INTO STRENGTHS

Notice how David used the five keys to goal setting. He counted the cost, he wrote them, he roped up with his friends, he set his goals during a momentous moment when he was sick of being a shrimp (sorry, lil bro), and he had the raw tenacity to "just do it." Now, I'm not endorsing being body-centered, as David was for a period. And I can't promise you that you can will your way into growing taller, no matter how much milk you drink. I'm only trying to demonstrate the power that goals can play in your life.

As David told me his story, it became clear that being a ninety-pound wimp might have been a blessing in disguise. His apparent weakness (skinny body) actually became his strength (forced him to develop discipline and perseverance). People who lack the native physical, social, or mental gifts they desire must fight just that much harder. And that uphill battle can produce qualities and strengths they couldn't develop any other way. That is how a weakness can become a strength.

So if you're not endowed with all the beauty, biceps, bucks, or brains that you covet—congratulations! You just may have the better deal. This poem by Douglas Malloch says it well:

> The tree that never had to fight
> For sun and sky and air and light,
> But stood out in the open plain
> And always got its share of rain,
> Never became a forest king
> But lived and died a scrubby thing . . .
> Good timber does not grow with ease,
> The stronger wind, the stronger trees.

Make Your Life Extraordinary Life is short. This point is emphasized in the classic movie *Friday Night Lights*. Coach Gary Gaines tells his team of struggling high school football players: "Being perfect is not about that scoreboard out there. It's not about winning. It's about you and your relationship with yourself, your family, and your friends. Being perfect is about being able to look your friends in the eye and know that you didn't let them down because you told them the truth. And that truth is you did everything you could. There wasn't one more thing you could've done. Can you live in that moment as best you can, with clear eyes, and love in your heart, with joy in your heart? If you can do that gentleman—you're perfect!"

Theologian Howard Thurman once said, "Don't ask yourself what the world needs. Ask yourself what makes you come alive and go do that, because what the world needs is people who have come alive." Carpe Diem! Sieze the day! Make your life extraordinary!

As you do this, remember, life is a mission, not a career. A career is a profession. A mission is a cause. A career asks, "What's in it for me?" A mission asks, "How can I make a difference?" Martin Luther King, Jr.'s mission was to ensure civil rights for all people, no matter their race. Gandhi's mission was to liberate 300 million oppressed

Car-pe. Car-pe. Car-pe. Car-pe. **Carpe diem.**

Indian citizens. Mother Teresa's mission was to clothe the naked and feed the hungry.

These are extreme examples. You don't have to change the world to have a mission. As educator Maren Mouritsen says, "Most of us will never do great things. But we can do small things in a great way."

COMING ATTRACTIONS

You've heard of willpower. But have you ever heard of won't power? That's up next!

1 Determine the three most important skills you'll need to succeed in your career. Do you need to be more organized, be more confident speaking in front of other people, have stronger computer programming skills?

The three most important skills I need for my career:

_____

 **2** Reread your mission statement daily for 30 days (that's how long it takes to develop a habit). Let it guide you in all your decisions.

3 Look in the mirror and ask, "Would I want to spend time with some-one like me?" If not, work to develop the qualities you're lacking.

4 Go to your school guidance or employment counselor and talk about college or career opportunities. Or, find an aptitude test online that'll help you evaluate your talents, abilities, and interests.

5 What's the key crossroad you are facing in your life right now? In the long run, what's the best path to take?

Key crossroad I am facing: _____

The best path to take: _____

6 Share some of The Great Discovery activity questions on your Facebook page or your blog. See what your friends' answers are. Share yours as well.

7 Think about your goals. Have you written them down? If not, take time to do it. Remember, a goal not written is only a wish.

8 Identify a negative label others may have given you. Think up a few things you can do to change that label.

Negative label: _____

How to change it: _____

Put First Things First

Will and Won't Power

I watched the Indy 500, and I was thinking that if they left earlier they wouldn't have to go so fast.

STEVEN WRIGHT, COMEDIAN

I was listening to a speech comparing the challenges faced by today's teens to those of teens who lived 150 years ago. I agreed with most of what the speaker said until this: "The challenge that teens faced 150 years ago was hard work. The challenge that teens face today is a lack of hard work."

Uh, ex-squeeze me! I mumbled to myself. *A lack of hard work? What are you smokin'?* I think teens are multitasking more than ever. I see it with my own eyes every day. Between school, socializing, extracurricular activities, clubs, athletics, part-time jobs, dealing with family, and on and on, there's barely time to breathe. A lack of hard work? Ha! Milking cows and mending fences doesn't sound any more difficult than juggling the multifaceted life of a twenty-first-century teen.

Let's face it. You've got a lot to do and there's just not enough time. After school there's rehearsal, followed by work. There's also that bio test tomorrow. And you've gotta text your friend relationship crisis advice. On top of that, you should exercise. The dog needs a walk. And your room's a disaster. What'll you do?

Habit 3, Put First Things First, can help. It's all about learning to prioritize and manage your time so that your first things come first, not last. But there's more to this habit than just time management. Putting first things first can also help you learn to overcome your fears and be strong during hard moments.

In Habit 2, you decided what your first things are. Habit 3, then, is putting them *first* in your life.

Sure we can have a nice list of goals and good intentions, but doing them, putting them into action is the hard part. That's why I call Habit 3 the habit of *willpower* (the strength to say yes to your most important things) and *won't power* (the strength to say no to less important things and to peer pressure).

The first three habits build upon each other. Habit 1 says, "You are the driver, not the passenger." Habit 2 says, "Decide where you want to go and draw up a map to get you there." Habit 3 says, "Now, get there! Don't let roadblocks knock you off course."

● PACKING MORE INTO YOUR LIFE

Have you ever packed a suitcase and noticed how much more you can fit inside when you neatly fold and organize your clothes instead of just throwing them in? It's really quite surprising. The same goes for your life. The better you organize yourself, the more you'll be able to pack in—more time for family and friends, more time for school, more time for yourself, more time for your first things.

I'd like to show you an amazing model called the Time Quadrants that can help you pack more in (especially important things). It's made up of two primary ingredients, "important" and "urgent."

Important—your most important things, your first things, activities that contribute to your mission and your goals.

Urgent—things that have to be done ASAP, in-your-face things, activities that demand immediate attention.

In general, we spend our time in four different time quadrants, as shown below. Each quadrant contains different kinds of activities and is represented by a type of person.

The Time Quadrants

	URGENT	NOT URGENT
IMPORTANT	**1** THE **PROCRASTINATOR** • TEST TOMORROW • FRIEND GETS INJURED • LATE TO CLASS • ESSAY DUE TODAY • CAR BREAKS DOWN	**2** THE **PRIORITIZER** • PLANNING & GOAL SETTING • ESSAY DUE IN A WEEK • WORKING OUT • RELATIONSHIPS • RELAXATION
NOT IMPORTANT	**3** THE **YES-MAN** • TEXTING ENDLESSLY • DISTRACTIONS • OTHER PEOPLE'S SMALL PROBLEMS • PEER PRESSURE	**4** THE **SLACKER** • STUCK ON FACEBOOK • NONSTOP XBOX • MALL MARATHONS • MINDLESS GOSSIP • TIME WASTERS

HABIT 3

If you haven't already noticed, we live in a society that's addicted to urgency. It's the NOW generation. That's why we have Internet on our phones, instant messaging, Instagram, crash diets, fast food, 140-character tweets, and online shopping. It reminds me of Veruca Salt, the spoiled rich girl in *Willie Wonka and the Chocolate Factory*, who keeps saying, "Now, Daddy! Now! I want an Oompa-Loompa now!"

Urgent things aren't bad, necessarily. The problem comes when we become so focused on *urgent* things that we put off *important* things that aren't urgent, like working on that report in advance, going for a walk in nature, or taking time to videochat with a long distance friend. All these *important* things get interrupted by *urgent* things, like texts, emails, deadlines, and other "in-your-face-do-it-this-second" things.

As we dig a little deeper into each quadrant, ask yourself, "What quadrant am I spending most of my time in?"

QUADRANT 1: *The Procrastinator*

Let's start with Q1, things that are both urgent and important. There will always be Q1 things that we can't control and that must get done, like helping someone who is sick or sticking to a due date. But we also cause many Q1 headaches because we procrastinate, like when we put off doing our homework and then have to cram all night for a test or when we neglect our bike for too long and then have to take it in to get repaired. Q1 is part of life, but if you're spending too much time in Q1, believe me, you'll feel like a hot mess and you'll seldom be performing to your potential.

Meet the Procrastinator, who hangs out in Q1. Perhaps you know her. Her motto is, "I'm going to stop procrastinating—sometime soon." Don't expect her to work on a paper or study for a test until the night before. And don't expect her to take time to get gas; she's usually too busy driving.

The Procrastinator is addicted to urgency. She likes to put things off and put things off and put things off . . . until it becomes a crisis. But she likes it that way because, you see, even though it's stressful, doing everything at the last minute gives her a rush. In fact, her mind won't kick into gear until there's an emergency. She thrives under pressure.

Planning ahead is simply out of the question for the Procrastinator because it would ruin the excitement of doing everything at the last possible moment.

I can relate to the Procrastinator because I was a cram artist in high school. I used to think it was impressive to not study all semester, then cram the night before and pull off a good grade. How stupid! Sure I got the grade, but I didn't learn a thing and I paid for it in college. In many ways I'm still paying for it.

One procrastinating teen said it this way:

"What I do is I slack off until the end of the term and kill myself for the last two weeks. When grades come out I get around a 3.7 to 3.8, but I don't feel I have earned it because everyone else turned stuff in on time and does what they're supposed to. They're not stressed. That's how I want to be."

The results of too much time in Q1 are:
- Stress and anxiety
- Feeling burnt out
- Mediocre performance

QUADRANT 2: *The Prioritizer*
We'll save the best for last—I'll keep you in suspense for now!

QUADRANT 3: *The Yes-man*
Q3 represents things that are urgent but not important. It is characterized by trying to please other people and responding to their every desire. This quadrant is deceptive because urgent, immediate things feel important. In truth, they're often not. I mean how many times do you drop something to check your phone, when the only text you got is from a friend responding "k" or "lol" and that's it! Not really worth the interruption. Q3 is loaded with activities that are important to other people but not important to you—things that you would like to say no to but can't because you're afraid you might offend someone.

Meet the Yes-man of Q3, who has a hard time saying no to anything or anyone. He tries so hard to please everyone that he usually ends up pleasing no one, including himself. He suffers from FOMO—Fear of Missing Out. He can't stop imagining that everyone's having fun without him, and so he tries to be a part of everything. He often caves to peer pressure because he likes feeling popular and he wouldn't want to stand out. His motto is, "Tomorrow, I'll be more assertive—if that's okay with you."

When his friends dropped by unexpectedly one evening and wanted him to go for a night ride, he just couldn't muster up the courage to turn them down. He didn't want to disappoint his buddies. It didn't matter that he was taking a massive test the next morning and needed to study and get some sleep.

He told his sister that he'd help her with math, but he couldn't resist getting distracted by a texting marathon for most of the night. Even though it wasn't that important.

He didn't really want to join the swimming team. He preferred graphic design. But his dad was a swimmer and, of course, he didn't want to let him down.

I think all of us, myself included, have a little Q3 inside of us. But we won't accomplish much if we say yes to everything and never learn to focus on what's most important. Comedian Bill Cosby has said it well: "I don't know the key to success, but the key to failure is to try to please everyone." Q3 is one of the worst quadrants to be in because it has no backbone. It's fickle and will blow whichever way the wind is blowing.

The results of spending too much time in Q3 are:
- Feeling like a follower rather than a leader
- Lack of discipline
- Feeling like a doormat for others to wipe their feet on

QUADRANT 4: *The Slacker*

Q4 is the category of waste and excess. These activities are neither urgent nor important.

Meet the Slacker who hangs out in Q4. He loves anything in excess, like too much TV, too much sleep, too much PlayStation, or too much time online. Two of his favorite pastimes include regular napping and binging on an entire TV series each weekend.

He's a professional slacker. Sleeping in until noon takes real skill, after all. School, of course, is the last thing on his mind, and a summer job is out of the question. He'd rather, you know, just hang out.

Yes, of course chilling out and watching

videos online are part of a healthy lifestyle. It's only when they're done in excess that they become a waste of time. You'll know when you cross that line. Watching that first episode of your favorite TV show might be just what you need to relax, and that's okay. But then watching the second, third, or even fourth show (a rerun that you've seen five times already) until 2 A.M. turns a relaxing evening into a wasted one.

The results of living in Q4 are:
- Lack of responsibility
- Guilt
- Flakiness
- Missing out on adventures

QUADRANT 2: *The Prioritizer*

Now back to Q2. Q2 is made of things that are important but not urgent—like relaxation, friendships, working out, planning ahead, and doing homework . . . on time! It's the quadrant of excellence—the place to be. Q2 activities are important. But are Q2 activities urgent? No! And that's why we have trouble doing them. For example, getting a good summer job may be very important to you. But since it's weeks away and not urgent, you may put off looking on Craigslist until it's too late and suddenly all the good jobs are filled. Had you been in Q2, you would have planned ahead and found a better job. It wouldn't take more time, just a little more planning.

Meet the Prioritizer. Although she's by no means perfect, she's basically got it together. She takes a look at everything she has to do and then prioritizes, making sure her first things get done first and her last things last. Because she has the simple but powerful habit of planning ahead, she's usually on top of things. By doing her homework on time and writing papers a little in advance, she does her best work and avoids the stress and burnout that come from cramming. She makes time to exercise and renew herself, even if it means pushing aside other things once in a while. The people who matter most in her life, like her friends and her family, come first. Although it's a struggle, staying balanced is important to her.

She changes the oil in her car regularly. And she doesn't wait until she's running on fumes to fill up with gas. She takes time to relax, but knows there's a time and a place to let loose.

She's learned how to say no with a smile. When her friends dropped by unexpectedly one evening to go to a party, she said, "Nah, I have a huge test tomorrow. How about Friday night? Let's go out then." Her friends were okay with that and secretly wished they'd had the courage to stick to their guns, too. She's learned that resisting peer pressure appears unpopular at first, but that people come to respect her for it.

The results of living in Q2 are:
- Control of your life
- Balance
- High performance

So in which quadrant are you spending the majority of your time? 1, 2, 3, or 4? Since, in reality, we all spend some time in each quadrant, the key is to shift as much time as possible into Q2. And the only way you'll find more time for Q2 is to reduce the amount of time you spend in the other quadrants. Here is how to do that:

Shrink Q1 by procrastinating less. You're always going to have lots to do in Q1. That's guaranteed. But if you can cut your procrastination in half by doing important things early, you'll be in Q1 far less often. And less Q1 time means less stress!

Say no to Q3 activities. Learn to say no to unimportant things that pull you away from more important ones. Don't be so interruptible. Trying to please everyone is like a dog trying to catch its tail. Remember, when you're saying no you're really saying yes to more important things.

Cut down on Q4, slacker activities. Don't stop doing these things, just do them less often. You don't have time to waste. Shift this time to Q2. You need to relax and kick back, but remember relaxation is Q2. Excessive relaxation is Q4.

In addition to spending more time in Q2, consider two other suggestions to help you better manage your time and put first things first: Start a calendar and plan weekly.

● GET A PLANNER

To start with, I highly recommend getting a planner or calendar—on your computer, phone, on paper, whatever works. Just somewhere with space to write down appointments, to-do lists, and goals. There are some great apps for calendars, or if you want you can buy a paper planner or make your own out of a spiral-bound notebook.

Some of you might be thinking, "I don't want my life to be tied to a planner. I like my freedom." If this is you, keep in mind that a planner wasn't designed to tie you down but to free you up. With a planner you'll no longer have to worry about forgetting things or double-booking yourself. It will remind you when your papers are due and tests are to be taken. You can keep all of your important information in one place instead of scattered all over. A planner is not meant to be your master but a tool to help you live your life.

Plan Weekly

Take a few minutes each week to plan your week and see what a difference it can make. Why weekly? Because we think in weeks and because daily planning is too narrow a focus and monthly planning is too broad a focus. Once you have a planner of some sort, follow this three-step weekly planning process.

Step 1: Identify Your Big Rocks. At the end or beginning of each week, sit down and think about what you want to accomplish for the upcoming week. Ask yourself, "What are the most important things I need to do this week?" I call these your big rocks. They are sort of like mini-goals and should be tied into your mission statement and longer-term goals. Not surprisingly, you'll find that most of them will be Q2's.

You might come up with a list of big rocks that looks something like this:

My Big Rocks for the Week
- Study for chemistry test
- Finish *The Great Gatsby* for English
- Attend Carly's game
- Finish summer job applications
- Party at Anjali's
- Workout 3 times

So how do you know which are your big rocks? Well, think through the key roles of your life—student, friend, family member, employee, individual, and whatever else you do and then come up with the one or two most important things you want to get done in each role. Planning your life around roles majorly helps you stay balanced.

ROLE	MY BIG ROCKS FOR THE WEEK
Student	Get started on history report
Friend	Julio's birthday Be more complimentary
Family	Get Mother's Day gift at the mall Call Grandma
Job	Get to work on time
Me	Go to Jayden's gig Write in journal every night
Debate Team	Research arguments Practice openings

Don't get carried away when you're identifying your big rocks for the week. Although you may feel you have forty big rocks that must get done, be realistic and narrow your focus to no more than seven to ten.

Step 2: Block Out Time for Your Big Rocks. Do you know the big rock experiment? You get a bucket and fill it half full of small pebbles. You then try to put several big rocks in the bucket, on top of the pebbles. But they don't all fit. So you empty the bucket and start over. This time you put the big rocks in the bucket first, followed by the pebbles. The pebbles neatly fill in the spaces around the big rocks. This time it all fits! The difference is the order in which the rocks and pebbles were placed in the bucket. If you put the pebbles in first, the big rocks don't all fit. But if you put the big rocks in first, everything fits, big rocks *and* pebbles. Big rocks represent your most important things. Pebbles represent all the little everyday things that suck up your time—such as chores, texting, errands, and interruptions, etc. Moral of the story? If you don't schedule your big rocks first, they won't get done.

During your weekly planning, block out time for your big rocks by putting them in your calendar. For example, you might decide that the best time to get started on your history report is Tuesday night and the best time to call your grandma is Sunday afternoon. Now block out those times. It's like making a reservation. If your big rock such as "give out three compliments each day this week" doesn't have a specific time attached to it, write it somewhere in your planner where it can be seen.

If you block out time for your big rocks first, the other everyday activities will fit in as well. And if they don't, who cares? You'd rather push aside pebbles than big rocks. Take care of 'em next week.

Step 3: Schedule Everything Else. Once you have your big rocks booked, schedule in all of your other little to-dos, daily tasks, and appointments. Here's where the pebbles go. Take note of upcoming events and activities, like a vacation, a friend's concert, or birthday.

Adapt Daily

You'll probably need to rearrange some big rocks and pebbles now and then. So adapt each day as needed. Try your best to follow your plan, but if you don't accomplish everything you set out to do, no big deal. Even if you only get a third of your big rocks accomplished, that's a third more than you might have accomplished without planning ahead.

If this weekly planning method feels too rigid or complicated, don't scrap it entirely, just do weekly planning *light*. For example, you may find you only want to schedule two or three big rocks for the week and that's about it.

The point is: The simple act of planning ahead each week will help you focus on your big rocks and consequently accomplish so much more.

Does It Really Work?

Does this time-management stuff really work? You bet it does. I have personally read numerous emails and letters from teens who have had great success with the above suggestions. Here are comments from two teens who were taught about the Time Quadrants and began using a planner and doing weekly planning:

Jacob:

I remember looking at the diagram of the Time Quadrants and saying, "Man, this is true. I do a lot of last-minute things." Like homework. If a paper was due, I'd do it Sunday night to turn in Monday, or if there was a test on Friday, I'd skip school on Thursday to study for my test. I was pretty much in crisis.

Once I figured out what was important to me, I started to prioritize and started using a planner. If I wanted to go fishing I would say, "Well, this other thing is more important. I'll do that first, and then maybe tomorrow I will have the whole day to fish." Eventually I started studying more effectively, aced my tests, and everything just fell into place. My life would have been less stressful if I only had used my time more effectively earlier.

Brooke:

My stress level has decreased because I am no longer constantly trying to remember what I have to do a few days ahead. Now I can just pull out my schedule and I'm all set. When I get in a bad mood and stressed out, I look at my schedule and realize that I still have time to do everything, especially the things just for me.

One of the few things that can't be recycled is wasted time. So make sure you treasure each moment. In the words of Queen Elizabeth I on her deathbed: "All my possessions for one moment of time."

● THE OTHER HALF

Time management isn't all there is to Habit 3. It's only half of it. The other half is learning to overcome fear and peer pressure. It takes courage and guts to stay true to your first things, like your values and standards, when the pressure is on. I once asked a group of kids, "What are your first things?" to which they answered, among other things: "family," "friends," "freedom," "excitement," "growth," "trust," "God," "stability," "belonging," "looks." I then asked, "What keeps you from putting these things first in your life?" Not surprisingly, "fear" and "peer pressure" were two of the top responses. So we're going to talk about how to deal with these.

The Comfort Zone and the Courage Zone

Putting your first things first takes courage and it'll often cause you to stretch outside your comfort zone. Take a peek at the Courage and Comfort Zone diagram.

Your comfort zone represents things you're familiar with, your regular haunts, friends you're at ease with, activities you love doing. Your comfort zone's risk free. It's easy. It doesn't cause you to stretch. Within these boundaries we feel safe and secure.

On the other hand, things like making new friends, speaking before a large audience, or sticking up for your values can totally freak you out. Welcome to the courage zone! Adventure, risk, and challenge included! Everything that makes us feel challenged (aka uncomfortable) is found here. In this territory waits uncertainty, pressure, change, the possibility of failure. But it's also the place to go for opportunity and the only place in which you'll ever reach your full potential. You'll never reach it by hanging out in your comfort zone. That's for sure.

What's that you asked? *"What's so wrong about enjoying your comfort zone?"*

Nothing. In fact, much of our time should be spent there. But there's something absolutely wrong with never venturing into unknown waters. You know as well as I do that people who seldom try new things or spread their wings live safe but boring lives! And who wants that? "You miss 100 percent of the shots you never take," said hockey great Wayne Gretzky. Why not show some faith in yourself, take a risk, and parachute into your courage zone from time to time? Remember, the risk of riskless living is the greatest risk of all.

It's not the mountain we conquer, but ourselves.

EDMUND HILLARY
(first person to climb Mount Everest)

Never Let Your Fears Make Your Decisions

There are a lot of sick emotions is this world, but perhaps one of the worst is *fear.* When I think about all I failed to do in my life because my fears got the best of me I ache inside. In high school I had a crush on a cool girl named Sherry but I never asked her out because my fears whispered, "She may not like you." I remember quitting my seventh-grade football team after one practice because I was afraid of competition. I'll never forget contemplating running for a student body office but chickening out because I was too scared of speaking in front of the whole school. Throughout my life there have been classes I never took, friends I never made, and teams I never played for—all because of these ugly, yet very real, fears. I like how Shakespeare put it in *Measure for Measure*:

> Our doubts are traitors,
> And make us lose the good we oft might win
> By fearing to attempt.

My dad once told me something I've never forgotten. "Sean," he said, "never let your fears make your decisions. You make them." That really stuck with me. Think of all the heroic acts that have been accomplished by people who acted in the face of fear. Think of Nelson Mandela, who was instrumental in ending the oppressive apartheid system in South Africa. Mandela was imprisoned for twenty-seven years (imagine that) for speaking out against apartheid before being elected as the first non-white president of South Africa. What if, because of his fears, he had never dared to fight the system? Or consider the unyielding courage of Susan B. Anthony as she led the long struggle that finally won women the right to vote under the U.S. Constitution. Or think of Winston Churchill, prime minister of England during World War II, who led the free world in its fight against Nazi Germany. What if, because of self-doubt, he had been fainthearted during the war? Surely all great, risky deeds, whether by famous people or by everyday people, were accomplished in the face of fear.

Acting in the face of fear will never be easy, but afterward you'll always be glad you did it. During my senior year in college I was short a few credits, and so I skimmed through the class schedule looking for something to fill the hours. When I came across "Private Voice Instruction," as in singing lessons, I thought, "Why not step outside my comfort zone and give it a try?"

I was careful to sign up for private lessons instead of group lessons because I didn't want to make a fool of myself by singing in front of other students.

Things went fine until the end of the semester when my singing professor brought the shocking news. "By the way, Sean, have you decided which song you want to sing at the recital?"

"What do you mean?" I asked in horror.

"Well, the class requirements state that you have to sing at least one time in front of the other private voice students."

TO BE OR NOT TO BE.

"Acting in the face of fear"

"That would not be a good idea," I said emphatically.

"Oh, it's no big deal. You'll do fine."

Well, to me it *was* a huge deal. The thought of singing in front of a group made me physically sick. "How am I going to get out of this one?" I thought. But I couldn't allow myself to do that because I had been speaking to various groups over the past year advising them to never let fears make their decisions. Now . . . I was up to bat.

"Courage, Sean." I kept rehearsing in my mind. "You've got to at least try."

That dreaded day finally arrived. As I entered the "room of doom" where I was to make my debut, I kept trying to convince myself, "Just chill, ok? This can't be that bad."

But it kept getting worse. I became increasingly intimidated as I discovered that nearly everyone in the room was either a music or theater major. I mean, these people really knew how to sing. Since childhood they'd been performing in musicals and choruses. My fear only increased when the first student called upon sang a song

HABIT 3

from *Les Misérables* that sounded better than on the soundtrack. The guy was incredible. Yet the class had the audacity to critique him. "I think that your tonality was a little flat," someone said. "Oh, no! What will they think of me?"

"Sean, you're up."

Now it was my turn.

As I stood in front of the class, three million light-years outside my comfort zone, I kept repeating to myself, "Courage! *Ugh, I can't believe I'm doing this.* Courage! *Ugh, I can't believe I'm doing this.*"

"I will be singing 'On the Street Where You Live' from *My Fair Lady*," I quivered.

As the accompanist began playing the prelude and all eyes fell upon me, I couldn't help but think, "How? How in the world did I get myself into this situation?" And from the smiles on everyone's faces it looked as if they were actually going to take me seriously.

"I have often walked down this street before . . ." I rang out.

Even before I reached the second line, the expressions of excitement on the students' faces turned to anguish. I was so nervous that my body felt as tight as jeans just pulled from the dryer. I had to squeeze each word out.

Near the end of the song is a really high note. It had always been difficult for me to reach, even in practice. Now I anticipated it with terror. But as that note approached I thought, "What the heck. Go for it!"

I don't recall if I hit that note or missed it. All I remember is that a few students were so embarrassed that they couldn't even look at me.

I finished and sat down quickly. Silence. No one knew what to say.

"That was great, Sean."

"Thanks a lot," I shrugged, as if I believed them. But do you know what? Although that experience nearly killed me, when I left that classroom and walked alone through the empty parking lot to my car I was so proud of myself. I felt a great sense of personal accomplishment, and I frankly didn't care what anyone else thought about my high note. I had survived and I was proud of it.

As gymnast and Olympic gold-medalist Gabby Douglas put it, "The hard days are the best because that's where champions are made—so if you can push through, you can push through any-thing!" So the next time you want to:

- make a new friend,
- resist peer pressure,
- break an old habit,
- develop a new skill,
- try out for a team,
- audition for a play,
- ask out the one and only,
- change your job,
- get involved,
- be yourself,

or even if you want to sing in public . . . Do it! . . . even when all your fears and doubts scream out, "You loser," "You'll fail," "Don't try." Never let your fears make your decisions. You make them.

Winning Means Rising Each Time You Fall

We all feel fear from time to time, and that's okay. "Feel the fear and do it anyway" goes the saying. One way I've learned to overcome fear is to keep this thought always in the back of my mind: *Winning is nothing more than rising each time you fall.* We should worry less about failing and more about the chances we miss when we don't even try. After all, many of the people we most admire failed many times.

For instance, Babe Ruth struck out 1,330 times. Albert Einstein didn't talk until he was four. Beethoven's music teacher said, "As a composer he is hopeless." Louis Pasteur was graded "mediocre" in chemistry. Rocket scientist Wernher von Braun failed ninth-grade al-gebra. Chemist Madame Marie Curie experienced near financial ruin before creating the field of nuclear chemistry and forever changing the course of science. Steve Jobs was fired by Apple after he founded it and later returned to run the company and invent the iPhone. Dr Seuss's first book was rejected by twenty-seven publishers.

Below are events in the life history of a man who failed many times but kept fighting back. See if you can guess who it is. This man:

- failed in business at age twenty-two
- was defeated for the state legislature at age twenty-three
- failed in business at age twenty-five
- coped with the death of his sweetheart at age twenty-six
- suffered a nervous breakdown at age twenty-seven
- was defeated for Speaker at age twenty-nine
- was defeated for congressional nomination at age thirty-four
- was elected to Congress at age thirty-seven
- lost renomination for Congress at age thirty-nine

- was defeated for the Senate at age forty-six
- was defeated for the vice presidency of the United States at age forty-seven
- and was defeated for the Senate at age forty-nine

This person was none other than Abraham Lincoln, elected president of the United States at age fifty-one. He rose each time he fell and eventually reached his destination, gaining the respect and admiration of all nations and peoples.

> Two roads diverged in a wood, and I—
> I took the one less traveled by,
> And that has made all the difference.
>
> ROBERT FROST
> POET

Be Strong in the Hard Moments

The poet Robert Frost wrote, "Two roads diverged in a wood, and I—I took the one less traveled by, And that has made all the difference." I have come to believe that there are certain hard moments, diverging-road moments, that, if we are strong in them, will make "all the difference" down the road of life.

So what exactly are hard moments? Hard moments are conflicts between doing the right thing and doing the easier thing. They are the key tests, the defining moments of life—and how we handle them can literally shape our forevers. They come in two sizes, small and large.

Small hard moments occur daily and include things like getting up when your alarm rings early, controlling your temper, or disciplining yourself to finish your homework. If you can conquer yourself and be strong in these moments your days will run so much more smoothly (also you won't have to stress about 'em anymore). For example, if I'm weak in a hard moment and sleep in (mattress over mind), it often snowballs and becomes the first of many little failures throughout the day. But if I get up when planned (mind over mattress), it often becomes the first of many little successes.

In contrast to small hard moments, larger ones occur every so often in life and include things like surrounding yourself with good friends, resisting negative peer pressure, and rebounding after a major setback: You may get cut from a team or dumped by your first love, your parents may get divorced or you may have a death in the family. These moments have huge consequences and often strike when you're least expecting them. If you recognize that these moments will come (and they will), then you can prepare for them and meet them head-on like a warrior and come out victorious.

Be courageous at these key junctures! Don't sacrifice your future happiness for one night of pleasure, a weekend of excitement, or a thrilling moment of revenge. If you are ever thinking about doing something really stupid, remember these lines from Shakespeare (Wow! Shakespeare twice in one chapter):

What win I, if I gain the thing I seek?
A dream, a breath, a froth of fleeting joy.
Who buys a minute's mirth to wail a week?
Or sells eternity to get a toy?
For one sweet grape who will the vine destroy?

These lines are about sacrificing your future for a brief moment of joy. Who would want to give up the rest of his or her life for a toy? Or who would want to buy a minute of happiness (mirth) for a week's worth of pain? Or who would destroy an entire vine for just one grape? Only a stupid person would.

Overcoming Peer Pressure

Some of the hardest moments come when facing peer pressure. Saying no when all your friends are saying yes takes raw courage. However, standing up to peer pressure, what I call "won't power," is a massive deposit into your PBA.

A counselor at a high school shared this:

A freshman girl rushed into my office before school with tears streaming down her face. "They hate me! They hate me!"

She had just been dumped by her group of friends who told her to get lost because she had been "too good" the day before to ditch school and ride up to Chicago for the day. She said at first she wanted to go but then thought how much it would hurt her mom when the school called home and told her that her daughter wasn't in school. She felt she just couldn't do that to her mom because she had made so many sacrifices for her. She couldn't let her down!

She stood up and said no I can't do it, and everyone just blew her off. She thought the next day that everything would be okay, but it wasn't— they all told her to find new friends because she was too good for them.

Through the tears and pain she began to see that she felt good inside, but lonely, as her friends didn't accept her. But she accepted herself and gained self-respect and inner peace despite outside rejection. A life lesson learned and a moment of standing up for herself.

Sometimes peer pressure can be so strong that the only way to resist it is to remove yourself entirely from the environment you're in. This is especially the case if you're involved with a gang, a fraternity or sorority, or a tight group of friends. For Heather, changing her environment was the best solution:

Even though I knew for a long time that I needed to change my friends, I just didn't know how. My "best friend" would encourage me to do the things she was, like sleeping around and doing drugs. Before long people at school started to call me easy.

I still wanted to be friends with her, and my other friends, because I would think about all the good times we'd had together. Yet when I went out with them at night we would get into stuff we weren't supposed to. I knew I was holding on to things that I shouldn't be.

I decided I needed to change my whole environment and get away from it all. I asked my mom if I could go and stay with my aunt to get a new start and find a better group of friends. She agreed, and since then I've moved in with my aunt.

Now, around my new friends, I say whatever I feel is right, and I am being more myself. I don't care what people say about me, and if they don't like me, then oh well! This is me, and I am not going to change just to fit in with them. I am going to change for me.

To overcome peer pressure, you've got to care more about what *you* think of you than what *other people* think of you, as this short poem by Portia Nelson reminds us:

> *Any day of the week*
> *I would choose to be "out"*
> *with others*
> *and in touch*
> *with myself . . .*
> *than to be "in" with others*
> *and out of touch*
> *with myself.*

Why is peer pressure so hard to resist? It's because sometimes you're just dying to belong. That's why teens are often willing to go through brutal hazing rituals to become a member of a club, or fraternity or sorority. Some get into drugs and violence to become a member of a gang. Some feel they have to suck up to certain people to be popular, then drop their old friends on the way up the social ladder.

At times you may need to take a risk, resist the peer pressure, and do the right thing.

Jon of Brooklyn told this story:

Some of my friends in sophomore year started a page on Facebook about hating one girl named in our class. It was really awful—they'd make memes out of her photos and write terrible messages about her.

There was really no reason to do this, she was just kind of an outsider and people were taking it so way out of control it wasn't even funny.

Some of my friends were pressuring me to participate, but I just refused. Finally, I reported the group for hate speech, anonymously, and it got shut down. I knew it was the right thing to do. I also told the principal, without naming names, that some people in the grade were cyberbullying, and we had an assembly about it. I was scared of having to face everyone the next day at school, but no one knew it was me who did it. In fact, I went up and talked to the girl in math class, just to get to know her a little and let her know she wasn't alone. Turns out she's a really cool, nice person. We've been friends ever since and she still doesn't know it was me who stopped the cyberbullying.

• THE GOOD KIND OF PRESSURE

Not all peer pressure is bad. In fact, much of it can be very good. If you can find a friend who puts positive pressure on you to be your best, then hang on to him or her, because you've got something very special—someone who's got your back.

If you find yourself wanting to stand up but instead you are continually caving in to peer pressure, here are two things you can do.

First, build your PBA (Personal Bank Account). If your self-confidence and self-respect are low, how can you expect to have the strength to resist? What can you do? You can begin today to build your PBA, little by little. Make a promise to yourself and keep it. Help someone in need. Develop a talent. Renew yourself. Eventually you'll have sufficient strength to forge your own path instead of following the beaten ones. (You may want to review the chapter on the personal bank account.)

Second, write your mission statement and set goals. If you haven't decided what your values are, how can you expect to stick up for them? It will be a whole lot easier to say no if you know what goals you're saying yes to. For example, it's easier to say no to cutting class when you are saying yes to your goal of getting good grades and making it to college. (You may want to review the chapter on Habit 2, Begin with the End in Mind.)

• THE COMMON INGREDIENT OF SUCCESS

In the final analysis, putting first things first takes discipline. It takes discipline to manage your time. It takes discipline to overcome your fears. It takes discipline to be strong in the hard moments and resist peer pressure. A man by the name of Albert E. Gray spent years studying successful people in an attempt to figure out that special ingredient that made them all successful. What do you think he found? Well, it wasn't dressing for success, or eating Greek yogurt, or having a positive mental attitude. Instead, this is what he found. Read it carefully.

Albert E. Gray's Common Denominator of Success:

All successful people have the habit of doing the things failures don't like to do. They don't like doing them either necessarily. But their disliking is subordinated to the strength of their purpose.

What does this mean? It means that successful people are willing to suck it up from time to time and do things they don't like doing. Why do they do them? Because they know these things will lead them to their goals.

In other words, sometimes you just gotta exercise your special human tool called *willpower* to get things done, whether you feel like it or not. Do you think a concert pianist always enjoys hours of practice each day? Does a person who is committed to earning her own way through college enjoy taking on a second job?

I remember reading a story about an all-American collegiate wrestler who was asked what the most memorable day of his career had been. He replied that it was the one day during his career when practice had been canceled. He hated practice, but was willing to endure it for a greater purpose, his love of being the best he could be.

● A FINAL WORD

We've surveyed thousands of people on the 7 Habits and guess which habit is the hardest one to live? You guessed it! It's Habit 3. So don't get discouraged if you struggle with it. You've got company.

If you don't know where to start with Habit 3, go to the baby steps. That's what they are there for—to help you get started.

Your teen years can be some of the most exciting and adventurous years of life. So value each moment, as this poem so beautifully communicates:

To realize the value of One Year,
Ask a student who failed his or her AP exams.
To realize the value of One Month,
Ask a mother who gave birth to a premature baby.
To realize the value of One Week,
Ask an editor of a weekly magazine.
To realize the value of One Day,
Ask a daily wage laborer who has six kids to feed.
To realize the value of One Hour,
Ask the lovers who are waiting to meet.
To realize the value of One Minute,
Ask a person who missed their train.
To realize the value of One Second,
Ask the person who survived an accident.
To realize the value of One Millisecond,
Ask the person who won a silver medal in the Olympics.

★★★

COMING ATTRACTIONS

Just up ahead we'll talk about the stuff that life is made of. I think you'll be surprised what that stuff is. So keep moving! By the way, you're halfway done with the book. Congratulations!

BABY STEPS

1 Do a search and get a planner app on your tablet or smart phone and use it to get more organized. Try it for 30 days before judging it.

2 Identify your biggest time-wasters. Do you really need to spend two hours checking out other people's Instagrams, or playing video games?

My biggest time-wasters: ....

3 Are you a "pleaser," someone who says yes to everything and everyone? If so, have the courage to say no today when it's the right thing to do.

4 If you have an important test in one week, don't procrastinate and wait until the day before to study. Suck it up; study a little each day.

5 Think of something you've procrastinated for a long time but that's very important to you. Block out time this week to get it done.

Item I've procrastinated forever: ....

6  Note your seven most important big rocks for the upcoming week. Now, block out time on your calendar to accomplish each one.

7 Identify a fear that's holding you back from reaching your goals— it could be fear of a person, fear of emotions, fear of getting hurt. Decide right now to jump outside your comfort zone and stop letting that fear get the best of you.

Fear that's holding me back: ....

8 How much impact does peer pressure have on you? Identify the person or people who have the most influence upon you. Ask yourself, "Am I doing what I want to do or what they want me to do?"

Person or people who most influence me: ....

....

PART III

The Public Victory

The Relationship
Bank Account

THE STUFF THAT LIFE IS MADE OF

One of my favorite quotes, which, by the way, always makes me feel guilty, is "On their deathbed nobody has ever wished they had spent more time at the office."

I've often asked myself, "What *do* they wish they'd spent more time doing?" I think the answer might be "Spent more time with the people they love." You see, it's all about relationships, the stuff that life is made of.

What's it like to be in a relationship with you? If you had to rate how well you're doing in your most important relationships, how would you score?

HOW ARE YOUR RELATIONSHIPS WITH . . .	LOUSY			EXCELLENT	
Your friends?	1	2	3	4	5
Your siblings?	1	2	3	4	5
Your parents or guardian?	1	2	3	4	5
Your girlfriend or boyfriend?	1	2	3	4	5
Your teachers?	1	2	3	4	5

Maybe you're doing pretty well. Maybe not. Either way, this chapter is designed to help you improve these key relationships. But before we go there, let's quickly review where we've just come from.

In the Private Victory, we learned about the personal bank account and Habits 1, 2, and 3. In the Public Victory section, we'll learn about the relationship bank account and Habits 4, 5, and 6. As we've already discussed, the key to mastering relationships is first mastering yourself, at least to some degree. You don't have to be perfect; you just need to be making progress.

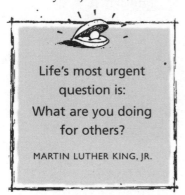

Life's most urgent question is:

What are you doing for others?

MARTIN LUTHER KING, JR.

Why is success with self so important to success with others? It's because the most important ingredient in any relationship is *what you are.* As the essayist and philosopher Ralph Waldo Emerson put it, "Who you are speaks so loudly I can't hear what you're saying." In many cases, if you're struggling in your relationships, you probably don't have to look much further than yourself for the answer.

The Private Victory will help you become independent so that you can say, "I am responsible for myself and I can create my own destiny." This is a huge accomplishment. The Public Victory will help you become interdependent, that is, help you learn to work cooperatively with others, so that you can say, "I am a team player, and I have the power to influence and inspire people." This is an even greater accomplishment. The long and short of it is, your ability to get along with others will largely determine how successful you are in your career and your level of personal happiness.

Now back to talking about relationships. Here's a practical way to think about them. I call it the relationship bank account (RBA). In an earlier chapter we spoke about your personal bank account (PBA), which represents the amount of trust and confidence you have in yourself. Similarly, the RBA represents the amount of trust and confidence you have in each of your relationships.

The RBA is very much like a checking account at a bank. You can make deposits and improve the relationship, or take withdrawals and weaken it. A strong and healthy relationship is always the result of steady deposits made over a long period.

Although there are similarities, the RBA is different from a financial account in three ways, as a colleague of mine, Judy Henrichs, once pointed out to me:

1. Unlike a bank where you may have only one or two accounts, you have an RBA with everyone you meet. Suppose you come across a new kid in school. If you smile and say hello, you've just opened an account with him. If you ignore him, you've just opened an account as well, although a negative one. There's kinda no getting around it.

2. Unlike a checking account, once you open an RBA with another person, you can never close it. That's why you can run into a friend you haven't seen in years and pick up right where you left off. Not a dollar's lost. It's also why people hang on to grudges for years.

3. In a checking account, ten bucks is ten bucks. In an RBA, deposits and withdrawals are not created equally. It usually takes many deposits to make up for one withdrawal. One subtle but demeaning comment, like "I didn't know you could fit into a size 4," can destroy weeks of deposits. So be careful when you open your mouth.

So how can you build a rich relationship or repair a broken one? It's simple. One deposit at a time. It's the same way you'd eat an elephant if you had to. One bite at a time. There is no quick fix. If my relationship with you is $5,000 in the hole, I'll need to make $5,001 worth of deposits to get it back in the positive.

I once asked a group of teens, "What's the most powerful deposit someone has made into your RBA?" These are some of their responses:

- "The steady stream of deposits my family makes that strengthen me."
- "When a friend, teacher, loved one, or employer takes the time to say, 'You look nice' or 'Great job.' A few words go a long way."
- "My friends made me a banner on my birthday."
- "Bragging about me to others."
- "When I have made mistakes, they forgive, forget, and help and love."
- "My friend told me, after I read some poems I wrote, that I was brilliant and I should write a book. It was hard to share some of those in the first place."
- "My mother called from California, as well as both of my sisters, to wish me a happy birthday, before I left for school."
- "My brother would always take me to hockey games with his friends."
- "Little things."

- "I have four really good friends, and just being together as friends and knowing that we're all doing good and are happy keeps me going."
- "Whenever Chris says 'Hi, how are you, Ryan?' it makes me feel so uplifted the way he does it."
- "I had a friend who told me he believed I was very sincere and always myself. It meant a lot that someone would recognize that."

As you can see, there are many kinds of deposits, but here are six that seem to work every time. Of course, with every deposit, there is an opposite withdrawal.

RBA DEPOSITS	RBA WITHDRAWALS
Keep promises	Break promises
Do small acts of kindness	Keep to yourself
Be loyal	Gossip and break confidences
Listen	Talk too much
Say you're sorry	Be arrogant
Set clear expectations	Set false expectations

- **KEEPING PROMISES**

"Sean, I don't want to ask you again. There are trash bags in the trunk of my car from the party the other night. Please throw them away."

"Okay, Dad."

As a carefree teenager, I somehow forgot to empty the trash bags in Dad's Ford, as I said I would, because I had a hot date that Saturday afternoon. I had asked my dad if I could use the Ford, but he said no because it wasn't his car. It was a loaner that his friend at the dealership had arranged for. But I took it anyway because he was busy and I was sure he wouldn't notice.

The date was awesome and I felt great. On the way home, though, I rammed into the back of a car doing thirty. No one was seriously hurt, but both cars were nearly totaled. I'll never forget the most miserable call of my life.

"Dad."

"What?"

"I had an accident."

"YOU WHAT? ARE YOU OK?"

"I got into a wreck. No one's hurt."

"IN WHICH CAR?"

"Your car."

"NOOOOOOOOOOO!!!" By this time I was holding the phone six inches away. And it still hurt.

I had the car towed to the Ford dealership to see if they could salvage it. Since it was Saturday, they told me they wouldn't be able to work on it until Monday. On Monday my dad received a call from the repair shop. The manager said that when his people opened the trunk to repair the car, the smell of rotting garbage (the garbage I forgot to empty) was so disgusting that they refused to work on the car. If you thought my dad was mad before, you shoulda seen him then.

For the next several weeks I was in the doghouse. It wasn't just the crash he was so mad about. He was angry because I'd broken two promises: "I won't take your car, Dad," and "Don't worry, Dad. I'll take the trash out of the trunk." It was a huge withdrawal, and it took me a long time to rebuild my RBA with my dad again.

Keeping small commitments and promises is vital to building trust. You just gotta do what you say you're going to do—otherwise, don't say you'll do it. If you tell your mom you're going to be home at 11:00 or that you'll do the dishes, then do it and make a deposit. Give out promises sparingly, and then do everything you can to keep them. If you find you can't keep a commitment for some reason (it happens), then let the other person know why. "Aaah sis, I'm really sorry I can't come to your play tonight. I didn't realize I have soccer later. Promise I'll be there tomorrow!" If you're sincere and try to keep your promises, people will understand when something else comes up.

If your RBA with your parents is low, try building it by keeping your commitments. When your parents trust you, everything goes *so* much better at home. But I guess I don't need to tell you what you already know.

● DO SMALL ACTS OF KINDNESS

Have you ever had a day where everything's going wrong and you feel totally bummed out . . . and then suddenly, out of nowhere, someone says something nice to you and it turns your whole day around? Sometimes the smallest things—a "hi," a smile, a compliment, a hug, a funny text from a friend—can make such a big difference. If you want to build friendships, start by doing the little things, because in relationships the little things *are* the big things. As Mark Twain put it, "I can live three months on a good compliment."

One kind word can warm three winter months.

JAPANESE SAYING

A friend of mine, Renon, once told me about a $1,000 deposit her brother made into her RBA:

When I was in ninth grade, my big brother Hans, who was a junior in high school, seemed to me to be the epitome of popularity. He was good in sports and dated a lot. Our house was always filled with his cool friends, guys I dreamed would someday think of me as more than just "Hans's dumb little kid sister."

Hans asked Rebecca Knight, the most popular girl in the school, to go with him to the junior prom. She accepted. He rented the tux, bought the flowers, and, along with the rest of his popular crowd, hired a limo and made reservations at a fancy restaurant. Then, disaster struck. On the afternoon of the prom, Rebecca came down with a terrible flu. Hans was without a date, and it was too late to ask another girl.

There were a number of ways Hans could have reacted, including getting angry, feeling sorry for himself, blaming Rebecca, even choosing to believe that she really wasn't sick and just didn't want to go with him, in which case he would have had to believe that he was a loser. But Hans chose not only to be proactive but to give someone else the night of her life.

He asked me—me! his little sister!—to go with him to his junior prom.

Can you imagine my ecstasy? Mom and I flew about the house getting me ready. But when the limo pulled up with all of his friends, I almost chickened out. What would they think? But Hans just grinned, gave me his arm, and proudly escorted me out to the car like I was the queen of the ball. He didn't warn me not to act like a kid; he didn't apologize to the others; he ignored the fact that I was dressed in a simple short-skirted piano-recital dress while all of the other girls were in elegant formals.

I was enchanted at the dance. Of course, I spilled punch on my dress. I'm sure Hans bribed every one of his friends to dance at least one dance with me, because I never sat out once. Some of them even pretended to fight over who got to dance with me. I had the greatest time. And so did Hans. While the guys were dancing with me, he was dancing with their dates! The truth is, everyone was wonderful to me the whole night, and I think part of the reason was because Hans chose to be proud of me. It was the dream night of my life, and I think every girl in the school fell in love with my brother, who was cool enough, kind enough, and self-confident enough to take his little sister to his junior prom.

If, as the Japanese saying goes, "one kind word can warm three winter months," think how many winter months were warmed by this single act of kindness.

You don't have to look far to find opportunities for small acts of kindness. A young man named Lee, who was taught about the RBA, related this:

I'm the junior class president at my school. I decided to try the small kindness deposit I learned about by putting a simple note in the boxes of just the student body officers I didn't know well. I told them that I appreciated the work they did. They took me about five minutes to write up.

The next day one of the girls I'd written a note to came up to me and abruptly gave me a big hug. She thanked me for the note, and handed me a letter and a candy bar. The note said that she had had a terrible day. She had a great deal of stress and was very depressed. My small note had turned her whole day around, helping her to happily accomplish the things that had caused her so much grief. The strange thing was that I had hardly known her when I gave her the note and I was sure that she didn't like me anyway because she never really paid any attention to me. What a surprise! I couldn't believe how much a simple note meant to her.

Small acts of kindness don't always have to be one-on-one. You can also team up with others to make a deposit. I remember reading about a deposit the kids at Joliet Township Central High School near Chicago made in the life of an unsuspecting teenage girl named Lori when they crowned her homecoming queen.

You see, unlike most of the students at Joliet, Lori was had a disability and made her way around the school in a motorized wheelchair. Because of cerebral palsy, her words were often difficult to understand and her movements uneasy. Everyone at school knew her as super sweet and friendly.

After being nominated for homecoming queen by students in Business Professionals of America, Lori made the first cut when students narrowed the slate to ten. At a pep rally soon after, it was announced that she had won. The entire student body of twenty-five hundred started chanting, "Lori! Lori!" A day later, people were still grinning at her in the hallways and leaving roses at her locker.

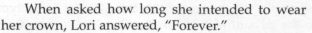

When asked how long she intended to wear her crown, Lori answered, "Forever."

Follow the Golden Rule and treat others as you would want them to treat you. Think about what a deposit means to someone else, not what *you* would want as a deposit. A nice gift may be a deposit for you, but a listening ear may be a deposit for another person.

If you ever have something nice to say, don't let that thought just rot, *say it.* As Ken Blanchard wrote in his book *The One Minute Manager*, "Unexpressed good thoughts aren't worth squat."

If you're unsure whether you should approach someone, just remember how good it'll make them feel to receive a compliment. Don't wait until people are dead to give them flowers.

- ## BE LOYAL

As a junior in high school, I'll never forget watching a high school basketball game with my friend Eric. I began making fun of one of the players who always sat on the bench. He was a nice guy and had always been good to me, but a lot of other people made fun of him so I thought I would, too. It made Eric laugh. After I'd dissed this kid for several minutes, I happened to turn around and, to my horror, saw this kid's younger brother sitting right behind me. He'd overheard everything. I'll never forget the look of betrayal on his face. Quickly turning back around, I sat quietly for the rest of the game. I felt like a total jerk, about one foot tall. I learned an important lesson about loyalty that night!

One of the biggest RBA deposits you can make is to be loyal to other people, not only when they're around but more especially when they aren't around, when they're not present. When you talk behind people's backs, you're only hurting yourself in two ways.

First, you make withdrawals from everyone who hears your comments. If you hear me trash Ethan when Ethan isn't there to defend himself, what do you think I'm going to be doing when you're not present? That's right, I may be gossiping about you, too.

Second, when you bad-mouth or gossip you make what I call an "invisible withdrawal" from the person you're attacking. Have you ever sensed that someone's been trashing you behind your back? You didn't hear it, but you can feel it. It's strange but true. If you sweet-talk people when they're facing you but trash-talk them when their backs are turned, don't think they won't feel it. It somehow gets communicated.

Gossiping is a huge problem among teens, stereotypically among girls, but guys do it, too—everyone does it. Guys often prefer other methods of attack (we call them *fists*), but girls seem to stick to *words*. Why is gossiping so popular? For one thing, you hold someone's reputation in the palms of your hands and that's a powerful feeling. For another, we gossip because we're insecure, afraid, or threatened. That's why gossipers usually like to pick on people who look different, think different, are self-confident, or stand out in some way. But isn't it kinda silly to think that tearing someone else down builds you up?

Gossip's rampant online. You see photos of what everyone's up to and it's easy to feel jealous or excluded. It can bring out a desire to tear other people down. Gossip and rumors probably have destroyed more reputations and relationships than every other bad habit combined. This story, told by my friend Annie, illustrates their venomous power:

The summer after high school graduation my best friend, Tara, and I were dating two really cool guys. They were best friends, we were best friends, and so we'd all go out together. One weekend Tara and my boyfriend, Sam, both went out of town with their families. Tara's boyfriend, Will, texted me and said, "Hey, let's go see a movie since Tara and Sam are out of town and we have nothing to do."

We truly went out only as friends—Will knew that and I knew that. Of course, someone saw us at the movies and misinterpreted the situation. Well, in a small town, things have a tendency to grow. When Tara and Sam returned, and even before I had a chance to talk to my best friend or my boyfriend, photos of us together were out. There was no pulling back the stories and rumors. When I called to say "hi" to them, I got a frigid blast of arctic air. There was no explaining. There was no communication. My best friend and my boyfriend chose to believe the pictures of us hanging out somehow proved that Will and I were cheating on them. I learned a really tough lesson about loyalty that summer that I have never forgotten nor even gotten over. And to this day, my once-best friend still won't talk to me.

In the above catastrophe, it seems to me that a little loyalty and trust would have solved a lot of problem. So just what is it that makes a loyal person?

Loyal people keep secrets. When people share something with you and ask you to keep it "just between you and me," then for goodness' sake, keep it "just between you and them" instead of running out and telling every last soul on Gchat every juicy detail as if you had no control of your bodily functions. If you enjoy being told secrets, then keep them secret, and you'll get more of 'em told to you.

Loyal people avoid gossip. Have you ever been hesitant to leave a party because you're afraid someone might start gossiping about you? Don't let others think that about you. Avoid gossip like the plague. Think well of others and give them the benefit of the doubt. This doesn't mean that you can't talk about other people, just do it in a constructive way. Remember, strong minds talk about ideas; weak minds talk about people.

Loyal people stick up for others. The next time a group starts gossiping about another person, either refuse to participate in the gossip or stick up for that person. You can do so without sounding self-righteous. Katie, a senior in high school, shared this story:

One day in my English class, my friend Matt started talking about a girl I knew in my neighborhood, although we'd never been close friends. His friend had taken her out to a dance and so he started saying things like "She is such a snot" and "She's so ditzy."

I turned around and said, "Excuse me, but Kim and I have grown up together and I think she's one of the sweetest people I have ever met." After I said it, I was kind of surprised at myself. I had actually been struggling to get along with her. Even though Kim never knew what I said about her, my attitude toward her changed and we became really close friends.

Matt and I still are good friends. I think he knows he can count on me to be a loyal friend.

Steering clear of a gossip pile-on takes courage. But after the initial discomfort it may cause you, people will admire you. They'll recognize that you're loyal to the core. I'd make an extra effort to be loyal to your family members, since these relationships will last a lifetime.

As illustrated so well in A.A. Milne's *Winnie-the-Pooh* classics, people need to feel safe and secure in relationships:

Piglet sidled up behind Pooh.

"Pooh," he whispered.

"Yes, Piglet?"

"Nothing," said Piglet, taking Pooh's paw. "I just wanted to be sure of you."

- ### LISTEN

Listening to someone can be one of the single greatest deposits you can make into another's RBA. Why? Because not enough people these days listen, furthermore, listening can heal wounds, as it did in the case of this fifteen-year-old named Tawni:

At the beginning of the year I was having communication troubles with my parents. They were not listening and I was not listening. It was one of those "I'm right and you're wrong" kind of things. I would come in late and just go to bed, and in the morning I would have breakfast and go to school and not say anything.

I went to see my cousin, who is older than me and in her twenties and said, "I need to talk to you." We went for a drive across town so we could be alone. She listened to me freak out and cry and scream for two and a half hours. She really helped me a lot because she just listened to all of it. She was optimistic that it would be all right and suggested that it might help if I tried to win back my parents' trust.

I have been trying to see things from their point of view lately. We are not fighting anymore, and things are getting back to normal.

People need to be listened to almost as much as they need food. And if you'll take time to feed them, you'll create some fantastic friendships. We'll talk about listening a lot more when we get to Habit 5: Seek First to Understand, Then to Be Understood. It's just up ahead.

• SAY YOU'RE SORRY

Saying you're sorry when you yell, overreact, or make a stupid mistake can quickly restore an overdrawn bank account. But it takes guts to go to a friend and say, "Look, I was wrong," "I apologize," or "I'm sorry." It's especially hard to admit that you made a mistake to your parents, because, of course, you know so much more than they do. Seventeen-year-old Lena had this to say:

I know from experience how much an apology means to my parents. It's like they forgive me for almost anything and are ready to start over if I admit my mistakes and apologize. But that doesn't mean it's easy to do.

I recall one night recently when my mother confronted me with something she didn't approve of that I had done. I didn't fess up to any of it; on the contrary I ended up acting like they were total jerks and slamming the door to my room right in front of my mother's nose.

As soon as I got inside my room I felt sick about it. I realized I probably had known all along I was wrong and that I had been extremely rude. Should I just stay in my room and go to bed and hope it would blow over, or should I go upstairs and apologize? I waited about two minutes and then took the high road and went straight to my mom, gave her a big hug, and told her how sorry I was for acting that way. It was the best thing I ever could have done. Immediately it was as though it had never happened. I felt light and happy and ready to concentrate on something else.

Don't let pride or a lack of courage stand in the way of saying sorry to people you may have offended. It's never as scary as it seems, and it'll make you feel so good afterward. In addition, apologies disarm people. Think about it: when people get offended their tendency is to take up a sword, so to speak, to protect themselves in the future. But when you apologize, you take away their desire to fight you and they will drop their swords. *Clank!*

Seeing that you and I will continue to make mistakes the rest of our lives, saying you're sorry ain't too bad a habit to get hooked on.

• SET CLEAR EXPECTATIONS

"I think that we should be seeing other people," your boyfriend or girlfriend might tell you.

"But . . . I thought we were starting to get serious," you might reply.

"Um, no offense . . . but, like, not really."

"Well what about everything you told me? About your feelings and stuff?"

"I didn't really mean it that way . . ."

How often have you seen someone get hurt because another person led them on by not communicating their real feelings? Our tendency is to want to flatter and please others, and, as a result, we often set unclear or unrealistic expectations.

To please your dad at the moment, you might say, "Sure, Dad, I can help you fix up the car this weekend." But, realistically, you're booked the entire weekend and don't have a second. In the end, you disappoint your dad. You would have been better off being realistic up front.

To develop trust we need to avoid sending vague messages or implying something that is not true or not likely to happen.

Maya says, "I had a great time, Jeff. Let's for sure do something next week!" What she really feels is: "I had a good time. Let's just be friends." But since she's created false expectations, Jeff will continue to ask her out and Maya will continue to turn him down saying, "Maybe next week." Everyone would have been better off if Maya had been honest from the get-go. It's hard to do, but don't be afraid to turn someone or something down. You'll be hurting them more in the long run if you string them along and *then* dump them.

Whenever you get into a new job, relationship, or setting, you're better off taking the time to lay all expectations out on the table so that everyone is on the same page. So many withdrawals are made because one party assumes one thing and another party assumes something else.

Your boss might say, "I need you to work this Tuesday night."

You might reply, "I'm sorry, but I babysit my brother on Tuesday nights for my mom."

"You should've told me that when I hired you. Now what am I going to do?"

Build trust through telling it like it is and laying out clear expectations right up front.

A Personal Challenge I'd like to leave you with a personal challenge. Pick one important relationship in your life that's damaged. It may be with a parent or a sibling or a friend. Now commit yourself to rebuilding that relationship one deposit at a time. The other person may be suspicious at first and think "What's up with you? Do you want something from me?" But be patient and stick with it. Remember, it may take months to build up what took months to tear down. But little by little, deposit by deposit, they'll begin to see that you are genuine and that you really want to be friends. I never said it would be easy, but I promise you it will be worth it.

COMING ATTRACTIONS

If you love a buffet (and who doesn't?),
you're gonna love the chapter that follows.

BABY STEPS

Keep Promises

1 The next time you go out for the night, tell your mom or dad what time you'll be home and stick to it. As a bonus, text 'em when you're heading back!

2 All day today, before giving out any commitments, pause and think about whether or not you can keep them. Don't say, "I'll email you the notes tonight," or "Let's go to the pool today," unless you can follow through.

Do Small Acts of Kindness

3 Buy a sandwich for a homeless person this week.

4 Handwrite a thank-you note to someone you've wanted to thank for a long time.

Person I need to thank: _____

Be Loyal

5 Pinpoint when and where it's most difficult for you to hold back from gossiping. Is it with a certain friend, in the locker room, on social media? Come up with a plan of action to avoid doing it.

6 Try to go one whole week saying only positive things about others online.

Listen

7 Take it easy and don't talk so much today. Spend the day listening.

8 Think of a family member you've never really taken the time to listen to, like your mom, your big brother, or grandpa. Take the time.

Say You're Sorry

9 Before you go to bed tonight, write a simple message of apology to someone you may have offended.

Set Clear Expectations

10 Think of a situation where you and someone else have different expectations. Put together a plan for how to get on the same page.

Their expectation: _____

My expectation: _____

HABIT 4

Think Win-Win

Life Is an All-You-Can-Eat Buffet

What do we live for, if it is not to make life less difficult for each other?
GEORGE ELIOT, AUTHOR

I attended a tough business school that utilized the infamous "forced curve" grading policy. Every class consisted of ninety students and in each class, 10 percent, or nine people, would receive what was called a category III. A category III was a nice way of saying "You flunked!" In other words, no matter how well or poorly the class performed as a whole, nine people would flunk the class. And if you flunked too many classes, you were kicked out of school. The pressure was insane.

> Pride gets no pleasure out of having something, only out of having more of it than the next man.
>
> C. S. LEWIS
> AUTHOR

The problem was, everyone in the class was smart. (I must have been an admissions error.) So the competition became very intense, which *influenced* me (notice I didn't say *made* me) and my classmates to act in funny ways.

Instead of aiming for good grades, as I did in college and high school, I found myself aiming not to be one of the nine people that would flunk. Instead of playing to win, I was playing not to lose. It reminds me of the story I once heard about two friends being chased by a bear, when one turned to the other and said, "I just realized that I don't need to outrun the bear; I only need to outrun you."

While sitting in class one day, I couldn't help but look around the room and try to count off nine people who were dumber than me. When someone made a stupid comment, I caught myself thinking, "Phew, he's guaranteed to flunk. Only eight more to go." Sometimes I found myself not wanting to share my best ideas with others during study groups because I was afraid they'd steal them and get all the credit instead of me. All these feelings were eating me up inside and making me feel real small, as if my heart were the size of a grape. The problem was, I was thinking Win-Lose. And Win-Lose thinking will always fill your heart with negative feelings. Luckily, there is a more excellent way. It's called Think Win-Win and it's Habit 4.

Think Win-Win is an attitude toward life, a mental frame of mind that says I can win, and so can you. It's not me or you, it's both of us.

Think Win-Win is the foundation for getting along well with other people. It begins with the belief that we are all equal, that no one is inferior or superior to anyone else, and no one really needs to be.

Now, you might say, "C'mon, Sean. It's a cutthroat, competitive world out there. Everyone can't always win."

I disagree. That's not how life really is. Life really isn't about competition, or getting ahead of others, or scoring in the 95th percentile. It may be that way in business, sports, and school, but those are merely institutions that we've created. It's certainly not that way in relationships. And relationships, as we learned just a chapter ago, are the stuff life's made of. Think how silly it is to say, "Who's winning in your relationship, you or your friend?"

So let's explore this strange idea called Think Win-Win. From my experience, the best way to do it is to see what Win-Win is not. Win-Win is not Win-Lose, Lose-Win, or Lose-Lose. These are all common but poor attitudes toward life. Climb aboard, strap yourself in, and let's take a look at each one.

HEY, TOM, I JUST REALIZED THAT I DON'T NEED TO OUTRUN THE BEAR; I ONLY NEED TO OUTRUN YOU.

• WIN-LOSE—THE TOTEM POLE

"Mom, there's a big game tonight and I need to take the car."

"I'm sorry Marina, but I need to get groceries tonight. Your friends can pick you up."

"But, *Mom*. My friends always have to pick me up. It's embarrassing."

"Listen, you've been complaining about not having any snacks in the house for a week. This is the only time I have to get groceries. I'm sorry."

"You're not sorry. If you were sorry you'd let me take the car. You're so unfair. You don't even care about me having friends."

"Look, fine. Go ahead. Take the car. But don't come whining to me when there's nothing to eat after school tomorrow."

Marina won and Mom lost. This is called Win-Lose. But has Marina really won? Maybe she has this time, but how does Mom feel? And what's she going to do the next time she has a chance to get even with Marina? That's why in the long run it never pays to think Win-Lose.

Win-Lose is an attitude toward life that says the pie of success is only so big, and if you get a big piece there is less for me. So I'm going to make sure I get my slice first or that I get a bigger piece than you. Win-Lose is competitive. I call it the totem pole syndrome. "I don't care how good I am as long as I'm a notch higher than you on the totem pole." Relationships, friendships, and loyalty are all secondary to winning the game, being the best, and having it your way.

Win-Lose is full of pride. In the words of C. S. Lewis, "Pride gets no pleasure out of having something, only out of having more of it than the next man . . . It is the comparison that makes you proud, the pleasure of being above the rest."

Don't feel too bad if you think Win-Lose at times, because we have been conditioned to do so from an early age. I think this is especially the case for those of us who've been raised in the U.S.A. where there are some amazing opportunities, but everyone's clawing to get at 'em.

To illustrate my point, let's follow Trey, an ordinary boy, as he grows up. Trey's first experience with competition begins in the third grade when he runs in the annual field day events and quickly discovers that ribbons are given only to first, second, and third place finishers. Trey doesn't win any races but is excited to at least receive a ribbon for *participation,* until his best friend tells him that "those ribbons don't really count 'cause everyone gets one."

When Trey enters middle school, his parents can't afford cool jeans and pricey sneakers, so Trey wears older, less cool stuff. He can't help but notice what his wealthier friends are wearing and feels as if he isn't quite measuring up.

In high school, Trey begins playing the violin and joins the orchestra. To his dismay, he learns that only one person can be first fiddle. Trey is disappointed when he's assigned second fiddle but feels very good about the fact that he's not third.

At home, Trey's been his mom's favorite child for several years. But now his younger brother, who happened to win a lot of trophies at Little League, is taking over as Mom's golden child. Trey begins studying extra hard at school for he figures that if he can get better grades than his brother, he might become Mom's chosen one again.

After four years of high school, Trey is ready for college. So he takes the SAT and scores in the 50th percentile, which means that he is smarter than half his peers but not as smart as the other half. Unfortunately, his score is not good enough to get into the college he wanted.

The college Trey attends uses forced-curve grading. In his first chemistry class of thirty students, Trey learns that there are only five A grades and five B grades available. The rest get C's and D's. Trey works hard to avoid a C or D and luckily earns the last B grade available.

And the story continues . . .

After being raised in this kind of world, is it any wonder then that Trey and the rest of us grow up seeing life as a competition and winning as everything? Is it any wonder that we often find ourselves looking around to see how we stack up on the totem pole? Fortunately, you and I are not victims. We have the strength to be proactive and rise above all of this Win-Lose conditioning.

A Win-Lose attitude wears many faces. The following are some of them:

- Using other people, emotionally or physically, for your own selfish purposes.
- Trying to get ahead at the expense of someone else.
- Gossiping or spreading rumors about someone else (as if putting someone else down builds you up).
- Always insisting on getting your way without thinking about other people's feelings.
- Getting jealous when something good happens to someone close to you.

In the end Win-Lose will usually backfire. You may end up on the top of the totem pole. But you'll be there alone and without friends. "The trouble with the rat race," said actress Lily Tomlin, "is that even if you win, you're still a rat."

● LOSE-WIN—THE DOORMAT

One teen wrote:

"I, for one, am a big peacemaker. I'd rather take the blame for just about anything than get into an argument. I constantly find myself saying that I'm dumb . . ."

Do you find yourself identifying with this statement? If so, you have fallen into the trap of Lose-Win. Lose-Win looks humble on the surface, but it's just as dangerous as Win-Lose. It's the doormat syndrome. Lose-Win says, "Have your way with me. Wipe your feet on me. Everyone else does."

Lose-Win is weak. It's easy to get stepped on. It's easy to be the nice guy or girl. It's easy to give in, all in the name of being a peace-maker. It's easy to let your parents have their way with you rather than try to share your feelings with them.

With a Lose-Win attitude you'll find yourself setting low expecta-tions and compromising your stan-dards again and again. Giving in to peer pressure is Lose-Win. Perhaps you don't want to ditch school, but the group wants you to. So you give in. What happened? Well, you lost and they won. That's called Lose-Win.

If you adopt Lose-Win as your basic attitude toward life, then people will wipe their dirty feet on you. And that's a real bummer. You'll also be hiding your true feelings deep inside. And that's not healthy.

There is a time to lose, of course. Lose-Win is just fine if the issue isn't that important to you, like if you and your sister can't agree on which show to watch or if your mom doesn't like the way you hold your fork. Let others win the little issues, and it will be a deposit into their RBA. Just be sure you take a stand on the important stuff.

If you're trapped in an abusive relationship, you're deep into Lose-Win. Abuse is a never-ending cycle of hurt and reconciliation, hurt and reconciliation. It *never* gets better. There's no win in it for you whatsoever, and you need to get out. Don't think that somehow the abuse is your fault or that somehow you deserve to be abused. That's how a doormat thinks. No one deserves to be abused, ever. (Please see the Abuse websites in the back of this book.)

● LOSE-LOSE—THE DOWNWARD SPIRAL

Lose-Lose says, "If I'm going down, then you're going down with me, sucker." After all, misery loves company. War is a great example of Lose-Lose. Think about it. Whoever kills the most people wins the war. That doesn't sound like anyone ends up winning at all. Revenge is also Lose-Lose. By getting revenge, you may think you're winning, but you're really only hurting yourself.

Lose-Lose is usually what happens when two Win-Lose people get together. If you want to win at all costs, and the other person wants to win at all costs, you're both going to end up losing.

Lose-Lose can also occur when someone becomes obsessed with another person in a negative way. This is especially likely to happen with those closest to us, like with Olivia, a high school junior.

My friend Maggie and I have been best friends since 7th grade. The second we met, it was like—boom, this is my new BFF. Right away she was so funny and great and opinionated. Deep down I also felt smart, and funny—but on the surface I came off as shy and a little self-conscious. Maggie could see the strength in me beneath the shy appearance, though, and that's why I felt so good around her.

The thing is, the older we got, like when we started freshman year, it started to weigh on me that I was still quiet and self-conscious, while Maggie was still bright and well liked. I started to feel like her sidekick and I really resented her. I got jealous because she got a lot of attention for being the smartest in class, and because guys were into her, and girls thought she was really cool. I tried to act like she did, and wanted everyone to treat me the way they treated her. I didn't know how to be myself.

I'd get snappy at her whenever she told me about something good going on in her life. Finally, one day I blew up at her over some little thing, but it turned into a huge fight and she was like "Why are you friends with me if you hate me?" I told her I didn't hate her, I just was jealous. And I felt like my own charm, and my own wit, and my own opinions were worthless compared to hers. And I felt bad about myself in comparison. As I heard myself saying all this, I knew how stupid it was, and also how unfair it was to Maggie. It wasn't her fault; she was just being herself. It was a rough patch in our friendship for a while, but she was able to forgive my jealousy and I feel like I've totally gotten over the competition. I realized I didn't have to drag her down with me to make myself feel better, I'm just glad to be around such a cool person. And I didn't have to go along with whatever she did to be liked, I could accomplish that by just being myself.

Luckily Olivia and Maggie's friendship turned from a Lose-Lose back into a Win-Win. But it's not just friendship that can be at risk; if you're not careful, boyfriend-girlfriend relationships can sour into Lose-Lose, too. You've seen it. Two good people begin dating and things go well at first. It's Win-Win. But gradually they become emotionally glued and codependent. They begin to get possessive and jealous. They constantly need to be together, to touch, to feel secure, as if they own the other person. Eventually, this dependency brings out the worst in both of them. They begin to fight and "get back at" each other, resulting in a downward spiral of Lose-Lose. It's not fun for anyone.

• WIN-WIN—THE ALL-YOU-CAN-EAT BUFFET

Win-Win is a belief that everyone can win. It's both nice and tough all at once. I won't step on you, but I won't be your doormat, either. You care about other people and you want them to succeed. But you also care about yourself, and you want to succeed as well. Win-Win is abundant. It is the belief that there's plenty of success to go around. It's not either you or me. It's  both of us. It's not a matter of who gets the biggest piece of pie. There's more than enough food for everyone. It's an all-you-can-eat buffet.

My friend Dawn shared how she discovered the power of thinking Win-Win in 10th grade:

In high school, I played on the girls' basketball team. I was pretty good for my age and tall enough to be starter on the varsity team even though I was just a sophomore. My friend Pam, another sophomore, was also moved up to be a starter on the varsity squad.

I had a sweet little shot I could hit quite regularly from ten feet out. Seriously, it worked every time. I began making four or five of those shots a game and began getting recognized for it. Pam, obviously, didn't like all the attention I was getting and decided, consciously or not, to keep the ball from me. It didn't matter how open I was for the shot, Pam flat out stopped passing the ball to me.

One night, after playing a terrible game in which Pam kept the ball from me most of the game, I was as mad as I had ever been. I spent many hours talking with my dad, going over everything, and expressing my anger toward my friend-turned-enemy, Pam. After a long discussion, my dad told me that the best thing he could think of would be to give Pam the ball every time I got it. Every time. I thought it was literally the stupidest thing he had ever told me. He simply told me it would work and left me at the kitchen table to think about it. But I didn't. I knew it wouldn't work and put it aside as silly fatherly advice.

At the next game I was determined to beat Pam at her own game. I planned and plotted and came out with a mission to ruin Pam's game. On my first possession of the ball, I heard my dad above the crowd. He had a booming voice, and though I shut out everything around me while playing basketball, I could always hear Dad's deep voice. At the moment I caught the ball, he yelled out, "Give her the ball!!" I hesitated for one second and then did what I knew was right. Although I was open for a shot, I found Pam and passed her the ball. She was shocked for a moment, then turned and shot, sinking the ball for two points. As I ran down the court to play defense, I got a feeling I'd never felt before: true joy for the success of another person. And, even more, I realized that it put us ahead in the game. It felt good to be winning. I continued to give her the ball every time I got it in the first half. Every time. In the second half, I did the same, only shooting if it was a designated play or if I was wide open for a shot.

We won that game, and in the games that followed, Pam began to pass me the ball as much as I passed it to her. Our teamwork was getting way stronger, and so was our friendship. We won the majority of our games that year and became kind of legendary at school. The local paper even did a write-up on our ability to pass to each other and sense each other's presence. Overall, I scored more points than ever before.

You see, Win-Win always creates more. An endless buffet. And as Dawn discovered, wanting another person to win fills you full of good feelings. By passing the ball, Dawn didn't score fewer points but eventually scored more. In fact, they both scored more points and won more games than if they had selfishly kept the ball from each other.

You probably do more Win-Win thinking than you give yourself credit for. The following are all examples of the Win-Win attitude:

- You recently got a promotion at the ice cream shop you work at. You share the praise and recognition with all of those who helped you get there.
- You were just elected to an important school office and make up your mind not to develop a "superiority complex." You treat everyone the same, including kids that are outsiders or sit alone in the cafeteria.

- Your best friend just got accepted at the college you wanted to get into. You didn't make it. Although you feel terrible about your own situation, you are genuinely happy for your friend.
- You want to get dinner. Your friend wants to see a movie. You jointly decide to download a movie and order in food to eat at home.

How to Think Win-Win

So how do you do it? How can you be happy for your friend when he just got accepted to a college and you didn't? How can you avoid feeling inferior to the girl next door who has those cheekbones? How can you find solutions to problems so that both of you can win?

Might I suggest two clues: Win the private victory first and avoid the tumor twins. Trust me, you'll see.

• WIN THE PRIVATE VICTORY FIRST

It all begins with you. If you are extremely insecure and haven't paid the price to win the private victory, it'll be difficult to think Win-Win. You'll still be threatened by other people. It'll be hard to be happy for their successes, or to share recognition or praise. Insecure people get jealous very easily. This chat between Austin and his girlfriend is typical of an insecure person:

"Amy, who's the dude who keeps liking all your posts on Tumblr?" asks Austin.

"Who? You mean Jon? He's an old friend I went to camp with," says Amy.

"Why do you respond to all his comments?"

"Because he's my friend. I've known him for a long time. We went to elementary school together."

"Then why's he all over you like that?" rants Austin.

"Austin, it's not a big thing. He liked, like, two pictures."

"Well he should leave you alone."

"Austin, you already know you're the one I wanna be with. My guy friends are just that—friends."

Can you see how impossible it would be for Austin to be comfortable in this situation when he's this insecure and emotionally dependent upon his girlfriend? Austin needs to start with himself. As he makes deposits into his PBA, takes responsibility for his life, and gets a plan in place, his confidence and security will increase and he'll start enjoying other people instead of being threatened by them. Personal security is the foundation for thinking Win-Win.

● **AVOID THE TUMOR TWINS**

There are two habits that, like tumors, can slowly eat you away from the inside. They are twins and their names are competing and comparing. It's virtually impossible to think Win-Win with them around.

Competing

Competition can be extremely healthy. It drives us to improve, to reach and stretch. Without it, we would never know how far we could push ourselves. For example: the glory of the Olympic Games is all about excellence and competition, and it motivates young men and women to work hard and become amazing athletes. In the business world, competition drives innovation and growth.

But there is another side to competition that isn't so nice. In the movie *Star Wars*, Luke Skywalker learns about a positive energy shield called "the Force," which gives life to all things. Later, Luke confronts the evil Darth Vader and learns about the "dark side" of the force. As Darth puts it, "You don't know the power of the dark side." So it is with competition. There is a sunny side and a dark side, and both are powerful. The difference is this: Competition is healthy when you compete against yourself, or when it challenges you to reach and stretch and become your best. Competition becomes dark when you tie your self-worth into winning or when you use it as a way to place yourself above another.

While reading a book called *The Inner Game of Tennis* by W. Timothy Gallwey, I found some words that say it perfectly. Tim wrote:

When competition is used as a means of creating a self-image relative to others, the worst in a person comes out; then the ordinary fears and frustrations become greatly exaggerated. It is as if some believe that only by being the best, only by being a winner, will they be eligible for the love and respect they seek. Children who have been taught to measure themselves in this way often become adults driven by a compulsion to succeed which overshadows all else.

A famous college coach once said that the two worst traits an athlete can have are a fear of failure and an inordinate desire to win, or a win-at-any-cost attitude.

I'll never forget an argument I had with my younger brother after his team beat mine in a game of beach volleyball.

"I can't believe you guys beat us," I said, shaking my head in disbelief.

"What's unbelievable about that?" he replied. "You think you're a better athlete than me?"

"I know I am. I mean, no offense, bro, but look at the evidence. I went way further than you in sports."

"But you're using your own narrow definition of what an athlete is. Frankly *I'm* a better athlete because I can jump higher and run faster."

"Bull! You're *not* faster than me. And what does jumping have to do with anything? I can kick your butt in every sport."

"Oh yeah? You wanna go there?"

"Yeah, I do actually!"

When we calmed down, we both felt like immature man-children. We'd been seduced by the dark side. And the dark side never leaves you with a good aftertaste.

Let's use competition as a benchmark to measure ourselves against, but let's stop competing over boyfriends, girlfriends, status, friends, popularity, attention, and just start enjoying life.

Comparing

Comparing is competition's twin. And it's just as cancerous. Comparing yourself to others is nothing but bad news. Why? Because we're all on different development timetables. Socially, mentally, and physically. Since we all bake differently, we shouldn't keep opening the oven door to see how well our cake is rising compared to our neighbor's, or our own cake won't rise at all. Although some of us are like the poplar tree, which grows like a weed the moment it's planted, others are like the bamboo tree, which shows no growth for four years but then grows ninety feet in year five.

I once heard it described this way: Life is like a great obstacle course. Each person has their own course, separated from every other course by tall walls. Your course comes complete with customized obstacles designed specifically for your personal growth. So what good does it do to climb the wall to see how well your neighbor is doing or to check out his obstacles in comparison to your own? That'll just distract you from your own obstacles.

Building your life based on how you stack up compared to others is never good footing. If I get my security from the fact that my GPA's higher than yours or my friends are more popular than yours, then what happens when someone comes along with a higher GPA or more popular friends? Comparing ourselves makes us feel

THE BAMBOO TREE

YEAR 1   YEAR 2   YEAR 3   YEAR 4   YEAR 5

like a wave of the sea tossed to and fro by the wind. We go up and down, feeling inferior one moment and superior the next, confident one moment and intimidated the next. The only good comparison is comparing yourself against your own potential.

Actress, singer, and songwriter Ariana Grande has taken Hollywood and the Internet by storm. But even with her fame, she's managing to maintain a healthy attitude when it comes to her body image and comparisons. As she says, "Too many young girls have eating disorders due to low self-esteem and a distorted body image . . . I think it's so important for girls to love themselves and to treat their bodies respectfully."

Ariana goes on to say that, "Sometimes, people can be extraordinarily judgmental and closed-minded to anyone different or special, which is why it's so hard for young people in this day and age to be comfortable enough in their own skin to not listen to the people picking on them. Be happy with being you. Love your flaws. Own your quirks. And know that you are just as perfect as anyone else, exactly as you are."

Maybe this refreshingly healthy attitude is why everyone loves her and her music and why she has so many Twitter followers. Let's hope this sweet actress-singer-dancer can continue to be such an inspiration.

I once interviewed a girl named Anne, who got caught in the web of comparisons for several years before managing to escape. She has a message for those who are caught:

My problems started in freshman year when I entered Clayton Valley High School. Most of the kids there had money. How you looked and dressed was everything. The big question was: Who is wearing what today? There were so many unspoken rules about clothes—you could never wear the same thing twice, and you could never wear the same thing as someone else. Brand names and expensive jeans were everything. You had to have every color, every style.

I had a boyfriend who was a junior and whom my parents didn't like. Our relationship was good at first, but after a while, he started making me feel self-conscious. He'd say stuff like, "Why can't you look like her?" "How come you're so fat?" "If you just changed a little bit you'd be just right."

I began to believe my boyfriend. I'd look at other girls and analyze all the reasons I wasn't as good as them. Even though I had a closet full of clothes, I remember having anxiety attacks because I couldn't decide what to wear. I even began shoplifting because I wanted to have the latest and best clothes. After a while, who I was hinged on who I was with, what I looked like, and what kind of clothes I had on. I never felt good enough, for anyone.

To cope, I started binging and purging. Eating gave me comfort and purging gave me some twisted kind of control. Although I wasn't fat, I was so scared of being fat. It soon became a big part of my life. I started throwing up thirty to forty times a day. I'd do it at school in the bathrooms, and anywhere else I could find. It was my secret. I couldn't tell my parents because I didn't want to let them down.

I remember being asked by the popular group one time to go to the football game. They were sixteen, one year older than me. I was so excited! My mom and I worked and worked to find me the perfect outfit. I waited by the window for hours, but they never came to pick me up. I felt worthless. I thought, "I wasn't picked up because I wasn't cool enough or didn't have the right look."

Finally, it all came to a head. While I was on stage performing in a play, I suddenly became totally disoriented and passed out. Waking up in the dressing room, I found my mom at my side. "I need help," I whispered.

Admitting that I had a problem was the first step to my recovery, which took several years. Looking back now, I can't believe I got into that state of mind. I had everything I needed to be happy but I was still so miserable. I was a cute, talented, healthy girl who got caught up in a world of comparisons and was made to feel not good enough. I want to shout out to all of us young people: "Don't ever do this to yourself. It's not worth it."

The key to my recovery was meeting some really special friends who made me feel that I mattered because of who I was and not what I wore. They told me, "You don't need this. You're better than that." I began to change for myself, not because someone else told me that I had to change to be worthy of their love.

The pearl of wisdom from the story is: Break the habit. Stop doing it. Comparing yourself can become an addiction as strong as drugs or alcohol. You don't have to look like or dress like a model to be good enough. You know what really matters. Don't get caught up in the game and worry so much about being popular during your teen years, because most of life comes after. (Please see the Eating Disorder website in the back of this book.)

- ## THE FRUITS OF THE WIN-WIN SPIRIT

I've learned never to underestimate what can happen when some-one thinks Win-Win. This was Andy's experience:

At first I could see no point to Win-Win. But I started applying it in my after-school jobs, and I was just blown away. I have used it now for two years and it's honestly scary how powerful this habit is—I wish I had known about it much sooner in my life. It's taught me to exercise my leadership ability and to approach my job with an attitude of "let's make this job more fun. Let's make it a win for both me and my employer." I now sit down with my manager monthly and tell her all the little things I can see in the company that aren't getting done that I am willing to do.

The last time we met she said to me, "I have always wondered how we could get all these little loose ends done. I am so impressed with how you look for opportunities and are so willing to perform." And then she gave me a dollar an hour raise.

Believe me, this Win-Win stuff's contagious. If you're big-hearted, committed to helping others succeed, and willing to share recognition, you'll be a magnet for friends. Think about it. Don't you just love people who are interested in your success and want you to win? It makes you want to help them in return, doesn't it?

The Win-Win spirit can be applied to just about any situation, from working out major conflicts with your parents to deciding who walks the dog, as Ben shared below.

My parents only let my sister and me use the family tablet for an hour each every day. At first we'd fight over who got to have first dibs, because we both wanted to use it—sometimes for looking up something for homework, or sometimes just to go on Twitter or watch a show. We decided to try something new. We'd alternate who got to go first every day, and then sometimes we'd even Tweet or watch a show together, which actually made it more fun.

Sometimes, no matter how hard you try, you won't be able to find a Win-Win solution. Or someone else may be so bent on Win-Lose that you don't even want to approach him or her. That happens. In these situations, don't get ugly yourself (Win-Lose) or get stepped on (Lose-Win). Instead, go for Win-Win or No Deal. In other words, if you can't find a solution that works for both of you, decide not to play. No Deal. For example, if you and your friend can't decide what to do one night, instead of doing an activity that one of you might resent, split up that night and get together another night.

Or if you and your girlfriend or boyfriend just can't develop a Win-Win relationship, it might be best to go for No Deal and part ways. It sure beats going for Win-Lose, Lose-Win, or, worst of all, Lose-Lose.

A fifteen-year-old named Bryan, who was taught Win-Win by his father, shared this interesting story:

Last year, my friend Steve and I wanted to make some money during summer break. So we started a window washing and lawn care business. We thought Green & Clean was kind of a cool name for our business.

Steve's parents had a friend who needed his windows washed, and before too long the word spread and we got a few jobs.

We used a program on my dad's computer to make a little sheet we call a Win-Win agreement. When we get to the house we go around and get the window measurements and write down an estimate. We make it totally clear that they are going to get clean windows for a set price. There is a line for them to sign on. If we don't do well, we know we won't get hired back. After we're done, we walk them around and show them our work for their approval. We want them to know we're accountable.

We have a little Green and Clean fund. Once we started making money, we split the money and then put some aside to buy window-washing equipment. As long as our customers are happy, and they get clean windows, they are winning. We win, because at fifteen, it's a way for us to make some extra money.

Watch How It Makes You Feel

Developing a Win-Win attitude is not easy. But you can do it. If you're thinking Win-Win only 10 percent of the time right now, start thinking it 20 percent of the time, then 30 percent, and so on. Eventually, it will become a mental habit, and you won't even have to think about. It will become part of who you are.

Perhaps the most surprising benefit of thinking Win-Win is the good feelings it brings on. One of my favorite stories that illustrates the power of *thinking* Win-Win is the true story of Jacques Lusseyran as told in his autobiography *And There Was Light*. The editors of *PARABOLA* magazine, who wrote the book's foreword, summarize Lusseyran's story this way:

"Born in Paris in 1924, [Jacques] was fifteen at the time of the German occupation, and at sixteen he had formed and was heading an underground resistance movement . . . which from a beginning of fifty-two boys . . . within a year had grown to six hundred. This would seem remarkable enough, but add to it the fact that from the age of eight, Jacques had been totally blind."

Although totally blind, Jacques could see, in a different way. As he put it: "I saw light and went on seeing it though I was blind . . . I could feel light rising, spreading, resting on objects, giving them form, then leaving them . . . I lived in a stream of light." He called this stream of light that he lived in "my secret."

Yet there were times when Jacques's light would leave him and he became cloudy. It was whenever he thought Win-Lose. As he put it:

"When I was playing with my small companions, if I suddenly grew anxious to win, to be the first at all costs, then all at once I could see nothing. Literally I went into fog or smoke.

"I could no longer afford to be jealous or unfriendly, because, as soon as I was, a bandage came down over my eyes, and I was bound hand and foot and cast aside. All at once a black hole opened, and I was helpless inside it. But when I was happy and serene, approached people with confidence and thought well of them, I was rewarded with light. So is it surprising that I learned to love friendship and harmony when I was very young?"

The true test of whether or not you are thinking Win-Win or one of the alternatives is how you feel. Win-Lose and Lose-Win thinking will cloud your judgment and fill you with negative feelings. You simply cannot afford to do it. On the other hand, just as Jacques discovered, thinking Win-Win will fill your heart with happy and serene thoughts. It will give you confidence. Even fill you with light.

★★★

COMING ATTRACTIONS

In the upcoming chapter, I'll share the secret to getting under your parents' skins in a positive way. So don't stop now!

BABY STEPS

1. Pinpoint the area of your life where you struggle with comparisons—clothes, physical features, friends, attention from boys/girls, talents, etc.?

   Where I'm struggling most with comparisons: _____

   _____

2. If you play sports or competitive games, show sportsmanship. Compliment someone from the opposing team after the match or game.

3. If someone owes you money, don't be afraid to mention it in a friendly way. "Hey, remember that $10 I loaned you last week? I could use it some-time this week." Think Win-Win, not Lose-Win.

4. Without caring whether you win or lose, play a game with others just for the fun of it.

5. Do you have an important test coming up soon? Form a study group and share your best ideas with each other. You'll all do better.

6. The next time someone close to you succeeds, be genuinely happy for them instead of feeling kinda jealous it didn't happen to you.

7. Think about your general attitude toward life. Is it based on Win-Lose, Lose-Win, Lose-Lose, or Win-Win thinking? How is that atti-tude affecting you?

8. Think of a person who you feel is a model of Win-Win. What is it about this person you admire?

   Person: _____

   What I admire about them: _____

   _____

9. Are you in a Lose-Win relationship with a member of the opposite sex? If you are, then decide what must happen to make it a Win for you. Otherwise, go for No Deal and get out of that toxic relationship.

HABIT 5

Seek First to Understand, Then to Be Understood

You Have Two Ears AND ONE MOUTH . . . **Hel-lo!**

Before I can walk in another's shoes, I must first remove my own.
UNKNOWN

Let's say you're buying a new phone. The salesman asks, "What kind of smartphone are you looking for?"

"Well, I'm looking for something that costs—"

"I think I know what you'd like," he interrupts. "Everyone is getting this new one. Trust me."

He rushes off and comes back with the sleekest, slimmest smartphone you've ever seen. "Just take a look at this baby," he says.

YOU'LL BE QUITE "THE BOMB" IN THESE...
AACK
SALE

"I mean, it's nice, but it's not what I need. I can't afford it."

"It's the hottest thing going right now, you gotta get it before it sells out."

"No thanks, I don't have the money."

"I promise you'll love it. Worth every penny."

"But I—"

"Listen. I've been selling phones for ten years and I'm telling you this phone is worth it."

After this experience, would you ever want to go to that store again? Definitely not. You can't trust people who give you solutions before they understand what your needs are. But did you know that we often do the same thing when we communicate?

"Hey, Missy. You look kinda bummed. What's up?"

"You wouldn't understand, Lily. You'd think it was stupid."

"No, I wouldn't. Tell me what's going on. I'm all ears."

"Oh, I dunno."

"C'mon. You can tell me."

"Well, okay . . . uuhm . . . things aren't the same between Tyrone and me anymore."

"I told you not to get involved with him. I just knew this would happen."

"Tyrone's not the problem."

"Listen, Missy, if I were you, I'd just forget about him and move on."

"But, Lily, that's not how I feel."

"Believe me. I know how you feel. I went through the same thing last year with Zack. Don't you remember? It practically ruined my entire year."

"Just forget it, Lily."

"Missy, I'm only trying to help. I really want to understand. Now, go on. Tell me how you feel."

It's our tendency to want to swoop out of the sky like Superman and solve everyone's problems before we even understand what the problem is. We simply don't listen. As the American Indian proverb goes, "Listen, or thy tongue will make thee deaf."

The key to communication and having power and influence with people can be summed up in one sentence: Seek first to understand, then to be understood. In other words, listen first, talk second. This is Habit 5, and it works. If you can learn this simple habit—to see things from another's point of view before sharing your own—a whole new world of understanding will be opened up to you.

OH, GOODY... HERE COMES "ANSWER MAN."

The Deepest Need of the Human Heart

Why is this habit the key to communication? It's because the deepest need of the human heart is to be understood. Everyone wants to be respected and valued for who they are—a unique, one-of-a-kind, never-to-be-cloned (at least for now) individual.

People won't expose their soft centers unless they feel genuine love and understanding. Once they feel it, however, they will tell you more than you may want to hear. The following story about a girl with an eating disorder shows the power of understanding:

I was a professional anorexic by the time I met Julie, Pam, and Lavon, my college roommates my freshman year. I had spent my last two years of high school concentrating on exercising, dieting, and triumphing in every ounce I lost. At eighteen years old and five foot eight, I weighed in at a breezy ninety-five pounds, a tall pile of bones.

I didn't have many friends. Constant deprivation had left me irritable, bitter, and so tired I couldn't carry on casual conversations. School social events were out of the question, too. I didn't feel like I had anything in common with any of the kids I knew. A handful of loyal friends really stuck it out with me and tried to help, but I tuned out their preachy lectures about my weight and chalked it up to jealousy.

My parents bribed me with new wardrobes. They badgered me and demanded that I eat in front of them. When I wouldn't, they dragged me off to a series of doctors, therapists, and specialists. I was miserable and convinced my whole life was going to be that way.

Then I moved away to attend college. The luck of the draw settled me into a dormitory with Julie, Pam, and Lavon, the three girls who made my life worth living again.

We lived in a tiny cinderblock apartment, where all my strange eating patterns and exercising neuroses were right out in the open. I know they must have thought I looked strange with my sallow complexion, bruises, thinning hair, and jutting hips and collarbones. When I see pictures of myself at eighteen, I'm horrified at how terrible I looked.

But they weren't. They didn't treat me like a person with a problem. There were no lectures, no force-feeding, no gossiping, no browbeating. I almost didn't know what to do.

Almost immediately, I felt like one of them, except that I didn't eat. We attended classes together, found jobs, jogged in the evenings, watched television, and hung out on Saturdays. My anorexia, for once, was not the central topic. Instead, we spent long nights discussing our families, our ambitions, our uncertainties.

I was absolutely amazed by our similarities. For the first time in literally years, I felt understood. I felt like someone had taken the time to understand me as a person instead of always trying to fix my problem first. To these three girls, I wasn't an anorexic needing treatment. I was just the fourth girl.

As my sense of belonging grew, I began to watch them. They were happy, attractive, smart, and occasionally they ate cookie dough right out of the bowl. If I had so much in common with them, why couldn't I eat three meals a day, too?

Pam, Julie, and Lavon never told me how to heal myself. They showed me every day, and they really worked to understand me before trying to cure me. By the end of my first semester in college, they were setting a place for me at dinner. And I felt welcome.

Think of the influence these three girls had on the fourth girl because they tried to understand her instead of judging her. Isn't it interesting that once she felt understood and not judged, she immediately dropped her defenses and was open to their influence? Contrast that with what might have happened had her roommates turned preachy on her.

Have you ever heard the saying "People don't care how much you know until they know how much you care"? So true. Think about a situation when someone didn't take the time to understand or listen to you. Were you open to what they had to say?

While playing college football I developed some severe arm pain in my bicep for a time. It was a complex condition and I had tried a number of techniques to fix it—ice, heat, massage, lifting weights, and anti-inflammatory pills—but nothing worked. So I went to see one of our more seasoned athletic trainers for help. Before I had described my condition, however, he said to me, "I've seen this thing before. This is what you need to do." I tried to explain more, but he was already convinced he knew the problem. I felt like saying, "Wait a minute. Hear me out, Doc. I don't think you understand."

As you might have guessed, his techniques actually made my arm hurt worse. He never listened, and I never felt understood. I lost confidence in his advice and avoided him at all costs whenever I had an injury. I had no faith in his prescriptions, because he never diagnosed the problem. I didn't care how much he knew, because he hadn't shown me that he cared.

You can show you care by simply taking time to listen without judging and without giving advice. This short poem captures how badly people just want to be listened to:

PLEASE LISTEN

When I ask you to listen to me
and you start giving me advice,
you have not done what I asked.
When I ask you to listen to me
and you begin to tell me why
I shouldn't feel that way,
you are trampling on my feelings.
When I ask you to listen to me
and you feel you have to do something
to solve my problem,
you have failed me,
strange as that may seem.
Listen! All I ask is that you listen.
Don't talk or do—just hear me.

• FIVE POOR LISTENING STYLES

To understand someone you must listen to them. Surprise! The problem is that most of us don't know *how* to listen.

Imagine this. You're trying to decide what classes to take next year. You open up your class schedule and look at what's available.

"Hmmm . . . Let's see . . . Geometry. Creative writing. Beginning

speech. English literature. Listening. Wait a minute. Listening? A class on listening? Is this a joke?"

This would be a weird surprise, wouldn't it? But it really shouldn't be, because listening is one of the four primary forms of communication, along with reading, writing, and speaking. And if you think about it, since birth you've been taking classes on how to read, write, and speak better, but when have you ever taken a class on how to listen better?

When people talk we seldom listen because we're usually too busy preparing a response, judging, or filtering their words through our own paradigms. It's so typical of us to use one of these five poor listening styles:

Five Poor Listening Styles

- Spacing out
- Pretend listening
- Selective listening
- Word listening
- Self-centered listening

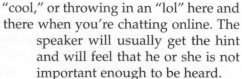

Spacing out is when someone is talking to us but we ignore them because our mind is wandering off in another galaxy. They may have something very important to say, but we're caught up in our own thoughts. We all zone out from time to time, but do it too much and you'll get a reputation for being out of it.

Pretend listening is more common. We still aren't paying much attention to the other person, but at least we pretend we are by making insightful comments at key junctures, such as "yeah," "uh-huh,"

"cool," or throwing in an "lol" here and there when you're chatting online. The speaker will usually get the hint and will feel that he or she is not important enough to be heard.

Selective listening is where we pay attention only to the part of the conversation that interests us. For example, your friend may be trying to tell you how it feels to be in the shadow of his talented brother in the army. All you hear is the word "army" and say, "Oh yeah, the army! I've been thinking a lot about it lately." Since you'll always talk about what you want to talk about, instead of what the other person wants to talk about, chances are you'll never develop lasting friendships.

Word listening occurs when we actually pay attention to what someone is saying, but we listen only to the words, not to the body language, the feelings, or the true meaning behind the words. As a result, we miss out on what's really being said. Your friend Kim might say to you, "What do you think of Ronaldo?" You might reply, "I think he's pretty cool." But if you had been more sensitive, and listened to her body language and tone of voice, you would have heard that she was really saying, "Do you think Ronaldo likes me?" If you focus on words only, you'll seldom be in touch with the deeper emotions of people's hearts.

Self-centered listening happens when we see everything from our own point of view. Instead of standing in another's shoes, we want them to stand in ours. This is where sentences like "Oh, I know exactly how you feel" come from. We don't know exactly how they feel, we know exactly how we feel, and we assume they feel the same way we do, like the salesman who thinks that you should buy the newest phone so he can make a buck. Self-centered listening is often a game of one-upmanship, where we try to one-up each other, as if conversations were a competition. "You think _your_ day was bad? That's nothin'. You should hear what happened to _me_."

When we listen from our point of view, we usually reply in one of three ways, all of which make the other person immediately close up. We _judge_, we _advise_, and we _probe_. Let's take a look at each.

Judging. Sometimes, as we listen to others, we make judgments (in the back of our minds) about them and what they're saying. If you're busy judging, you're not really listening, are you? People don't want to be judged, they want to be heard! In the conversation below, notice how little listening and how much judging is going on in the mind of the listener. (The listener's judgments are enclosed in parentheses.)

Peter: *I had literally the best time with Katherine last night.*

Karl: *Oh, sweet! (Katherine? Why would you want to go out with her?)*

Peter: *I had no idea how hilarious and awesome she is.*

Karl: *Oh, yeah? (Here you go again. You think every girl who gives you the time of day is great.)*

Peter: *Yeah, man. I'm thinking about asking her to prom!*

Karl: *I thought you were going to ask Jessica. (Are you crazy? Jessica's way cuter than Katherine.)*

Peter: *I mean I was, you know? But now I think I'm really into Katherine.*

Karl: *Well, ask her out then. (You'll obviously change your mind tomorrow.)*

Karl was so busy judging that he didn't hear a word Peter was saying and missed out on an opportunity to make a deposit into Peter's RBA.

Advising. This is when we give advice drawn from our own experience. This is the when-I-was-your-age speech you often get from your elders.

A sister who needs a listening ear says to her brother:

"I hate our new school. Ever since we moved I'm like the biggest outcast. I wish I could find some new friends already."

Instead of listening to understand, the brother reflects upon his own life and says:

"No, you need to start meeting new people and get involved in sports and clubs like I did."

Little sister didn't want any advice from a well-intentioned brother, no matter how good it was. She just wanted to be listened to, for heaven's sake. Once she felt understood, only then would she be open to his advice. Big brother blew a big chance for a big deposit.

Probing. Probing occurs when you try to dig up emotions before people are ready to share them. Have you ever been probed? Parents do it to teens, like, all the time. Your mom, with every good intention, tries to find out what's going on in your life. But since you're not ready to talk, her attempts feel intrusive, and so you shut her out.

"Hi, honey. How was school today?"

"Fine."

"How'd you do on that test?"

"OK."

"How're your friends?"

"Good."

"Do you have any plans tonight?"

"Not really."

"Have you been seeing any cute girls lately?"

"No, Mom, c'mon. Just leave me alone."

No one likes to be interrogated. If you're asking a lot of questions and not getting very far, you're probably probing. Sometimes people just aren't prepared to open up and don't feel like talking. Learn to be a great listener and offer an open ear when the time's right.

● GENUINE LISTENING

So much of our communication happens through text messaging or online, doesn't it? But I think, if you have something major to say, say it in person—that way someone won't take it the wrong way. Luckily, you and I never exhibit any of these five poor listening styles. Right? Well, maybe just occasionally. There's a higher form of listening, fortunately, which leads to real communication. We call it "genuine listening." And it's the kind of practice we want to put to use. But to do genuine listening, you need to do three things differently.

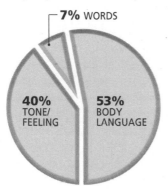

7% WORDS

40% TONE/FEELING

53% BODY LANGUAGE

First, listen with your eyes, heart, and ears. Listening with just your ears isn't good enough, because only 7 percent of communication is contained in the words we use. The rest comes from body language (53 percent) and how ve say words, or the tone and feeling reflected in our voice (40 percent). For example, notice how you can change the meaning of a sentence just by emphasizing a different word.

I didn't say you had an attitude problem.
I didn't say *you* had an attitude problem.
I didn't say you had an *attitude* problem.

That's why when you have something major to say, it is better to do it in person, rather than texting or online, so the other person really understands what you mean. Too often texting someone about an emotional issue creates more problems than it solves because people start jumping to conclusions and "hearing" things you didn't intend. So, when what you have to say is sensitive or complicated, go face-to-face.

To hear what other people are really saying, you also need to listen to what they're *not* saying. No matter how hard people may appear on the surface, most everyone is tender inside and has a desperate need to be understood. The following poem (one of my all-time favorites) captures this need.

PLEASE . . . HEAR WHAT I'M NOT SAYING
Don't be fooled by me. Don't be fooled by the mask I wear. For I wear a mask, I wear a thousand masks, masks that I'm afraid to take off, and none of them is me. Pretending is an art that is second nature with me, but don't be fooled.
. . . I give the impression that I'm secure, that all is sunny and unruf-

HABIT 5

fled with me, within as well as without; that confidence is my name and coolness is my game; that the waters are calm and that I'm in command and I need no one. But don't believe it; please don't.

I idly chatter with you in the suave tones of surface talk. I tell you everything that's really nothing, nothing of what's crying within me. So when I'm going through my routine, don't be fooled by what I'm saying. Please listen carefully and try to hear what I'm not saying; what I'd like to be able to say; what, for survival, I need to say but I can't say. I dislike the hiding. Honestly I do. I dislike the superficial phony games I'm playing.

I'd really like to be genuine, spontaneous, and me; but you have to help me. You have to help me by holding out your hand, even when that's the last thing I seem to want or need. Each time you are kind and gentle and encouraging, each time you try to understand because you really care, my heart begins to grow wings. Very small wings. Very feeble wings. But wings. With your sensitivity and sympathy and your power of understanding, I can make it. You can breathe life into me. It will not be easy for you. A long conviction of worthlessness builds strong walls. But love is stronger than strong walls, and therein lies my hope. Please try to beat down those walls with firm hands, but with gentle hands, for a child is very sensitive, and I am a child.

Who am I, you may wonder. For I am every man, every woman, every child . . . every human you meet.

<u>Second, stand in their shoes.</u> To become a genuine listener, you need to take off your shoes and stand in another's. In the words of Robert Byrne, "Until you walk a mile in another man's moccasins you can't imagine the smell." You must try to see the world as they see it and try to feel as they feel.

Let's pretend for a moment that everyone in the world wears tinted glasses and that no two shades are exactly alike. You and I are standing on the banks of a river. I am wearing green lenses and you are wearing red. "Wow, look how green the water is," I say.

"Green? Are you crazy, the water is red," you reply.

"Hello. Are you colorblind? That's as green as green gets."

"It's red, you idiot!"

"Green!"

"Red!"

Many people look at conversations as a competition. It's my point of view versus yours; we can't both be right. In reality, since we're both coming from a different point of view, we both can be. Furthermore, it's silly to try to *win* conversations. That usually ends up in Win-Lose or Lose-Lose and is a withdrawal from the RBA.

My little sister was once told this story by a friend of hers named Toby. Notice what a difference standing in another's shoes made:

The worst part about going to school was riding the bus. I mean most of my friends had cars but we couldn't afford a car for my own personal use, so I had to either take the bus or find a ride. Sometimes I'd call my mom after school to pick me up, but she would take so long it drove me crazy. I remember many times screaming at my mom, "What took you forever? Don't you even care that I've been waiting for hours?!" I never noticed how she felt or what she'd been doing. I only thought about myself.

One day I overheard my mom talking to my dad about it. She was crying and said how much she wished they could afford a car for me and how hard she had been working to try to earn the extra money.

Suddenly my whole perspective changed. I saw my mom as a real person with feelings—fear, hopes, doubts, and a great amount of love for me. I vowed never to treat her bad again. I even started talking more to her, and together we figured out a way I could get a part-time job and earn my way to a car. She even volunteered to drive me to work and back. I wish I had listened to her earlier.

Third, practice mirroring. Think like a mirror. What does a mirror do? It doesn't judge. It doesn't give advice. It reflects. Mirroring is simply this: *Repeat back in your own words what the other person is saying and feeling.* Mirroring isn't mimicking. Mimicking is when you repeat exactly what the other person says, like a parrot:

"Ugh, Tom. I'm having the worst time in school right now."

"You're having the worst time in school right now."

"I'm basically flunking all of my classes."

"You're basically flunking all of your classes."

"Man, stop saying everything I'm saying. What's wrong with you?"

Mirroring is different from mimicking in the following ways:

MIMICKING IS:	MIRRORING IS:
Repeating words	Repeating meaning
Using the same words	Using your own words
Cold and indifferent	Warm and caring

Let's take a look at an everyday conversation to see how mirroring works.

Your dad might say to you: "No! You can't take the car tonight, Son. And that's final."

A typical seek-first-to-talk response might be: "You never let me take the car. I always have to get a ride. And I'm sick of it."

This kind of response usually ends up in a big yelling match where neither side feels very good afterward.

Instead, try mirroring. *Repeat back in your own words what the other person is saying and feeling.* Let's try it again.

"No! You can't take the car tonight, Son. And that's final."

"I can see that you're upset about this, Dad."

"You bet I'm upset. The way your grades have been dropping lately, you don't deserve the car."

"So, you're worried about my grades then?"

"I am. You know how badly I want you to get into college."

"College is really important to you, isn't it?"

"I never had the chance to go to college. And I've never been able to make much because of it. I know money's not everything, but it sure would help right now. I just want a better life for you."

"Okay, I see what you're saying."

"You are so capable that it just drives me crazy when you don't take school seriously. I guess you can take the car if you promise me you'll do your homework later tonight. That's all I'm asking. Promise?"

Did you notice what happened? By practicing the skill of mirroring, the boy was able to uncover the real issue. Dad didn't care so much about him taking the car; he was more worried about his future and his casualness toward school. Once he felt that his son understood how important grades and college were to him, he dropped his defenses.

I can't guarantee that mirroring will always lead to such perfect outcomes. It's usually, but not always, more complicated than this. Dad might have replied, "I'm glad you understand where I'm coming from, Son. Now go do your homework." But I can guarantee that mirroring will be a deposit into another's RBA and that you'll get farther than you'd get using the "fight or flight" approach. If you're still a skeptic, I challenge you to give it a try. I think you'll be pleasantly surprised.

<u>Disclaimer.</u> If you practice mirroring but don't really desire to understand others, they will see through it and feel manipulated. Mirroring is a skill, the tip of the iceberg. Your attitude or desire to really understand another is the lurking mass of ice underneath the

surface. If your attitude is right but you don't have the skill, you'll be okay. But it doesn't work the other way around. If you have both the attitude and the skill, you'll become a powerful communicator!

Here are a few mirroring phrases you can use when trying to practice genuine listening. Remember, your goal is to *repeat back in your own words what another person is saying and feeling.*

> Listen, or thy tongue will make thee deaf.
>
> NATIVE AMERICAN PROVERB

Mirroring Phrases
- "It sounds like you feel . . ."
- "So, as I see it . . ."
- "I can see that you're feeling . . ."
- "You feel that . . ."
- "So, what you're saying is . . ."

Important note: There is a time and a place for genuine listening. You'll want to do it when you're talking about an important or sensitive issue, like if a friend really needs help or if you're having a communication problem with a loved one. These conversations take time and you can't rush them. However, you don't need to do it during casual conversations or everyday small talk:

"Man, where's the bathroom? I gotta go real bad."

"So what you're saying is you're worried you won't find a bathroom in time."

Genuine Listening in Action
Let's take another look at the sister who needs a listening ear from her big brother to illustrate how different genuine listening is.

Sister says, "I don't like our new school at all. Ever since we moved I've felt like the biggest outcast. I wish I could find some new friends."

The brother could use any one of the following responses:

"Pass the chips?" (Spacing out)

"Yeah, yeah, sounds great." (Pretend listening)

"Speaking of friends, my friend Julio . . ." (Selective listening)

"What you need to do is start meeting new people." (Advising)

"You're not trying hard enough." (Judging)

"Are you having trouble with your grades, too?" (Probing)

But if big bro is smart, he'll try mirroring:

"You feel that school's kind of tough right now." (Mirroring)

"It's the worst. I mean I don't have any friends. And this girl Tabatha has been so rude to me. She is literally like the queen bee in *Mean Girls.* Oh, I just don't know what to do."

"Sounds like you feel confused." (Mirroring)

"I mean, yeah! I've always been popular and then suddenly no one knows my name. I've been trying to get to know people, but it's not really working."

"I can see you're frustrated." (Mirroring)

"Yeah. I probably sound like I'm psycho or something. Anyway, thanks for listening."

"No problem."

"What do you think I should do?"

By listening, big brother made a huge deposit into his sister's RBA. In addition, little sister is now open to his advice. The time is now right for him to seek to be understood, to share his point of view.

A guy named Andy shared this:

I was going through communication problems with my girlfriend whom I cared very much about. We had been going out for a year and we were starting to fight a lot. I was really scared to maybe lose her. When I learned about seeking first to understand and then to be understood, and how to apply the relationship bank account to relationships, I took it very personally. I realized that I always had been trying to interpret what she was saying, but never really listened with an open mind. It saved our relationship and we are still together two years later. Our relationship is much more mature than most couples because we both believe in Habit 5. We use it for big decisions as well as little ones like going out to dinner. Every time I am together with her, I honestly keep saying to myself, "Now shut up and try to understand her."

• COMMUNICATING WITH PARENTS

Communication is hard enough by itself, but throw Mom or Dad into the mix and then you've got storms ahead. I got along pretty well with my parents as a teenager, but there were times when I was convinced they had aliens living inside their bodies. I felt they

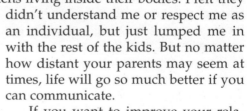

didn't understand me or respect me as an individual, but just lumped me in with the rest of the kids. But no matter how distant your parents may seem at times, life will go so much better if you can communicate.

If you want to improve your relationship with Mom or Dad (and shock 'em in the process), try listening to them, just like you would a friend.

Now, it may seem kind of weird to treat your parents as if they were normal people and all, but it's worth trying. We're always saying to our parents, "You don't understand me. No one understands me." But have you ever stopped to consider that maybe you don't understand *them*?

They have pressures, too, you know? While you're worrying about your friends and your upcoming history test, they're worrying about their bosses and how they're going to pay for your braces. Like you, they have days when they get offended at work and go in the restroom to cry. They have days when they don't know how they're going to pay the bills. Your mom may have too much work stress to just sit down and relax at night. Your dad may get laughed at by the neighbors because of the car he drives. They may have unfulfilled dreams they've had to sacrifice so that you can reach yours. Hey, parents are people, too. They laugh, they cry, they get their feelings hurt, and they don't always have their act together, just like me and you.

If you take the time to understand and listen to your parents, two incredible things will happen. First, you'll gain a greater respect for them. When I turned nineteen, I remember reading one of my dad's books for the first time. He was a successful author and everyone had always told me how great his books were, but I'd never taken the time to even look at one until then. "Wow," I thought after finishing that first book, "Dad is *smart*." And for all those years I was convinced I was smarter.

Second, if you take time to understand and listen to your parents, you'll get your way much more often. This isn't a manipulative trick, it's a principle. If they feel that you understand them, they'll be way more willing to listen to you, they'll be more flexible, and they'll trust you more. One mother once told me, "If my teenage daughters simply took time to understand my hectic world and did little things around the house to help me, I'd give them so many privileges they wouldn't know what to do with them."

I FEEL YOUR PAIN, DAD.

So how can you better understand your parents? Start by asking them some questions. When's the last time you asked your mom or dad, "How was your day today?" or "Tell me what you like and don't like about your job" or "Is there anything I could do to help around the house?"

You can also begin to make small deposits into their RBA. To do that, ask yourself, "What do my parents consider a deposit?" Jump into their shoes and think about it from their point of view, not yours. A deposit to them might mean taking out the recycling without being asked, or keeping a commitment to be home on time, or, if you're living away from home, calling them on weekends.

Then Seek to Be Understood

I saw the results of a survey in which people were asked what their greatest fears were. "Death" came out as number two. You'll never guess what the number-one fear was. It was "speaking in public." People would actually rather die than speak in public!

It takes boldness to speak up in public, no doubt about it. But it also takes boldness to speak up in general. The second half of Habit 5, Then Seek to Be Understood, is as important as the first half but requires something different of us. Seeking first to understand requires consideration, but seeking to be understood requires courage.

Practicing only the first half of Habit 5, Seek First to Understand, is weak. It's Lose-Win. It's the doormat syndrome. Yet it's an easy trap to fall into, especially with parents. "I'm not going to tell Dad how I feel. He won't listen and he'd never understand." So we harbor these feelings inside while our parents carry on never knowing how we truly feel. But this isn't healthy. Remember, unexpressed feelings never die. They are buried alive and come forth later in uglier ways. You've got to share your feelings or they'll eat your heart out.

Besides, if you have taken the time to listen, your chances of being listened to are very good. In the following story, notice how Leigh practiced both halves of the habit:

I was sick and missed a day of school. My parents were concerned that I wasn't getting enough sleep and that I was staying out too late. Instead of coming up with a bunch of excuses, I tried to understand their reasoning. And I agreed with them. But I also explained to them that I am trying to have a fun senior year, and this includes spending time with my friends. My parents were willing to look at the situation from my point of view, and we reached a compromise. I was to stay in one of the days that weekend and rest. I don't think my parents would have been as lenient if I hadn't tried to understand them first.

Giving feedback is an important part of seeking to be understood. If done in the right way it can be a deposit in the RBA. If someone's fly is open, for instance, give feedback. They'll be very grateful, believe me. If you have a close friend who has bad breath (to the point of developing a reputation for it), don't you think he or she would appreciate some honest feedback, delivered gently? Have you ever returned home from a date only to discover that you had a big piece of meat between your teeth the whole evening? With terror you immediately recall every smile you made that night. Don't you wish your date had told you?

If your RBA with someone is high, you can give feedback openly without hesitation. My younger brother Joshua, a senior in high school, shared this:

One nice thing about having older brothers or sisters is the feedback they give you.

When I come home from a high school basketball or football game, Mom and Dad will meet me at the door and go over all the key plays I made. Mom will rave about the talent that I have, and Dad will say it was my leadership skills that directed the team to victory.

When my sister Jenny comes in the kitchen to join us, I'll ask her how I did. She'll tell me how ordinary I played, and I'd better get my act together if I want to keep my starting position, and she hopes I'll play better the next game and not embarrass her.

Since Jenny and Josh are very close, they can share feedback candidly. Keep these two points in mind as you give feedback.

First, ask yourself the question "Will this feedback really help this person or am I doing it just to suit myself and fix them?" If your motive for the feedback isn't with *their* best interest at heart, then it's probably not the time or place to do it.

Second, send "I" messages instead of "you" messages. In other words, give feedback in the first person. Say, "*I'm* concerned that you have a temper problem" or "*I* feel that you've been acting selfish lately." "You" messages are more threatening because they sound as if you're accusing. "*You* are so self-centered." "*You* have a terrible temper." The other person will feel like they're getting attacked!

Well, that should pretty much wrap it up. I don't have a lot more to say about this habit, except to end with the thought that we began with: You have two ears and one mouth—use 'em accordingly.

COMING ATTRACTIONS
Next up, find out how I plus I can sometimes equal 3.
I'll see you there!

1 See how long you can keep eye contact with someone while they are talking to you. Yes it feels intense at first but it's a powerful way to communicate with someone. (Especially with a crush, btw.)

2 People-watch once in a while. See how others communicate with each other. Observe what their body language is saying.

3 In your interactions today, try mirroring one person and mimicking another, just for fun (maybe just do the mimicking in your head, though). Compare the results.

4 Ask yourself, "Which of the five poor listening styles do I have the biggest problem with—Spacing Out, Pretend Listening, Selective Listening, Word Listening, or Self-Centered Listening (judging, advising, probing)? Now, try to go one day without doing it.

The poor listening style I struggle with most: ....

....

5 Sometime this week, ask your mom or dad, "How's it going?" Open up your heart and practice genuine listening. You'll be surprised by what you learn.

6 If you're a talker, take a break and spend your day listening. Only talk when you have to.

7 The next time you find yourself wanting to bury your feelings deep inside you, don't do it. Instead, express them in a responsible, honest way.

8 Think of a situation where your constructive feedback would really help another person. Share it with them when the time is right.

Person who could benefit from my feedback: ....

....

HABIT 6

Synergize

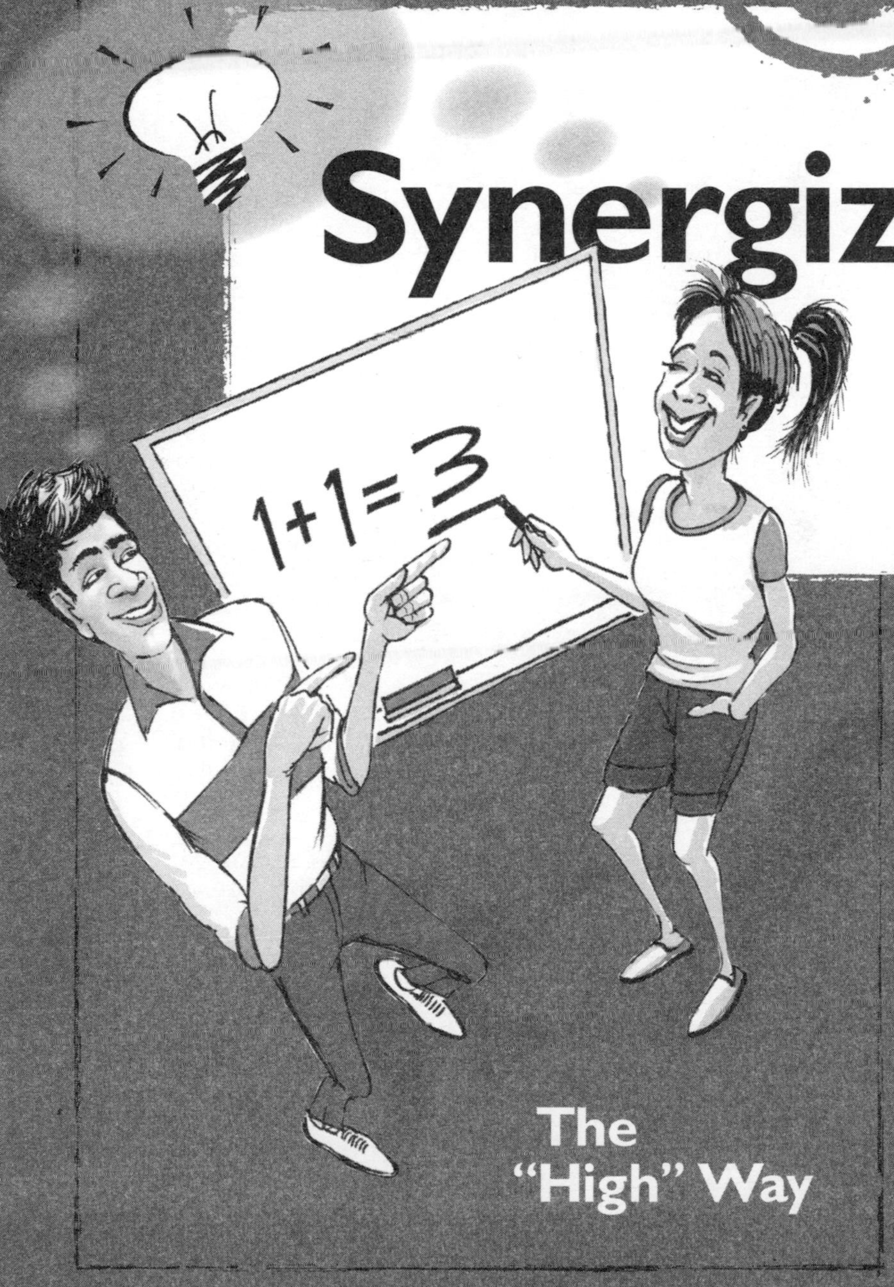

The "High" Way

Alone we can do so little: together we can do so much.
HELEN KELLER

Have you ever seen a flock of geese heading south for the winter flying along in a **V** formation? Scientists have learned some amazing things about why they fly that way:

...HONK!...

...HONK!...

...HONK!...

- By flying in formation, the whole flock can fly 71 percent farther than if each bird flew alone. When a goose flaps its wings, it creates an updraft for the goose that follows.

- As the lead goose gets tired, he will rotate to the back of the **V** and allow another goose to take the lead position.

- The geese in the back honk to encourage those in the front.

- Whenever a goose falls out of formation, it immediately feels the resistance of trying to fly alone and quickly gets back into formation.

- Finally, when one of the geese gets sick or is wounded and falls out of formation, two geese will follow it down to help and protect it. They will stay with the injured goose until it is better or dies and then will join a new formation or create their own to catch up with the group.

Smart birds, those geese! By sharing in each other's draft, taking turns in the lead position, honking encouragement to each other, staying in formation, and watching out for the wounded, they accomplish so much more than if each bird flew solo. It makes me wonder if they took a class in Habit 6, Synergize. Hmmm . . .

So, what does "synergize" mean? Basically, *synergy is achieved when two or more people work together to create a better solution than either could alone. It's not your way or my way but a better way, a higher way.*

Synergy is the reward, the delicious fruit you'll taste as you get better at living the other habits, especially at thinking Win-Win and seeking first to understand. Learning to synergize is like learning to form **V** formations with others instead of trying to fly through life solo. You'll be amazed at how much faster and farther you'll go!

To better understand what synergy is, let's see what synergy is not.

SYNERGY IS:	SYNERGY IS NOT:
Celebrating differences	Tolerating differences
Teamwork	Working independently
Open-mindedness	Thinking you're always right
Finding new and better ways	Compromise

● SYNERGY IS EVERYWHERE

Synergy is everywhere in nature. The great sequoia trees (which grow to heights of 300 feet or more) grow in clumps and share a vast array of intermingled roots. Without one another, they would blow over in a storm.

Many plants and animals live together in symbiotic relationships. If you have ever seen a picture of a small bird feeding off the back of a rhinoceros, you've seen synergy. Each benefits: The bird gets fed and the rhino gets cleaned.

Synergy isn't anything new. If you've ever been on a team of any kind, you've felt it. If you've ever worked on a group project that really came together or been on a really fun group date, you've felt it.

A good song is a great example of synergy. It's not just the beats, or the vocals, or the lyrics—it's all of them together that make up the "sound." Each musician and producer brings his or her strengths to the table to create something better than each could alone. No part is more important than another, just different.

● CELEBRATING DIFFERENCES

Synergy doesn't just happen. It's a process. You have to get there. And the foundation of getting there is this: Learn to celebrate differences.

I'll never forget encountering in high school a kid from Tonga named Fine (pronounced Fee-Nee) Unga. At first, I was *totally* intimidated by him. I mean the guy was built like a tank, strong as a bull, and there were rumors going around that he was a street fighter. We looked, dressed, talked, thought, and ate differently (you shoulda seen this guy eat). The only thing we had in common was football. So how in the world did we become best friends? Maybe it was because we were so different. I never quite knew what Fine was thinking or what he would do next, and vice versa. That was seriously refreshing. I especially enjoyed being his friend when a fight broke out. He had strengths I didn't have and I had strengths he didn't have. Together we made a great team.

Boy, am I glad that the world isn't full of a bunch of clones who act and think exactly like me. Thank goodness for diversity.

The word *diversity* usually calls to mind racial and gender differences, but there's so much more to it. As you've probably already noticed, human beings have a wide variety of physical features—hair textures, nose sizes, clothing styles. There are also endless differences in language, wealth, family backgrounds, religious beliefs, lifestyle, education, interests, skills, age, and on and on and on.

As Dr. Seuss said in *One Fish, Two Fish, Red Fish, Blue Fish*:

We see them come.
We see them go.
Some are fast.
And some are slow.
Some are high.
And some are low.
Not one of them
is like another.
Don't ask us why.
Go ask your mother.

The world is a great melting pot of cultures, races, religions, and ideas. Since this diversity around you is always expanding, you've got an important decision to make regarding how you're going to handle it. There are three possible approaches you can take:

Level 1: Shun diversity
Level 2: Tolerate diversity
Level 3: Celebrate diversity

Shunner's Profile

Shunners are afraid (sometimes even scared to death) of differences. It disturbs them that someone may have a different skin color, worship a different God, or wear a different brand of jeans than they do, because they're convinced their way of life is the "best," "right," or "only" way. They enjoy ridiculing those who are different, all the while believing that they are saving the world from some terrible pestilence. They won't hesitate to get physical about it if they have to and will often join gangs, cliques, or anti-groups because, as we've mentioned, there's strength in numbers.

Tolerator's Profile

Tolerators believe that everyone has the right to be different. They don't shun diversity but don't embrace it, either. Their motto is: "You keep to yourself and I'll keep to myself. You do your thing and let me do mine. You don't bother me and I won't bother you."

Although they come close, they never *get to synergy* because they see differences as hurdles, not as potential strengths to build upon. They "put up" with your differences, but never try to understand or learn from them. They don't know what they're missing.

Celebrator's Profile

Celebrators value differences. They see them as an advantage, not a weakness. They've learned that two people who think differently can achieve more than two people who think alike. They realize that celebrating differences doesn't mean that you necessarily agree with those differences, such as being a Democrat or a Republican, only that you value them. In their eyes, Diversity = Creative Sparks = Opportunity.

So where do you fall on the spectrum? Take a hard look. If someone's clothes are "different," do you value their unique clothing styles or do you think they're "out of touch"?

Think about a group that has contrary religious beliefs to yours. Do you respect their beliefs or do you write them off as a bunch of weirdos?

If someone lives on a different side of town than you, do you feel they could teach you a thing or two or do you label them because of where they live?

The truth is, celebrating diversity is a struggle for most of us, depending on the issue. For example, you may appreciate racial and cultural diversity and in the same breath look down on someone because of the clothes they wear.

• WE ARE ALL A MINORITY OF ONE

It's much easier to appreciate differences when we realize that in one way or another, we are all a minority of one. And we should remember that diversity isn't just an external thing, it's also internal. Everyone has their own unique way of thinking—even about the same topic. Think about how different you are from your friends or family members. Do you all react to life problems in the same way? Hardly! Think about it: some people, for example, are more easygoing and some are more tightly strung. How else do we differ on the inside? Well . . .

We learn differently. As you've probably noticed, your friend's or sister's brain doesn't work the same way yours does. Dr. Thomas Armstrong has identified seven kinds of smarts and says that kids may learn best through their most dominant intelligence:

- *LINGUISTIC:* learn through reading, writing, telling stories
- *LOGICAL-MATHEMATICAL:* learn through logic, patterns, categories, relationships
- *BODILY-KINESTHETIC:* learn through bodily sensations, touching
- *SPATIAL:* learn through images and pictures
- *MUSICAL:* learn through sound and rhythm
- *INTERPERSONAL:* learn through interaction and communication with others
- *INTRAPERSONAL:* learn through their own feelings

One type isn't better than another, only different. You may be logical-mathematical dominant and your sister may be interpersonal dominant. Depending on your approach to diversity, you might say she's weird because she's so talkative, *or* you could take advantage of those differences and get her to help you in your speech class.

We see differently. Everyone sees the world differently and has a different paradigm about themselves, others, and life in general. To understand what I mean, let's try an experiment. Look at the picture below for a few seconds. Now look at the picture on the bottom of page

194 and describe what you see. You might say that the picture on page 194 is a squiggly drawing of a small mouse with a long tail.

But what if I told you that you were wrong? What if I told you that I don't see a mouse at all, but that I see a squiggly drawing of a man with glasses? Would you value my opinion or would you think I'm a dork because I don't see the way you do?

To understand my point of view, turn to page 201 and check out the picture in the middle of that page for a second. Then look at page 194 again. Now can you see what I see?

It goes to show that all the events of your past have formed a lens, or paradigm, through which you see the world. And since no one's past is exactly like anyone else's, no two people see alike. Some see mice and some see men, and both are right.

Once you catch on that everyone views the world differently, and that everyone can be right, it will increase your understanding and respect for differing viewpoints. You might want to try this same experiment with a friend.

We have different styles, traits, and characteristics. The following exercise is not meant to be an in-depth diagnosis but a fun look at some of your general characteristics and personality traits. This exercise was developed by the Legislator's School in North Carolina and was adapted from *It's All in Your Mind* by Kathleen Butler.

Read across each row and place a 4 in the blank that best describes you. Now place a 3 in the blank for the second word that best describes you. Do the same for the final words using a 2 and a 1. Do this for each row.

EXAMPLE:

Imaginative	2	Investigative	4	Realistic	1	Analytical	3

COLUMN 1		COLUMN 2		COLUMN 3		COLUMN 4	
Imaginative		Investigative		Realistic		Analytical	
Adaptable		Inquisitive		Organized		Critical	
Relating		Creating		Getting to Point		Debating	
Personal		Adventurous		Practical		Academic	
Flexible		Inventive		Precise		Systematic	
Sharing		Independent		Orderly		Sensible	
Cooperative		Competitive		Perfectionistic		Logical	
Sensitive		Risk-Taking		Hard-Working		Intellectual	
People-Person		Problem Solver		Planner		Reader	
Associate		Originate		Memorize		Think Through	
Spontaneous		Changer		Wants Direction		Judger	
Communicating		Discovering		Cautious		Reasoning	
Caring		Challenging		Practicing		Examining	
Feeling		Experimenting		Doing		Thinking	

Now add up your totals (don't include the example, of course) for each column and place the total in the blanks below.

COLUMN 1 **Grapes**		COLUMN 2 **Oranges**		COLUMN 3 **Bananas**		COLUMN 4 **Melons**	

If your highest score was in column 1, consider yourself a grape.
If your highest score was in column 2, consider yourself an orange.
If your highest score was in column 3, consider yourself a banana.
If your highest score was in column 4, consider yourself a melon.
Now find your fruit below and review what this may mean to you.

GRAPES

Natural abilities include:

- Being reflective
- Being sensitive
- Being flexible
- Being creative
- Preference for working in groups

Grapes may have trouble:

- Giving exact answers
- Focusing on one thing at a time
- Organizing

Grapes learn best when they:

- Can work and share with others
- Balance work with play
- Can communicate
- Are noncompetitive

To expand their style, Grapes need to:

- Pay more attention to details
- Not rush into things
- Be less emotional when making some decisions

ORANGES

Natural abilities include:

- Experimenting
- Being independent
- Being curious
- Creating different approaches
- Creating change

Oranges may have trouble:

- Meeting time limits
- Following a lecture
- Having few options or choices

Oranges learn best when they:

- Can use trial and error
- Produce real products
- Can compete
- Are self-directed

To expand their style, Oranges need to:

- Delegate responsibility
- Be more accepting of others' ideas
- Learn to prioritize

BANANAS

Natural abilities include:
- Planning
- Fact-finding
- Organizing
- Following directions

Bananas may have trouble:
- Understanding feelings
- Dealing with opposition
- Answering "what if" questions

Bananas learn best when they:
- Have an orderly environment
- Have specific outcomes
- Can trust others to do their part
- Have predictable situations

To expand their style, Bananas need to:
- Express their own feelings more
- Get explanations of others' views
- Be less rigid

MELONS

Natural abilities include:
- Debating points of view
- Finding solutions
- Analyzing ideas
- Determining value or importance

Melons may have trouble:
- Working in groups
- Being criticized
- Convincing others diplomatically

Melons learn best when they:
- Have access to resources
- Can work independently
- Are respected for intellectual ability
- Follow traditional methods

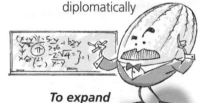

To expand their style, Melons need to:
- Accept imperfection
- Consider all alternatives
- Consider others' feelings

• CELEBRATE YOUR OWN DIVERSITY

Our tendency is to ask, *Which fruit is best?* The answer is, *That's a dumb question.*

I have three brothers. We have some stuff in common, like nose size and parents, but we are very different. When I was younger, I was always trying to prove to myself that my talents were better than theirs: "So what if you're more outgoing than me. I've always been better at school than you and that's more important anyway." I've since seen the stupidity of that kind of thinking and am *still* learning to appreciate the fact that my brothers have their strengths and I have mine. No one's better or worse, only different.

That's why you shouldn't feel so bad if a member of the opposite sex (whom you're just dying to go out with) doesn't go for you. You may be the must luscious and mouth-watering grape around, but he or she may be looking for an orange. And no matter how much you want a change of fruit, you're a grape and they want an orange. But don't worry. A grape seeker is bound to drop by. It all balances out.

Instead of trying to blend in and be like everyone else, be proud of and celebrate your unique differences and qualities. A fruit salad is delicious precisely because each fruit maintains its own flavor.

• ROADBLOCKS TO CELEBRATING DIFFERENCES

Although there are many, three of the largest roadblocks to synergy are ignorance, cliques, and prejudice.

Ignorance. Ignorance means you're clueless. You don't know what other people feel or believe, or what they've been through. Ignorance often abounds when it comes to understanding people with disabilities, as Crystal Lee Helms explained in an article submitted to *mirror,* a Seattle-area newspaper:

My name is Crystal. I'm 5'1" with blond hair and hazel eyes. Big deal, right? What if I told you I was deaf?

In a perfect world, it wouldn't/shouldn't matter. We don't live in a perfect world, though, and it does matter. The moment someone knows I'm deaf, their whole attitude changes. Suddenly they look at me differently. You'd be surprised how people act.

The most common question I get is, "How'd you become deaf?" When I tell them, their reaction is as common as the question itself: "Oh, I'm so sorry. That's so sad." Whenever that happens I simply look them in the eye and I calmly inform them, "No, really, it's not sad at all. Don't apologize." No matter how good the intentions are, pity always makes my stomach churn.

Not all attitudes put me on the defensive. Some are just plain funny. I was signing with my friends and some dude I didn't know came up to me and started talking.

"What's it like being deaf?"

"I don't know. What's it like being hearing? I mean, it isn't like anything. It just is."

You see, the thing is this: if you meet someone who is deaf, don't write them off as disabled or disadvantaged. Instead take the time to get to know them and find out what being deaf is all about. By doing this, you open yourself to understanding not only others, but, more important, yourself.

Cliques. There's nothing wrong with hanging out with guys or girls you're comfortable with; it only becomes a problem only when your group of friends becomes so exclusive that they reject everyone who isn't just like them. It's kind of hard to value differences in a close-knit clique. Those on the outside feel like second-class citizens, and those on the inside often suffer from superiority complexes. But breaking into a clique isn't hard. All you have to do is lose your identity, be assimilated, and become part of the Borg collective.

Prejudice. Have you ever felt stereotyped, labeled, or prejudged by someone because of your skin, your gender, your accent, or where you live? Isn't it a sick feeling?

Although we're all created equal, unfortunately, we're not all *treated* equally. It's a sad fact that minorities and women often have additional hurdles to leap in life because of prejudices held by so many. The United States elected an African American president, but racism is *still* a huge problem. This is Natarsha's experience:

Racism can make succeeding tougher. When you're a black student in the top 10 percent of your class, maintaining a 4.0 grade point average, some people have a tendency to feel threatened. I just wish that people would realize that everyone, no matter where they're from or what color they are, deserves the same opportunities. As far as my friends and I are concerned, prejudice will always be a battle.

We aren't born with prejudices. They're learned. Kids, for instance, are color-blind. But as they mature they begin to pick up on the prejudices of others and form walls, as is explained in Rodgers and Hammerstein's lyrics to a song from the old classic musical *South Pacific:*

> *You've got to be taught to be afraid*
> *Of people whose eyes are oddly made,*
> *And people whose skin is a diff'rent shade,*
> *You've got to be carefully taught.*
>
> *You've got to be taught before it's too late,*
> *Before you are six or seven or eight,*
> *To hate all the people your relatives hate,*
> *You've got to be carefully taught!*

The following poem by an unknown source tells the sad tale of what happens when people prejudge one another.

THE COLD WITHIN

> *Six humans trapped by happenstance, in bleak and bitter cold,*
> *Each one possessed a stick of wood, or so the story's told.*
>
> *Their dying fire in need of logs, the first man held his back,*
> *For of the faces 'round the fire, he noticed one was black.*
>
> *The next man looking 'cross the way saw one not of his church,*
> *And couldn't bring himself to give the fire his stick of birch.*
>
> *The third one sat in tattered clothes, he gave his coat a hitch,*
> *Why should his log be put to use to warm the idle rich?*
>
> *The rich man just sat back and thought of the wealth he had in store,*
> *And how to keep what he had earned from the lazy, shiftless poor.*
>
> *The black man's face bespoke revenge as the fire passed from sight,*
> *For all he saw in his stick of wood was a chance to spite the white.*
>
> *The last man of this forlorn group did naught except for gain,*
> *Giving only to those who gave was how he played the game.*
>
> *Their logs held tight in death's still hand was proof of human sin,*
> *They didn't die from the cold without—they died from the cold within.*

● STICKING UP FOR DIVERSITY

Fortunately, the world is full of people who are warm within and who value diversity. The following story by Bill Sanders is a wonderful example of sticking up for diversity and showing courage:

A couple of years ago, I witnessed courage that ran chills up and down my spine.

At a high school assembly, I had spoken about picking on people and how each of us has the ability to stand up for people instead of putting them down. Afterwards, we had a time when anyone could come out of the bleachers and speak into the microphone. Students could say thank-you to someone who had helped them, and some people came up and did just that. A girl thanked some friends who had helped her through family troubles. A boy spoke of some people who had supported him during an emotionally difficult time.

Then a senior girl stood up. She stepped over to the microphone, pointed to the sophomore section and challenged her whole school. "Let's stop picking on that boy. Sure, he's different from us, but we are in this thing together. On the inside he's no different from us and needs our acceptance, love, compassion, and approval. He needs a friend. Why do we continually brutalize him and put him down? I'm challenging this entire school to lighten up on him and give him a chance!"

> Differences create the challenges in life that open the door to discovery.
>
> American Sign Language symbol for
> **"WE ARE DIVERSE"**

All the time she shared, I had my back to the section where that boy sat, and I had no idea who he was. But obviously the school knew. I felt almost afraid to look at his section, thinking the boy must be red in the face, wanting to crawl under his seat and hide from the world. But as I glanced back, I saw a boy smiling from ear to ear. His whole body bounced up and down, and he raised one fist in the air. His body language said, "Thank you, thank you. Keep telling them. You saved my life today!"

If you've ever been bullied yourself you know how it feels. It's a terrible thing that no one should ever have to go through. So watch out for those courageous moments when you can stop the bullying of another person right in its tracks, whether live or online.

Finding the "High" Way   Once you've bought into the idea that differences are a strength and not a weakness, and once you're committed to at least trying to celebrate differences, you're ready to find the High Way. The Buddhist definition of the Middle Way does not mean compromise; it means higher, like the apex of a triangle.

Synergy is more than just compromise or cooperation. Compromise is $1 + 1 = 1\frac{1}{2}$. Cooperation is $1 + 1 = 2$. Synergy is

1 + 1 = 3 or more. It's creative cooperation, with an emphasis on the word *creative*. The whole is greater than the sum of the parts.

Builders know all about it. If one 2" x 4" beam can support 607 pounds, then two 2" x 4"s should be able to support 1,214 pounds. Right? Actually, two 2" x 4"s can support 1,821 pounds. If you nail them together, two 2" x 4"s can now support 4,878 pounds. And three 2" x 4"s nailed together can support 8,481 pounds. Musicians know how it works, too. They know that when a C and G note are perfectly in tune, it produces a third note, or an E.

Finding the High Way always produces more, as Laney discovered:

In my physics lab the teacher was demonstrating the principle of momentum and our assignment was to construct a catapult, like in medieval times. We called it a pumpkin launcher.

There were three of us in our group, two boys and me. We are all quite different, so we came up with a lot of different ideas.

One of us wanted to use bungee cords to make the launcher flip. Someone else wanted to use tension and ropes. We tried each without much success and then we figured out a way to use both of them together. It gave a lot more spring than either would have alone. It was cool because it doubled the length of our shot.

Synergy occurred as the founders of the United States were forming their government structure. William Paterson proposed the New Jersey Plan, which said that states should get equal representation in government regardless of population size. This plan favored the smaller states. James Madison had a different idea, known as the Virginia Plan, which argued that states with greater populations should have greater representation. This plan favored the larger states.

After several weeks of debate, they reached a decision that all  parties felt good about. They agreed to have two branches of Congress. In one branch, the Senate, each state would get two representatives, regardless of population size. In the other branch, the House of Representatives, each state would get representatives based on population.

Although it is called the Great Compromise, this famous decision could really be called the Great Synergy, because it has proved to be better than either of the original proposals.

- **GETTING TO SYNERGY**

Whether you're arguing with your parents over dating and curfew guidelines, picking teams to shoot hoops, or simply not seeing eye to eye with your best friend there's a way to *get to synergy.* Here's a simple five-step process to help you get there.

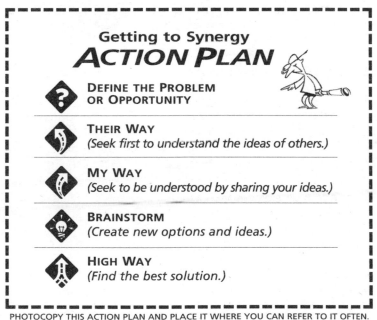

Getting to Synergy
ACTION PLAN

? DEFINE THE PROBLEM OR OPPORTUNITY

) THEIR WAY
(Seek first to understand the ideas of others.)

(MY WAY
(Seek to be understood by sharing your ideas.)

💡 BRAINSTORM
(Create new options and ideas.)

🛣 HIGH WAY
(Find the best solution.)

PHOTOCOPY THIS ACTION PLAN AND PLACE IT WHERE YOU CAN REFER TO IT OFTEN.

Let's give the action plan a try on a problem to see how it works.

The Vacation

Dad: *I don't care how you feel. You're going on this vacation whether you like it or not. We've had this planned for months, and it's important that we spend some time together as a family.*

Mom: *I don't want you staying here by yourself. I'd worry about what you're doing and who you're hanging out with. We want you with us.*

DEFINE THE PROBLEM OR OPPORTUNITY

In this case, we have a problem. It's this:

My parents want me to vacation with the family, but I would rather stay home and go out with my friends.

THEIR WAY *(Seek first to understand the ideas of others.)*

Try using the listening skills you learned in Habit 5 so that you can really understand your mom and dad. Remember, if you want to have power and influence with your parents, they need to feel understood.

By listening, you learn the following:

This vacation is very important to my dad. He wants to have a family bonding time. He feels it won't be the same without me. Mom feels that she would worry so much about me being home alone that she wouldn't enjoy the vacation.

MY WAY *(Seek to be understood by sharing your ideas.)*

Now practice the second half of Habit 5 and have the courage to share your feelings. If you've taken the time to listen to them, they'll be much more likely to listen to you. So you tell your parents how you feel.

Mom and Dad, I want to stay home and be with my friends. They are very important to me. We have a lot of things planned, and I don't want to miss out on any of the fun. Besides, I go crazy when I have to drive in a car all day with a little sister.

BRAINSTORM *(Create new options and ideas.)*

This is where the magic happens. Utilize your imagination and create new ideas together that you could never think of alone. As you brainstorm, keep these tips in mind:

- *GET CREATIVE:* Throw out your wildest ideas. Let it flow.
- *AVOID CRITICISM:* Nothing kills the flow of creativity like criticism. Resist.
- *PIGGYBACK:* Keep building upon the best ideas. It's called piggybacking. One great idea leads to another, which leads to another.

Brainstorming produces the following ideas:

- *Dad said we could go to a vacation spot that I would enjoy more.*
- *I mentioned that I could stay with relatives close by.*
- *Mom suggested I could take a friend with me.*
- *I mentioned using my savings and busing out to meet them, so I wouldn't have to drive in a crowded car.*
- *Mom was willing to cut the vacation short so it would be easier for me.*
- *I suggested staying home for part of the vacation and joining them later.*

- *Dad was willing to let me stay home if I would clean up his computers so they'd run faster while they were gone.*

HIGH WAY *(Find the best solution.)*

After brainstorming for a while, the best idea will usually surface. Now it's just a matter of going with it.

We all agreed that I could stay home during the first half of the week and then bus out with a friend to join the family for the second half. They even offered to pay the bus fare for my friend and me if I would clean up the computers. It's not hard work, so I will still have time to hang out with my friends. They're happy, and so am I.

If you will follow the basics of the above formula, you'll be amazed at what can happen. But it takes a lot of maturity to get to synergy. You have to be willing to listen to the other point of view. You then need to have the courage to express your point of view. Finally, you've got to let your creative juices flow. See how this eleventh grader named Erica got to synergy:

HEY, WILBUR, THIS SYNERGY STUFF IS GREAT! YOU PUSH, AND I'LL FLY!

As a senior editor of the school paper, I had a lot of responsibility to delegate. I wanted to add in a new section this year, to switch things up a little, so I came up with this idea: we'd do a feature on a different kid every week, and interview them about their talents and interests. My co-editor wanted to just pick popular kids from the older grades, but I said, why don't we reach a bigger crowd? What if there are some freshmen with awesome talents who are too shy to show off their skills?

So I posted on the newspaper's Twitter page about how we were looking for kids in school with unique stories and skills, and people started posting and Tweeting at us right away. One guy was a really amazing break-dancer and he sent in a video for us to upload. Another girl showed us how she is completely bilingual in Spanish and English and translated a poem for us to publish in the paper. This shy kid in my art class sent in a video of himself playing bass in his band, and it turns out he's a really good musician!

My co-editor really came around to this open call—I think he caught on pretty quickly how limited we would have been if we'd just sought out popular kids. Last week, he and I suggested to the student council to start a talent show so everyone could do this stuff in person, not just online! Overall, it's been a surprisingly awesome way to see how the student body is a synergy of each individual with unique talents and personalities.

Go for It

The Getting to Synergy Action Plan can be used in all kinds of situations:

- You've just been assigned a group project for biology with three people you don't even know.
- You're in charge of social media at your summer job and you have to juggle multiple opinions.
- You want to go to college, but your parents aren't willing to help you pay for it.
- As a student body officer, you and your team are in charge of planning Homecoming.
- You and your stepmom disagree on your curfew.
- You're always fighting with your brother about who gets to use your mom's laptop.

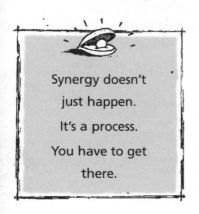

Synergy doesn't just happen. It's a process. You have to get there.

The Getting to Synergy Action Plan is a guideline, nothing more. The steps don't always have to be in order, and you don't always have to do all of them. If your RBA is extremely high with someone, you can virtually skip the first three steps and jump right into brainstorming. On the other hand, if your RBA is low, you may need to take more time listening. It may take several conversations to solve some problems. Be patient.

Despite herculean efforts on your part to find the High Way, sometimes the other party won't make any effort at all. You may just have to keep building the RBA in these situations.

How do you normally solve conflicts? Most of the time it's usually fight (with words or fists) or flight (you don't speak up or you take off). Well things are looking up . . . The Getting to Synergy Action plan offers an alternative.

Pretend you and your best friend have just run for different Student Council offices in your high school. You won. She lost. Ever since the election she's hardly talked to you. Each of you feels the other person isn't doing enough to stay in touch, dispel the jealousies, or keep the friendship going. It's creating tension. Having recently learned about synergy, you decide to give the Getting to Synergy Action Plan a try while on a phone call with this best friend.

❓ DEFINE THE PROBLEM OR OPPORTUNITY

YOU: *I feel like it's been pretty hard since the election, you know. I guess I don't know what's really going on. (only silence) It just seems like whenever we see each other there's this weird energy, you know, either we don't talk at all or things turn into some sort of argument. (more silence) You wanna try and figure this out?*

THEM: *I guess.*

THEIR WAY (Seek first to understand the ideas of others.)

YOU: *Well, to start with, how are you feeling about everything?*

THEM: *That's easy. Ever since you won you just think you're better than me. You got this meeting and this club and this game . . .*

YOU: *It's just that things got so crazy so fast, you know?*

THEM: *No, I don't know, wish I did, but I didn't win, remember?*

YOU: *Look, I'm sorry you didn't win, I really am, but—*

THEM: *Whatever. I mean, are you really too busy to text me?*

YOU: *You're feeling that I'm too busy for you?*

THEM: *Totally. It's like you're a different person or something. And you're always hanging out with all these Student Council kids and I feel like a total loser.*

YOU: *This whole thing has really hurt you.*

THEM: *You have no idea. How would you feel if you lost and I won and I stopped talking to you all of sudden?*

YOU: *I'd feel bad, too.*

THEM: *Yeah, sure.*

YOU: *So, it's like your best friend suddenly thinks she's better than you and doesn't have time for you and you're totally left out of everything. Is that it?*

THEM: *You got it.*

MY WAY (Seek to be understood by sharing your ideas.)

YOU: *I'm sorry you feel like that. Would you mind if I shared what I'm going through?*

THEM: *I think I already know, but go ahead.*

YOU: *It's just that I'm so tired after school and meetings and everything I just get home and collapse. It's not you. I don't really feel like talking to anyone.*

THEM: *That busy, huh?*

YOU: *And then it's like your punishing me for winning.*

THEM: *You're probably right. I shouldn't take it out on you.*

BRAINSTORM (Create new options and ideas.)

YOU: *Well why don't we figure out how to get together more?*

THEM: *Hey, how 'bout you come over after school Friday, we could hang out like we used to?*

YOU: *I would if I could but I have a meeting with my committee and then we all gotta go to the game, ride some goofy float. Hey, you could come to the game?*

THEM: *I have to work.*
YOU: *Starting when?*
THEM: *An hour or so after the game starts.*
YOU: *And you can't get it off?*
THEM: *No way, I just started.*
YOU: *So I guess I'm not the only one who's busy?*
THEM: *Huh, good one, guess not.*
(long pause)
YOU: *Hey . . .*
THEM: *What?*
YOU: *Well, it's just an idea, and you might not want to, but what if you joined my committee? We need another girl and then we'd be seeing each other a lot.*
THEM: *Really? I can just do that? I don't have to run or anything?*
YOU: *I'm in charge now, remember, I can do anything.*
(you both laugh)

HIGH WAY *(Find the best solution.)*

THEM: *Well, that'd be awesome.*
YOU: *In fact, how about just coming to the meeting Friday, then come to the game for a while until you have to work?*
THEM: *That'd be perfect.*
YOU: *I think so.*
THEM: *Hey, thanks so much for taking the time to talk, I'd hate it if I wasn't your friend.*
YOU: *Same.*

It's not always this easy. But, on the other hand, sometimes it is.

• TEAMWORK AND SYNERGY

Great teams are usually made up of five or more different types of people, with each member playing a different but important role.

Plodders. Sure and steady, they stick to a job until it's done.

Followers. They are very supportive of leaders. If they hear a great idea, they can run with it and follow through on making it work.

Innovators. They are the creative, idea people. They offer the sparks.

Harmonizers. They provide unity and support and are great synergizers as they work with others and encourage cooperation.

Show-offs. Fun to work with, they can be tough at times. They often add the spice and momentum needed to bring the team overall success.

Great teamwork is like a great piece of music. All the voices and instruments may be singing and playing at once, but they aren't competing. Individually, the instruments and voices make different sounds, play different notes, pause at different times; yet they blend together to create a whole new sound. This is synergy.

The book you are holding is dripping with synergy. When I first decided to write it, I felt overwhelmed. So I started in the only way I knew how. I got help. I immediately asked a friend for assistance. I soon put together a bigger team. I identified a few schools and educators from around the country who agreed to give feedback on drafts at different stages. I began interviewing teens one-on-one and in groups. I hired an artist. I put together contests asking for stories dealing with teens and the 7 Habits. By the end, there were well over 100 people involved in the creation of this book.

Slowly but surely it all came together. Each person brought his or her talents to the table and contributed in a different way. While I focused on writing, others focused on what they were good at. One was good at collecting stories. One could find great quotes. Another knew how to edit. Some were plodders, some innovators, some show-offs. It was teamwork and synergy to the max.

The wonderful by-product of teamwork and synergy is that it builds relationships. Basketball Olympian Deborah Miller Palmore said it well: "Even when you've played the game of your life, it's the feeling of teamwork that you'll remember. You'll forget the plays, the shots, and the scores, but you'll never forget your teammates."

★ ★ ★

COMING ATTRACTIONS

If you keep reading, you'll discover the real reason why
Beyoncé looks like a million bucks.
Just a few more pages and you're done!

1 When you're around someone with a disability or impairment, don't feel sorry for them or avoid them because you don't know what to say. Instead, get acquainted—it'll make everyone more comfortable.

2 The next time you are having a disagreement with a parent, try out the Getting to Synergy Action Plan. 1. Define the problem. 2. Listen to them. 3. Share your views. 4. Brainstorm. 5. Find the best solution.

3 Use your influence to create synergy in your school this week by using your social media presence to bring people together.

4 This week, look around and notice how much synergy is going on all around you—on a team, in nature, between friends, in the business world. What kind of creative problem solving do they use?

5 Think about someone who irritates you. What is different about them?

Now, what are their positive attributes and what can you learn from them?

6 Brainstorm with your friends and come up with something fun, new, and different to do this weekend, instead of doing the same old thing again and again.

7 Rate your openness to diversity in each of the following categories. Are you a shunner, tolerator, or celebrator?

	SHUNNER	TOLERATOR	CELEBRATOR
Race			
Gender			
Religion			
Age			
Dress			

What can you do to become a celebrator in each category?

PART IV

Renewal

Habit 7—Sharpen the Saw
It's "Me Time"

Keep Hope Alive!
Kid, You'll Move Mountains

HABIT 7

Sharpen the Saw

It's "Me Time"

The time to repair the roof is when the sun is shining.
U.S. PRESIDENT JOHN F. KENNEDY

Do you ever feel imbalanced, stressed-out, or empty inside? If so, Habit 7 is going to be a huge help, because it's been specially designed to deal with these problems. Why do we call it "Sharpen the Saw"? Well, imagine that you're going for a walk in the forest when you come upon a guy furiously sawing down a tree.

"What're you doing?" you ask.

"I'm sawing down a tree," comes the curt reply.

"How long have you been at it?"

"Four hours so far, but I'm really making progress," he says, sweat dripping from his chin.

"Your saw looks pretty dull," you say. "Why don't you take a break and sharpen it?"

"I can't, you idiot. I'm too busy sawing."

We all know who the real idiot here is, now, don't we? If the guy were to take a fifteen-minute break to sharpen the saw, he'd probably finish three times faster.

Have you ever been too busy driving to take time to get gas?

Have you ever been too busy living to take time to renew yourself?

Habit 7 is all about keeping your personal self sharp so that you can better deal with life. It means regularly renewing and strengthening the four key dimensions of your life—your body, your brain, your heart, and your soul.

BODY **The Physical Dimension**
Exercise, eat healthy, sleep well, relax.

BRAIN **The Mental Dimension**
Read, educate, write, learn new skills, create.

HEART **The Emotional Dimension**
Build relationships (RBA, PBA), give service, laugh, learn to love yourself.

SOUL **The Spiritual Dimension**
Meditate, keep a journal, pray, take in quality media.

• BALANCE IS BETTER

The ancient Greeks' famous saying "Nothing overmuch" reminds us of the importance of balance and doing everything in moderation. Some people spend countless hours building the perfect body but neglect their minds. Others have minds that can bench-press 400 pounds but let their bodies go to pot or forget about having a social life. To perform at your peak, you need to strive for balance in all four dimensions of life.

Why is balance so important? It's because how you do in one dimension of life will affect the other three. Think about it: if one of your car's tires is out of balance, all four will wear unevenly. It's hard to be friendly (heart) when you're exhausted (body). It also works the other way. When you're feeling motivated and in tune with yourself (soul), it's easier to focus on work (mind) and to be friendlier (heart).

During my school years, I studied some great artists, authors, and musicians, like van Gogh, Hemingway, Mozart, and Beethoven. Many of them were known for being emotionally messed up. Why? Your guess is as good as mine, but I think it was because they were out of balance. It seems they focused so hard on just one thing, like their music or art, that they neglected the other dimensions of life and lost their bearings. As the saying goes, *Balance and moderation in all things.*

• TAKE TIME FOR A TIME-OUT

Just like a car, you too need regular tune-ups and oil changes. You need time out to rejuvenate the best thing you've got going for yourself—you! Time to relax and to treat yourself to a little tender loving care is essential. This is what sharpening the saw is all about.

Over the next several pages, we'll take a look at each dimension, the body, mind, heart, and soul, and talk about specific ways to get your saw razor sharp. So read on!

Caring for Your Body

TRY IT AGAIN, SEAN.

I hated junior high. I felt awkward and unsure about who I was, and my body started undergoing all sorts of weird changes. I remember my first day in gym class. I had bought my first jock ever, but I had no idea how to put it on. And all of us boys were so embarrassed at seeing each other naked for the first time that we just stood around in the showers and giggled.

You may have already found that during your teenage years your voice changes, your hormones run rampant, and curves and muscles start springing up all over. Welcome to your new body!

Actually, this ever-changing body of yours is really quite an amazing machine. But you only get *one,* and you can either handle it with care, or you can abuse it.

There are so many ways to stay physically sharp. You can eat good food, get enough sleep, keep good hygiene, do push-ups or crunches in your room (you don't have to pay for a gym membership), lift weights, take time to relax, go for a walk, dance, do yoga, or try a hundred other things.

For now, let's focus on nutrition and exercise.

• YOU ARE WHAT YOU EAT

There's much truth to the expression "You are what you eat." I'm not an expert in nutrition, but I have found two rules of thumb to keep in mind.

First rule of thumb: Listen to your body. Pay careful attention to how different foods make you feel and, from that, develop your *own* handful of do's and don'ts. For example, whenever I eat a big meal right before bed I feel horrible in the morning. And whenever I eat *too* many nachos or *too much* pizza I get a "grease rush." (Have you ever had one of those?) These are my *don'ts.* On the other hand, I've learned that eating lots of fruit and drinking tons of water makes me feel on top of my game. These are my *do's.*

Second rule of thumb: Be moderate and avoid extremes. For

many of us, it's often easier to be extreme than moderate, and so we find ourselves jumping back and forth between eating like a rabbit and eating like a pig. A little junk food on occasion isn't going to hurt you. (I mean, what would life be like without an occasional Slurpee?) Just don't make it your everyday fare.

JUNK-FOOD PLATE
(Extreme)

Teen obesity is on the rise and it comes with a boatload of health risks, including type 2 diabetes, asthma, high blood pressure, and other problems you don't want. If you are overweight, it doesn't have to get in the way of the rest of your life. You can take control. It's simply a matter of a healthy diet and moderate exercise. Talk with a doctor or health expert for advice. Read up on nutrition and exercise. For starters, just try losing 10 percent of your body weight at a healthy rate (1–2 pounds a week and no more) and watch how good you'll feel.

RABBIT-FOOD PLATE
(Extreme)

The USDA MyPlate is a balanced approach to nutrition that I recommend. As you can see, it encourages us to fill half our plate with fruits and vegetables. The other half should be filled up with whole grains (like oatmeal or whole wheat bread) and healthy proteins (like fish, chicken, nuts, or beans). On the side is a smaller circle for a cup of low fat milk or yogurt. It also tells us to eat *less* fast food and processed food, which are often loaded with fat, sugar, salt, and other gook and to drink 6–8 glasses of water every day, which is essential to your body. Just make sure you're near a bathroom a lot.

• USE IT OR LOSE IT

One of my favorite classic movies is *Forrest Gump*. It's the story of a naive young man from Alabama with a good heart who keeps stumbling into success in spite of himself. At one point in the movie, Forrest is frustrated and confused about his life. So what does he do? He starts to run, and keeps on running. After running back and forth from one coast to the other two and a half times, Forrest feels better and is finally able to sort his life out.

We all feel depressed, confused, or apathetic at times. It's at times like these when perhaps the best thing we can do for ourselves is to do what Forrest did: exercise ourselves better. Besides being good for your heart and lungs, exercise has an amazing way of giving you a shot of energy, melting stress away, and clearing your mind.

There's no single best way to exercise. Some teenagers play competitive sports; some prefer running, walking, biking, skateboarding, dancing, doing yoga, or lifting weights. Still others just like to just get outside and move around.

"Pain" doesn't have to be the first thing that comes into your mind when you hear the word "exercise." Find something fun that you enjoy doing, so that it's easy to maintain a consistent workout schedule. For best results, you should exercise for thirty minutes or so, at least three times a week.

GARFIELD © 1982 Paws, Inc. Reprinted with permission of UNIVERSAL PRESS SYNDICATE. All rights reserved.

• IT'S ALL ABOUT HOW YOU FEEL, NOT HOW YOU LOOK

But be careful. In your quest for a better physique, make sure you don't get too obsessed with your appearance. As you've probably noticed, our society is hung up on "looks." To prove my point just look at how celebrities are viewed in the public eye: gossip tabloids praise their beauty, and then criticize their every flaw and bit of cellulite. By comparison, it can really make a person feel self-conscious about his or her appearance!

As a kid, I was very self-conscious about my fat cheeks. My dad told me that when I was born my cheeks were so fat the doctors didn't know which end to spank.

I clearly remember a neighbor—a girl—making fun of my cheeks. My brother David heroically tried to defend me by saying they were made out of muscle. It backfired and "Muscle Cheeks" became my least favorite nickname of all.

I lost the baby-fat in my cheeks in eighth grade. But as my teen-age years unfolded, I became self-conscious about other things, such as not having a perfect smile, like some of my friends did, or those zits that kept resurfacing like a bad habit that won't go away.

Before you start comparing yourself to the beautiful, fit men and women in magazines and movies and hating everything about your body and looks, remember that there are millions of healthy, happy teens who *don't* have high cheekbones, big breasts, rock-hard abs, or buns of steel. There are many successful singers, talk show hosts, dancers, athletes, actors, and actresses who have all kinds of physical imperfections. You don't have to pop steroids or get plastic surgery to be happy. If you don't have the "look" or body type our society has stamped "ideal," so what? What's popular today will change tomorrow anyhow. And the grass is always greener—someone in your class might wish they had your dimples, even while you're wishing they'd just disappear.

Embrace the way you look naturally. Even if you don't find it beautiful right now, there's always someone who will. Seriously! There are lots of people who love curly hair or crooked noses or gap teeth—and find these "eccentricities" beautiful and unique.

The important thing is feeling good physically—and not so much your appearance. Oprah Winfrey said it best: "You have to change your perception. It's not about weight—it's caring for yourself on a daily basis."

Real Life or Art?

Besides, if you didn't already know it, what you see on screen or on paper isn't real. They're "images." They're tweaked to make the already-ripped guys look even more ripped, and the already-thin women look even thinner. Thing is, those celebs are just like us— they get the occasional pimple, their hair frizzes, and their stomachs spill over their waistbands sometimes. The only difference is they have a crew of retouchers to cover these "flaws." Beyoncé has been known to criticize magazines and clothing brand companies that try to crop out her curves and make her look like a stick figure, knowing full well how much is distorts beauty expectations of her fans.

As a *The New York Times* article by Steve Lohr points out:

The photographs of celebrities and models in fashion advertisements and magazines are routinely buffed with a helping of digital polish.

The retouching can be slight— colors brightened, a stray hair put in place, a pimple healed. Or it can be drastic—shedding 10 or 20 pounds, adding a few inches in height and erasing all wrinkles and blemishes, done using Adobe's Photoshop software, the photo retoucher's magic wand.

They're setting up some pretty unrealistic expectations, huh? Some argue that any retouched photos should be marked, so audiences know that what they're looking at is about as real as a computer-generated image.

Remember, our fetish with skinny and chiseled bodies hasn't always been trendy. Wouldn't it be nice to have lived in eighteenth-century Europe, when being overweight was "in"; or during the Dark Ages, when everyone wore baggy robes and no one really knew what your body looked like? Boy, those were the days.

Of course, you want to look your best and be presentable, but be careful: becoming obsessed with looks can be dangerous. It can lead to severe eating disorders such as compulsive eating, bulimia, or anorexia, or to addictions to performance-enhancing drugs, like steroids. Abusing your body in order to be accepted by someone else is never worth it.

If you're struggling with an eating disorder, you don't have to feel alone. It's a very common problem among teens. Humble yourself and admit you have a problem and get help, from friends, family, or groups that specialize in this kind of thing. (At the back of the book I have listed some organizations that can help.)

• I CAN QUIT WHENEVER I WANT

There are ways to care for your body, and there are ways to destroy it. Using addictive substances such as alcohol, drugs, and tobacco is a speedy way to do the latter. Alcohol, for example, is often associated with the three leading causes of death among teens: car accidents, suicide, and homicide. And then there's smoking, which has been proven to cloud your eyes, cause your skin to prematurely age, yellow your teeth, cause bad breath, triple your cavities, cause receding gums, discolor the skin on your fingertips, create tiredness, and, of course, cause cancer. There are no reasons left to smoke, besides thinking it looks "cool"—but even that logic is out of date. According to the Massachusetts Department of Public Health:

Smoking isn't as attractive as you think. In a study, 8 out of 10 guys and 7 out of 10 girls said they wouldn't date someone who smokes. So if you smoke, you better get used to kissing that cigarette.

According to the American Lung Association, the top 5 tobacco companies spend $34 million *every single day* on advertising. They want your money. After all, a pack of cigarettes a day adds up to about $2,500 a year (or more). Just think about how much you could buy with that. Cigarette companies are especially known for targeting teenagers, as if young people could be more easily tricked. Don't let them sucker you!

Now, of course, no one *plans* on getting addicted. It usually starts innocently enough. Too often, though, "gateway drugs" like alcohol and tobacco lead to marijuana, and then eventually on to deadly drugs like cocaine, heroin, opiates, acid, and crystal meth. Some people start using these substances to display their freedom, only to find that addictive drugs *destroy* their freedom. Believe me, there are far better ways to assert your individuality.

Perhaps the worst thing about picking up an addiction is this: You're no longer in control—your addiction is. When it says *jump*, you *jump*. Say good-bye to the whole idea of being proactive. I always feel sorry for people at work who have to go outside to smoke, no matter what the weather is. It's sad to see them standing outside in the pouring rain, puffing away, unable to control their urge.

It's easy to think that addiction is something that only happens to other people, and that we could quit anytime. But in reality, it's *hard*. As an example, only 25 percent of teen tobacco users who try to quit are successful. I like what Mark Twain said about how easy it was for him to quit smoking: "I've done it a hundred times."

Here's a story of the struggle one teenage guy went through to overcome his drug addiction:

The first time I used any kind of drug or alcohol was when I was fourteen. I didn't even know what drugs were. I really didn't care. Everyone just told me how bad they were. My friend said, "Here, take this. It's pretty cool." So I took it. When I started, I wanted to be cool. After that, it wasn't peer pressure anymore. It was just me.

I started doing drugs and drinking more and more and my schoolwork started slipping. My relationships started to decrease. I was losing touch with my family, and I hated that. My attitude toward things turned around, you know—just a lot of negativity. I also started to see my girlfriend less.

Right after I started drinking and drugging, I noticed some physical problems, too. I felt real tired all the time. I also lost a lot of weight— about thirty pounds in two months.

The other thing was that I would go home and run out of tooth- paste or something like that, and I'd cry. I was overreacting big time. My temper was really short.

About a month after my seventeenth birthday, I got caught with drugs in school. They suspended me for a week, and I knew that was the time I needed to get myself back together. So I tried to stop, but I couldn't. It's like when you smoke cigarettes. You can put one down and say you're going to quit, you're going to quit, but it is real hard to stop.

So I stopped hanging around my old friends and started going to Alcoholics Anonymous (AA) meetings and I got a sponsor. AA is a life-long thing. You take one drink and it messes up everything you had built up to that point. A lot of my friends who came to AA have relapsed. But my sponsor really helped me out. Without this program, I know I wouldn't have stopped.

Since I've been in this program, it's been the greatest life. I don't drink. I don't drug. My schoolwork is going back up. My family is closer than ever now. Before, I worked at almost every fast-food place there is in town because I'd quit within two weeks at each one. Now, I've had just one job for about two months. I came back to school and I started to care. I was nice to people even when they weren't nice to me. I've totally changed my life around. I'm starting to think about college and doing all these things I would never think of before. It's real confusing to me why anyone would spend their high school years drinking. It's a scary life.

● THE REFUSAL SKILL™

Steering clear of drugs is easier said than done. Here are *The Refusal Skill*™* steps that you might want to consider the next time you feel pressured to drink, smoke, or do drugs, and don't really want to.

1. *Ask questions.* Ask tough questions that really make you think about what you're doing.
"Why would I want to smoke?"
"What will happen to me if I get stoned tonight?"

2. *Name the trouble.* Put a face on what you're doing.
"Drugs are illegal."
"Smoking will ruin my breath."

3. *State the consequences.* Think through the consequences of your actions.
"I could get arrested if I'm caught with drugs."
"If I get wasted tonight, someone might try to take advantage of me."

4. *Suggest an alternative.* Have your own list of fun alternatives ready to go whenever you're being lured in.
"Hey, why don't we go see a movie instead?"
"Nah, I'd rather play basketball."

5. *Take off.* If you get caught in a situation that just doesn't look good or makes you uncomfortable, don't worry about what everyone might think of you, just get out of there.
"Sorry, everyone, but I'm heading off."
Use your creativity to develop your own approach to avoiding the entire scene, as Jim did:

My friends and I just didn't want all that trouble that came from drinking and doing drugs, so we formed a group. We were about ten people who were committed to helping our friends stay out of trouble. We hung out a lot together, and weekly would go to pasta dinners and plan how we could support each other. The support mostly came in the form of talking to others when we saw them being tempted or floundering, and assuring them that they really didn't need to do those things to be cool, and then inviting them to come join us in our fun instead. It worked and really was very powerful.

Believe me, you're not missing out on anything if you stay away from this stuff. "Life itself," said TV chef Julia Child, "is the proper binge." You don't need to even experiment. The short-term bang's never worth the long-term devastation that often follows. If you don't smoke, drink, or do drugs, why even start? If you do, why not get help and quit? There are much better and more natural ways to get a high from life. Why not give them a try? (See Info Central in the back of the book for more information.)

Caring for
Your Brain

 There's a folklore story about a young man who came to Socrates, the great philosopher and said, "I want to know everything you know."

"If this is your desire," said Socrates, "then follow me to the river." Full of curiosity, the young man followed. As they sat on the riverbank, Socrates said, "Take a close look at the water and tell me what you see."

"I don't see anything," said the man.

"Look closer," replied Socrates.

As the man peered over the bank and leaned closer to the water, Socrates grabbed the man's head and shoved it under the water. The man's arms flailed wildly as he attempted to escape, but Socrates's strong grip kept him submerged. About the time the man was about to drown, Socrates pulled him from the river and laid him on the bank.

Coughing, the man gasped, "Are you crazy, old man? What are you trying to do, kill me?"

"When I was holding you under the river, what did you want more than anything else?" asked Socrates.

"I wanted to breathe. I wanted air!" he cried out.

"Don't ever make the mistake of thinking wisdom comes so easily, my young friend," said Socrates. "When you want to learn as badly as you wanted air just now, then come to me again."

The point here is clear. Nothing in life comes easy. You have to pay the price! Everyone has to pay the price. Write that down. Memorize it. Underline it. I don't care what people say, there are no free lunches! What a naive young man to think that he could gain a lifetime of learning without paying the price. But are we any less naive when we think that we can secure a good job and a promising future if we haven't paid the price to develop a strong mind?

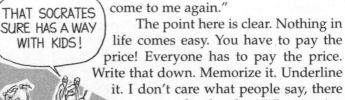

THAT SOCRATES SURE HAS A WAY WITH KIDS!

In fact, getting a good education may just be the most important price you can pay—because, perhaps more than anything else, what you do with that mass of gray material between your ears will determine your future. In fact, unless you want to be flipping burgers and living with your parents when you're thirty years old, you'd better start paying the price now.

The mental dimension of Habit 7, Sharpen the Saw, means developing brainpower through your schooling, extracurricular activities, hobbies, jobs, and other mind-enlarging experiences.

The Key to Unlocking Your Future When researching this book, I asked a group of teenagers in a survey "What are your fears?" I was surprised by how many spoke about the stress of doing well in school, going to college, and getting a good job in the future. Said one, "What can we do to be certain that we can get a job and support ourselves?" The answer is really rather simple. You could try to win the lottery. Your chances of doing that are about 1 in 175 million. Or you could develop an educated mind. By far, this offers your best chance of securing a good job and making a life for yourself.

What does it take to have an educated mind? It's more than earning a diploma, though that's an important part of it. It's more than looking up a fact on Wikipedia, then thinking you're an expert. An educated mind is like a well-conditioned ballerina. A ballerina has perfect control over her muscles. Her body will bend, twist, jump, and turn perfectly, according to her command. Similarly, an educated mind can focus, synthesize, write, speak, create, analyze, imagine, and so much more. To do that, however, it must be trained. It won't just happen automatically.

I'd suggest you get as much education as you can. Any further education beyond high school—a college degree, vocational or technical training, an apprenticeship, or training in any of the armed forces—will be well worth your time and money. See it as an investment in your future. Statistics have shown that a college graduate earns about twice as much as a high school graduate. And the gap seems to be widening. Don't let a lack of money be the reason you don't get more education. "If you think education is expensive, try ignorance," said Derek Bok, a former president of

Harvard University. You'd also be amazed at the number of scholarships, grants, loans, and student-aid options that are available if you search them out. In fact, millions of dollars of grant and scholarship money goes unclaimed each year because no one bothered to apply for it. (Refer to the back of the book for more information on grants and scholarships.) Even if you have to sacrifice and work your tail off to pay for your education, it's well worth it.

• SHARPEN YOUR MIND

There are countless ways to expand your mind. The simplest, most straightforward approach is to *read*. As the saying goes, reading is to the mind what exercise is to the body. Reading is foundational to everything else. Books transport you to other worlds, and you don't have to pay the travel costs. The following are twenty possible ways to sharpen your mind. I'm sure you can come up with another fifty if you try.

- Set a trusted news source as your Internet homepage
- Follow blogs that cover topics you're curious about
- Travel
- Plant a garden
- Observe wildlife
- Attend lectures at a local college
- Watch documentaries
- Visit a library
- Read or listen to the news
- Research your family history
- Write a story, poem, or song
- Play challenging, solitary games, like crossword puzzles or Sudoku
- Debate
- Play a game of chess with someone who challenges you
- Visit a museum
- Speak up in class
- Attend a ballet, opera, or play
- Learn to play a musical instrument
- Ask your friends questions about different topics
- Start a blog by yourself or with friends about your interests

• FIND YOUR NICHE

While you may need to endure some subjects you don't enjoy at school, find the subjects you do enjoy and build upon them. Take additional classes, check out books, and see movies about the topic. Don't let school be your only form of education. Let the world be your campus.

Of course some classes are trickier than others. Unless you're an Einstein, not every subject will be easy for you. Actually, I take back what I just said—the famous Albert Einstein himself didn't speak until he was four and his parents thought he was retarded It's understandable to get discouraged by school sometimes, but please don't drop out. (You'll live to regret it.) Just keep plugging away. You're bound to eventually find something you enjoy about it or something you can excel at. I once interviewed a heavily right-brained kid named Chris who shared how long it took him to fit in at school and find his niche:

Up until I went to school I was a happy child. Then kids found out that learning was difficult for me and they would point and call me names. I was slow at math, English, and grammar. I remember sitting in class one day, divided up into groups, when a girl in my group stood up and said, "I'm not going to work with that retard," pointing to me. It made me feel terrible.

Through grade school and middle school, I could hardly read. A professional came to our home one day and after putting me through a number of tests told my mother that I would never be able to read. My mother was so angry that she told him to leave the house.

Years later, as a new high school student, I picked up a science fiction book one day, and to my surprise it was suddenly easy to read. The stories in the book stimulated my imagination and then the words weren't words anymore but became pictures in my head and I started to read other books and really got excited about reading and learning. I started speaking better and using larger words.

It was about at this time that I began to excel at the arts. I learned that I have an incredible eye for shapes and color. I've become skilled with watercolor, oil, painting, drawing, and design. I write about my experiences. I write poetry. Toward the end of high school, I won a lot of art gallery shows and gained a lot of confidence.

- ### DON'T LET SCHOOL GET IN THE WAY OF YOUR EDUCATION

Grades are important: they're a way to measure how well you're doing in school. A strong school transcript opens the door to other education options and work opportunities. But there is so much more to an education than good grades.

My family is composed of a bunch of technical incompetents. I blame the bad gene on my dad. Several times I've seen him in "technically-challenging" situations, like when he lifts up the hood of the car (as if he could actually fix something) or when he attempts to change a light bulb. In these tough situations, it seems like his brain literally shuts down and ceases to function. It's a phenomenon! Being the proactive person that I am, I decided I wanted to overcome my inherited weakness, so I signed up for an auto mechanics class during my senior year of high school. I was going to learn how to do an oil change if it killed me.

Believe it or not, I wound up getting an A in that class, but I'm ashamed to admit that I hardly learned a thing. You see, instead of really paying the price to learn, I did a lot of watching and not a lot of doing. I never did my assignments. And I crammed for all the tests, only to forget what I had learned two hours after taking them. I got the grade, but I failed to get an education.

Although grades are important, *learning* is more important, so make sure you don't forget why you're in school to begin with.

Over the years, I've seen people sacrifice their educations for so many stupid reasons, like thinking they don't need an education, or becoming obsessed with a part-time job, a girlfriend, a car, or a band.

I've also seen many athletes sacrifice their education on the altar of sports. I've often been tempted to write letters to these young men and women who become so sports-centered that they entirely forget about school. In fact, I actually wrote one, to an imaginary athlete, though it applies to anyone who needs to be convinced that it's all about the mind.

A LETTER TO AN

UNKNOWN
ATHLETE

Dear _____:

I'm a big believer in the benefits of athletics. However, after visiting with you, I'm shocked to learn about your attitude toward school.

You say you're banking on a pro career and don't feel the need for an education. I say your chances of making the pros are about as good as my dad's chances of growing his hair back. Studies have shown that only one out of every one hundred high school athletes will play Division I college sports, and that the chances of a high school player making the pros are one in ten thousand.

Of the hundreds of college athletes I played with in college who hoped to make the pros, I can think of only a handful who made it. On the other hand, I can think of many who wasted their minds in the name of sports, and who were then thrown into the workforce without a chance or a clue.

I'll never forget the time one of my teammates delivered a psyche-up speech to our team the night before we played a rival university. Having never learned to express himself, all he could do was uncork a barrage of vulgarities that could have cut down a forest. In a matter of three minutes it seemed he managed to use the f-word as a noun, a verb, an adjective, a pronoun, a conjunction, and a dangling participle. I left that meeting thinking, "Man, get a brain!"

Open your eyes! Your education is the key to unlocking your future.

You say you don't like school. I say, What does that have to do with it? Does anything good in life come easy? Do you like working out every day? Does a medical student enjoy studying for four years? Since when does liking something determine whether or not you should do it? Sometimes you just have to discipline yourself to do things you don't feel like doing because of what you hope to gain from it.

HABIT
7

You say that you try to sit down and study but can't because your mind wanders. I say that unless you learn to control your mind you won't amount to squat. It is one thing to train your body to perform at peak levels; it is quite another to control your thoughts, to concentrate for sustained periods, to synthesize, and to think creatively and analytically.

At times saying "I try" is a lame excuse. Imagine how absurd it would sound if I asked you, "Are you going to eat today or are you going to try to eat?" Discipline yourself to do the thing.

You say you can get by without studying, that by cramming and finding ways to beat the system you can pass. I say you reap what you sow. Can the farmer cram? Can he or she forget to plant crops in the spring, loaf all summer long, and then work real hard in the fall to bring in the harvest? Can you improve your bench press by lifting weights once in a while? Your brain is no different than your bicep. To improve the strength, speed, and endurance of your mind, you must work it out. There are no shortcuts.

Imagine five sets of hands. One set belongs to a concert pianist who can enthrall audiences with beautiful renditions of the classics. Another to an eye surgeon who can restore lost vision through microscopic surgery. Another to a professional golfer who consistently makes the clutch shot under pressure. Another to a blind man who can read tiny raised markings on a page at incredible speeds. Another to an artist who can carve beautiful sculptures that inspire the soul. On the surface, the hands look the same, but behind each set are years and years of sacrifice, discipline, and perseverance. These people paid a price! Do you think they crammed?

One of my biggest regrets in life is that instead of reading 100 novels during high school, I read a bunch of Cliff Notes summaries.

In contrast, I have a friend who during his teen years must have read hundreds of books. His brain can benchpress over four hundred pounds. Now, decades later, I'd cut off one . . . no, two toes for such a brain.

If you don't pay the price you may earn a degree but fail to get an education. And there is a big difference between the two. Some of our best thinkers were degreeless, self-educated men and women. How did they do it? They read. It's only the single greatest habit you could ever develop. Yet few do it regularly. And many stop reading and learning when they finish school. That spells brain atrophy. Education's a lifelong pursuit. The person who doesn't read is no better off than the person who can't.

You say you live for today and don't think about the future. I say the major difference between you and your dog is that you can think about tomorrow and he can't. Don't make long-term career decisions based on short-term emotions, like the student who chooses his or her major based on the shortest registration line. Make decisions with the end in mind. To have a good job tomorrow, you must do your homework tonight.

The Proverb sums up the whole matter: "Take fast hold of instruction; let her not go: keep her; for she is thy life."

You seem to be saying you don't need a brain. I say, get one!

I hope I haven't offended you. I mean well. It's just that ten years from now, I don't want you to find yourself singing, as did our friend the Scarecrow:

> I would not be just a nothin',
> My head all full of stuffin',
> . . . If I only had a brain.

Think about it,

SEAN

HABIT
7

• POST-HIGH SCHOOL EDUCATIONAL OPTIONS

Don't get too worried about your major in school. If you can simply learn to think well, you'll have plenty of career and education options to choose from. Admissions offices and employers don't necessarily care about what you majored in, as long as they see evidence that you've got a sound mind. They will be looking at several different areas:

1. _Desire_—How badly do you want to get into this particular school or program? How much do you want this job?

2. _Standardized test scores_—How well did you score on your ACT, SAT, GRE, LSAT, etc.?

3. _Extracurricular_—What other activities (sports, work, clubs, student government, theatre, community, church/synagogue/mosque/temple, etc.) were you involved in?

4. _Letters of recommendation_—What do others—your teachers, employers, peers—think of you? Who would recommend you as a good candidate?

5. _Grade point average_—How well did you do in school?

6. _Communication skills_—How well can you communicate in writing (based on your application essays) and verbally (based on an interview)?

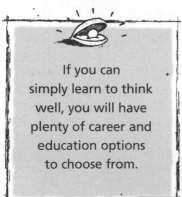

If you can simply learn to think well, you will have plenty of career and education options to choose from.

Most important, they just want to see evidence that you will succeed at the next level. Even if your GPA and standardized test scores swing low, you don't have to settle for second best. You can still get admitted to great programs or get a good job if you're strong in other areas.

Also, don't be scared off by rumors of how hard it is to get into college. It's usually not as hard as you might think if you're willing to put some effort into your application. However, it will be harder than the following college entrance exam would lead you to believe. (Hey, since I was a football player, I have the right to poke fun at myself.)

COLLEGE ENTRANCE EXAM
(Adapted for Football Players)

1. What language is spoken in France?

2. Would you ask William Shakespeare to
   ☐ build a bridge
   ☐ sail the ocean
   ☐ lead an army
   ☐ WRITE A PLAY

3. What religion is the pope?
   ☐ Jewish
   ☐ Catholic
   ☐ Hindu
   ☐ Polish
   ☐ Agnostic

4. What are the people in America's far north called?
   ☐ Westerners
   ☐ Southerners
   ☐ Northerners

5. Six kings of England have been called George, the last one being George the Sixth. Name the previous five.

6. How many commandments was Moses given (approximately)?

7. Can you explain Einstein's Theory of Relativity?
   ☐ yes
   ☐ no

8. What are coat hangers used for?

9. Explain Le Chatelier's Principle of Dynamic Equilibrium *or* spell your name in CAPITAL LETTERS.

10. Advanced math: If you have three apples, how many apples do you have?

You must correctly answer three or more questions to qualify.

HABIT 7

● **MENTAL BARRIERS**

There are a few barriers to overcome when you're expanding and building up your brain. Here are three to consider:

Screentime. Screentime is any time spent in front of a screen—this includes a computer, smartphone, tablet, video game, movie screen, or TV. *Some* time is healthy, but *too much* time texting, scanning through Facebook or Twitter, playing video games, or watching TV can numb the mind. The average teen watches more than twenty hours of TV a week—that's forty-three days a year, and a total of eight years over a lifetime! Just think how productive you could be in those forty-three days of the year—learn Mandarin, take a hip-hop dance class, or grasp computer programming. Set guidelines for your screen time, and don't let it get out of hand. Or try losing your remote control. That works, too.

The Nerd Syndrome. Some teens don't want to do too well in school because they could be labeled "nerds." Often, young women are made to feel that being brainy is bad because it intimidates guys. What will we think of next, for crying out loud?! If being smart and opinionated intimidates someone, that just tells you they're intim-idated—and not worth your time. Take pride in your mental abili-ties and the fact that you've got your bearings. I, for one, can think of a lot of wealthy, successful people who were once considered nerds.

Pressure. Sometimes we're scared of doing well in school because of the high expectations it creates. If we bring home a good report card and get praised for it, we've suddenly established the expecta-tion that we'll do it again and again. And the pressure builds. If we do poorly, there's no expectation and no pressure.

Just remember this: The stress that results from success is much more tolerable than the regret that results from not trying your best. Don't sweat the pressure. You *can* handle it.

● **YOU GOTTA WANNA**

In the end, the key to honing your mind lies in your desire to learn. You've gotta really want it. You've gotta get turned on by learning. You've gotta pay the price. The following story is an example of someone who had an irresistible drive for learning and who paid a huge price for the simple joy of reading. Reading to this person was "air."

The kitchen door opened—and I was caught, cold. It was too late to hide the evidence; the proof was in the open, plain as could be, right there in my lap. My father, drunk, his face flushed, reeled before me, glowering, menacing. My legs started to tremble. I was nine years old. I knew I would be beaten. There could be no escape; my father had found me reading . . .

An alcoholic like his parents before him, my father had hit me before, many times and harder, and in the years that followed he would hit me again, many times and harder, until finally I quit high school at sixteen and left home. His persistent rage about my reading when I was a boy, though, frustrated me more than all other abuse; it made me feel squeezed in the jaws of a terrible vise, because I would not, I could not, stop reading. I was drawn to books by curiosity and driven by need—an irresistible need to pretend I was elsewhere . . . Thus I defied my father—and, as I've recalled here, sometimes I paid a price for that defiance. It was worth it.

This account was written by Walter Anderson in his book *Read with Me.* Walter is now a successful editor, serves on the boards of many literacy organizations, and is the author of four books. Walter goes on to write:

When I was a child, I lived in a violent household, in a violent neighborhood. But there was a place that I could go—a library— and all the librarians did was encourage me to read. I could open a book, and I could be anywhere. I could do anything. I could imagine myself out of a slum. I read myself out of poverty long before I worked myself out of poverty.

In the back of the book, I have compiled a list of lots of great books for teens. Take a look.

It's never too late to start educating yourself. If you can learn to think well, the future will be full of open doors of opportunity. It's all about brain waves. Get some.

EXERCISE <u>YOUR</u> MIND...

Caring for
Your Heart

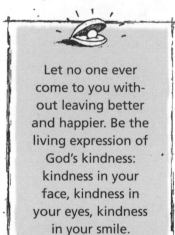

Late one afternoon there came a knock at the door.

"Who could that be?"

I opened the door and there stood my nineteen-year-old younger sister, heaving and sobbing.

"What's wrong?" I asked, leading her in, although I knew exactly what was wrong. This was the third sob-episode that month.

"He is so rude," she sniveled, wiping her red, swollen eyes. "I can't believe he did that to me. It was so mean."

"What did he do this time?" I asked.

"Well . . . you know, he asked me to come over to his house to study," she whimpered. "And while we were studying some other girls came to visit him. And he acted like he didn't even know me."

> Let no one ever come to you without leaving better and happier. Be the living expression of God's kindness: kindness in your face, kindness in your eyes, kindness in your smile.
>
> MOTHER TERESA

"I wouldn't worry about it," I said. "I used to do that kind of thing all the time."

"But I've been dating him for two years," she blubbered. "And when they asked him who I was, he told them that I was his sister."

Ouch!

She was devastated. But I knew that in just a matter of hours or days she'd be thinking he was the greatest thing since sliced bread. Sure enough, a few days later she was crazy about him all over again.

Do you ever feel that, like my sister, you're riding an emotional roller coaster, up one day and down the next? Do you ever feel that you're the moodiest person in the world and that you can't control your emotions? If you do, then welcome to the club, because those feelings are pretty normal. You see, the heart's a very temperamental thing. It needs constant nourishment and care, just like your body.

The best way to sharpen the saw and nourish your heart is to focus on building relationships or, in other words, to make regular deposits into your relationship bank accounts and into your own personal bank account. Let's review what those deposits are.

RBA (Relationship Bank Account) Deposits

- Keep promises
- Do small acts of kindness
- Be loyal
- Listen
- Say you're sorry
- Set clear expectations

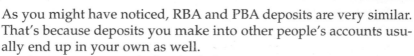

PBA (Personal Bank Account) Deposits

- Keep promises to yourself
- Do small acts of kindness
- Be gentle with yourself
- Be honest
- Renew yourself
- Magnify your talents

As you might have noticed, RBA and PBA deposits are very similar. That's because deposits you make into other people's accounts usually end up in your own as well.

As you set out each day, look for opportunities to make deposits and build lasting friendships. Listen deeply to a friend, parent, brother, or sister without asking for anything in return. Give out ten compliments today. Stick up for someone. Come home when you told your parents you would.

I like how Mother Teresa put it: "Let no one ever come to you without leaving better and happier. Be the living expression of God's kindness: kindness in your face, kindness in your eyes, kindness in your smile." If you look for ways to build instead of ways to tear down, you'll be amazed at how much happiness you can give to others and find for yourself.

As you think about caring for your heart, here are a few other points to consider.

● **SEX AND RELATIONSHIPS**

Said one young girl, "I don't care what kind of relationship you're in or how devout you are . . . sex is always in the air. No matter if you're sitting in the car alone with that person or at home watching TV—the question hangs in the air."

Sex is about a whole lot more than your body. It's also about your heart. In fact, what you do about sex may affect your self-image and your relationships with others more than any other decision you make. Before you decide to have sex or to continue having it, search your heart and think about it . . . carefully. The following excerpt from a pamphlet, published by Journeyworks Publishing, should help.

Think you're ready to go all the way? Are you sure? Sexually transmitted infections, unplanned pregnancy, and emotional doubts are all good reasons to wait! Before you go too far, take a look at this list. Or make up your own ways to finish the sentence:

You're not ready to have sex if . . .

1. You think sex equals love.
2. You feel pressured.
3. You're afraid to say no.
4. It's just easier to give in.
5. You think everyone else is doing it. (They're not!)
6. Your instincts tell you not to.
7. You don't know the facts about pregnancy.
8. You don't understand how birth control works.
9. You don't think a woman can get pregnant the first time. (She can.)
10. It goes against your moral beliefs.
11. It goes against your religious beliefs.
12. You'll regret it in the morning.
13. You feel embarrassed or ashamed.
14. You're doing it to prove something.
15. You can't support a child.
16. You can't support yourself.
17. Your idea of commitment is an online subscription.
18. You believe sex before marriage is wrong.
19. You don't know how to protect yourself from HIV—the virus that causes AIDS.
20. You don't know the signs and symptoms of sexually transmitted infections (STIs, also called STDs).
21. You think it will make your partner love you.
22. You think it will make you love your partner.
23. You think it will keep you together.
24. You hope it will change your life.
25. You don't want it to change your life.

26. You're not ready for the relationship to change.
27. You're drunk.
28. You wish you were drunk.
29. Your partner is drunk.
30. You expect it to be perfect.
31. You'll just die if it's not perfect.
32. You can't laugh together about awkward elbows and clumsy clothes.
33. You're not ready to take off your clothes.
34. You think HIV and AIDS only happen to other people.
35. You think you can tell who has HIV by looking at them.
36. You don't think teens get HIV. (They do.)
37. You don't know that abstinence is the only 100% protection against sexually transmitted infections and pregnancy.
38. You haven't talked about tomorrow.
39. You can't face the thought of tomorrow.
40. You'd be horrified if your parents found out.
41. You're doing it just so your parents will find out.
42. You're too scared to think clearly.
43. You think it will make you more popular.
44. You think you "owe it" to your partner.
45. You think it's not OK to be a virgin.
46. You're only thinking about yourself.
47. You're not thinking about yourself.
48. You can't wait to tell everyone about it.
49. You hope no one will hear about it.
50. You really wish the whole thing had never come up.

It's OK to Wait.

You're Gonna Make It   It's totally normal to feel depressed at times. But there's a big difference between the occasional blues and sustained depression. If life's been feeling painful for a long period of time, and you can't shake off feeling hopeless, then things are serious. Fortunately, depression is treatable. Don't hesitate to get help, either from prescription medication or from talking with someone who is trained to deal with these issues.

If you are having thoughts of suicide, please listen closely to what I'm saying. Hold on for dear life. You're gonna make it. Life will get better . . . I promise. You are priceless and you are needed. You have so much to contribute. Bad times will pass . . . they always do. Someday you will look back on your situation and be glad you held on, as was the case with this young lady:

I am one of the many young people who comes from a wonderful home and really don't have any reason to have gotten into trouble. But I did. Friends became very important to me in junior high and high school, and home life seemed very boring. I couldn't wait to get out of there every day just to be with my buddies and hang out. Within two years I probably tried every vice in the book, and it didn't make me feel any better. On the contrary.

I began having trouble even coming home. It was almost too painful to walk into that sunny, peaceful house with aromas of good cooking. They all seemed so darn good and perfect, and I felt like I couldn't fulfill their expectations. I somehow didn't fit in. I was not living a life they were proud of, and I would just make them unhappy. I began to wish I was dead. Then the thought led to actual suicide attempts.

I kept a journal and it really scares me today to see how close I came to ending it all. Today, just a few years later, I am in college getting straight A's, I have a happy social life, I have a boyfriend who loves me very much, and I have a great relationship with my family. I have so many plans, so many things I am going to do. I love life, I have so much to live for, I cannot believe that I ever felt different, but I did. It took several serious wake-up calls to make me realize that I could be different. Thank heavens I'm still here.

Remember that what feels like a struggle now, will eventually bring you strength. As the philosopher Kahlil Gibran wrote: "That self-same well from which our laughter rises was often times filled with our tears. The deeper that sorrow carries into our being, the more joy it can contain." (Please refer to the hotlines and websites in the back of this book if you need help.)

● LAUGH OR YOU'LL CRY

After all is said and done, there is one last key to keeping your heart healthy and strong. Just laugh. That's right . . . laugh. *Hakuna matata!* Don't worry, be happy! Sometimes life just stinks and there's not much you can do to change it, so you might as well laugh.

It's too bad that as we age we tend to forget what made childhood so magical. One study showed that by the time you reach kindergarten, you laugh about 300 times a day. In contrast, the typical adult laughs a wimpy seventeen times a day. No wonder children seem so much more happier! Why are we so serious? Maybe it's because we've been taught that laughing is childish. To quote the great Jedi Master, Yoda, "You must unlearn what you have learned." We must learn to laugh again.

A fascinating article by Peter Doskoch in *Psychology Today* spoke to the power of humor. Here are his main points:

Laughter:

- Loosens up the mental gears and helps us think creatively
- Helps us cope with the difficulties of life
- Reduces stress
- Relaxes us as it lowers our heart rate and blood pressure
- Connects us with others and counteracts feelings of alienation, a major factor in depression and suicide
- Releases endorphins, the brain's natural painkillers

Laughter has also been shown to promote good health and speed healing. I've heard several accounts of people who healed themselves from serious sickness through heavy doses of laughing therapy. Laughter can also help heal injured relationships. As the great entertainer Victor Borge once put it, "Laughter is the shortest distance between two people."

If you want to bring more laughter into your life, I suggest creating your own "humor collection," a collection of funny books or comics, memes, YouTube videos, comedy podcasts—whatever's funny to you. When you're feeling low or taking yourself way too seriously, visit your collection. For example, I like stupid movies. There are a few actors who make me laugh just at the thought of them. I watch their movies whenever I need to "lighten up." Similarly, my brother Stephen has one of the largest collections of *The Far Side* cartoons ever known to man. He swears that these cartoons have kept him from going insane during high-stress periods.

Learn to laugh at yourself when strange or stupid things happen to you, because they will. As someone once said, "One of the best things people can have up their sleeve is a good funny bone."

Caring for
Your Soul

What moves your soul? A great song? A good book? Have you ever seen a movie that made you cry? What was it that got to you?

What deeply inspires you? Does listening to music? Drawing? Being in nature? Writing?

By soul, I mean that inner self that lurks below the surface of your everyday self. Your soul is your core, wherein lies your deepest convictions and values. It is the source for purpose, meaning, and inner peace. Sharpening the saw in the spiritual area of life means taking time to renew and awaken that inner self. As the famous author Pearl S. Buck wrote, "Inside myself is a place where I live all alone and that's where you renew your springs that never dry up."

**How to Feed
Your Soul**   As a teenager, I got strength from writing in my journal, listening to good music, and spending time alone in the mountains. This was my way of renewing my soul, although I didn't think of it that way at the time. I personally also got strength from inspiring quotes, such as this one by past U.S. Secretary of Agriculture Ezra Taft Benson:

"Men and women who turn their lives over to God will find out that He can make a lot more out of their lives than they can. He will deepen their joys, expand their vision, quicken their minds, strengthen their muscles, lift their spirits, multiply their blessings, increase their opportunities, and pour out peace."

Your soul's a very private area of your life. Naturally, there are many different ways to feed it. Here are a few ideas shared by teens:

- Meditating
- Helping others
- Writing in a journal
- Taking walks
- Reading inspiring articles and books
- Drawing
- Praying
- Writing poetry or music

- Thinking deeply
- Listening to music that speaks to you
- Playing a musical instrument
- Practicing a religion
- Talking to friends I can be myself with
- Reflecting on my goals or mission statement

Here are a couple of soul-nourishing techniques to especially consider.

● GETTING BACK TO NATURE

There's something magical and unbeatable about being in nature. Even if you live in a downtown area far removed from rivers, mountains, or beaches, there will usually be a park nearby that you can visit. I once interviewed a young man named Ryan who learned about the healing powers of Mother Nature in the midst of a really messed up home life.

During high school, I went through a dark period where it seemed that everything just caved in. That's when I found the river hole. It was just a bank off in some trees in the back of an old farmer's place and didn't look like much. But it became my escape. There was no one around, you couldn't hear people. It was beautiful. Just swimming around made me feel at peace with nature. Anytime I was stressed out I'd go there. It was like my life could come back to normal.

Some people turn to organized religion for direction, but it's been hard for me to turn to religion. I do have a religion and I'm strong in it. But sometimes it's just hard for me to get up and go to church, because I go and everyone says, "Oh, just be happy. It will all work out. Just have faith. Things will work out with your family." I just think that's bull. C'mon. Families don't always work out. My family's all messed up.

But by going to the river, that place didn't judge me. That place didn't tell me what to do. It was just there. And by following its example, the peacefulness and the serenity that existed there, that's all I needed to calm things down. It made me feel like everything was going to work out.

● A TEEN'S BEST FRIEND

Keeping a journal can do wonders for your soul. A journal or diary can become your solace, your best friend, the only place where you can fully express yourself no matter how angry, happy, scared, love crazed, insecure, or confused you feel. You can pour your heart out and it will just listen; it won't talk back. And it won't talk behind your back. A blog is necessarily not as private as a journal, since it's on the Internet, but it, too, can become a great way to express yourself. Writing down your unedited thoughts can clear your mind, boost your confidence, and help you find yourself.

Keeping a journal will also strengthen your tool of self-awareness. It's enlightening to read past entries and realize how much you've grown, how stupid and immature you once sounded, or how caught up you were with some boy or girl. One young woman told me about how reading old journal entries gave her the insight to keep from returning to her former abusive boyfriend.

There's no formal way to keep a journal. It doesn't even have to have words—it can be a scrapbook or collage of mementos, ticket stubs, love notes—anything that will preserve memories and experience. My old journals are full of poor art, bad poetry, and strange smells. A journal is just a formal name for putting your thoughts down on paper. There are other names and forms. Allison writes little notes to herself that she keeps in a special box she calls her sacred box. Kaire renews herself by keeping a "gratitude book":

I have a book that helps me to be more positive in life. I call it my gratitude book. In this book, I write down something I'm grateful for or something positive that happened to me during the day. This book has changed my life and totally put things into perspective, because I try to pick out all the good things that happen and not the bad. I still keep a journal, but this is different. I have a page of my favorite songs, favorite touches (brother's hug), favorite sounds (Mom's laugh), favorite feels (cool breeze), and so on. I also write down small things like, "Brian offered to clear the table for me," or "John went out of his way to say hello to me today." These things make you feel good. I look back at this book and remember these good things and the bad things are forgotten, erased and gone. They can't affect me anymore.

I've given a book to others and they say it has really helped them. It's my way of saying, "You're the only one who can make you happy—no one else can."

● **YOUR SPIRITUAL DIET**

I've often wondered what would happen to someone who drank and ate only soft drinks and chocolate for several years straight.

What would they look and feel like after a while? Probably burnt out. But why do we think the result would be any different if we fed our souls trash for several years straight? You're not only what you eat, you're also what you listen to, read, and see. More important than what goes into your body is what goes into your soul.

So what's your spiritual diet? Are you feeding your soul nutrients, or are you loading it with nuclear waste? Have you ever even thought about just how much media you take in every day? This includes videos online and on TV, social media, Internet ads, as well as books, magazines, and even billboards you see on the street.

These days, it feels impossible to go "media-free" for even one day. Try it and you'll see what I mean! Dare yourself to go a day without searching Google, looking at a magazine, listening to music, or watching any TV. You'll find it's virtually impossible. At this point, our society is so addicted to technology and pop culture that you'd probably start feeling severe withdrawal pains.

Now, if you think the media doesn't affect you, just think about your favorite song and what it does to your emotions. Or think about the last time you saw half-naked models strutting across the screen. Or think back to the last bottle of shampoo you bought. Why did you buy it? Maybe because of the influence of a thirty-second TV commercial or a one-page magazine ad. And if a one-page ad can sell a bottle of shampoo, don't you think a full-length movie, magazine, or CD can sell a lifestyle?

Like with most things, there's a light and a dark side to the media. And you need to choose what you're going to allow in. My only suggestion is to follow your conscience and to treat your soul with the same respect that an Olympic athlete would treat his or her body. For example, if the music you listen to or the movies you watch make you feel depressed, angry, dark, violent, or like you're in heat, then guess what? That's probably a sign that they're trash, and you don't need trash. On the other hand, if they make you feel relaxed, happy, inspired, hopeful, or peaceful, then keep taking them in. You'll eventually become what you view, hear, and read, so continually ask yourself the question "Do I want this to be part of me?"

• YOU'RE DISTURBING MY SLEEP

I ran across a letter from the Youth Outlook website written by a girl named Ladie Terry who was fed up with all the trashy music videos coming out lately. She addressed the letter to "the sisters who like to grind their way across my TV screen." By permission, I've included parts of it here.

I guess it's exciting being in a music video. But do you know how you are affecting the minds and lives of your sisters? Do you think about the younger sisters, who learn fast and emulate you? Have you noticed the 12- and 13-year-olds dolled up to look like 20-year-olds? Or are times so hard that you don't care who you hurt?

I used to argue with my ex-boyfriend about watching BET and MTV, because the majority of the videos consisted of not-even-half-naked girls wiggling and jiggling like a bowl of Jell-O . . .

it hurt me to see my ex-boyfriend in a daze with his eyes moving up and down . . .

THAT'S IT! WE'RE SWITCHING TO NICKELODEON.

My neighbor used to tell me when she would watch music videos with her boyfriend he would say to her, "That's how your body should look." Another friend, who is 16, says boys ask her, "Why can't you dance like that?"

Why are you onscreen in tight, short clothing, moving your bodies around like you are freaks? . . . You sisters are very, very beautiful. You don't have to undress for success, or to get some attention. You want brothers to respect you? Show them why they should through your elegant, conservative dress—then back up your reasoning with your words. The way you dress tells people what is on your mind . . . when you upgrade your appearance and your mind-set, a lot of brothers will upgrade their treatment of you. So stop competing to see who is freakier than the next, and get your mind out of the bedroom, because you are disturbing my sleep.

• FRIED FROGS

Addictions of all kinds—whether it's to drugs, gossiping, shopping, overeating, or gambling—have common characteristics.

Addiction:
- Creates short-term pleasure
- Temporarily eliminates pain
- Gives an artificial sense of self-worth, power, control, security, and intimacy
- Worsens the problems and feelings you are trying to escape from
- Becomes the primary focus of your life

One of the more subtle but dangerous addictions is pornography, and it's available everywhere online. Now, you can argue all you want about what pornography is and isn't, but I think that deep in your heart you know. Porn may taste sweet for the moment, but it will gradually dull your finer sensitivities to romance, to the feelings of other people, and to life in general, until you can't feel much anymore. It'll also wear down that inner voice called your conscience, until it's smothered.

You may be thinking, "Take it easy, Sean. A little skin isn't going to hurt me." The problem is that porn, like any other addiction, sneaks up on you. It reminds me of a story I once read about frogs. If you put a frog in boiling water, it will immediately jump out. But if you put it in lukewarm water and then slowly turn up the heat, the frog will get cooked before it has the sense to jump out. It's the same with pornography. What you look at today may have shocked you a year ago. But because the heat was ever so slowly turned up, you didn't even notice that your conscience was being fried.

Have the courage to walk away, to turn it off, to throw it away. You are better than that. A boy shared this:

During the summer between my junior and senior years of high school, I worked for a construction company. One day the boss asked me to check on something with the building supervisor who had his office on the job site in a work trailer.

When I walked into the trailer there were pornographic pictures posted on all the walls. For a minute, I forgot what I had gone in there to ask the guys, because my attention was drawn to the pictures. It struck an interest in me. When I left the trailer I started thinking, where can I buy this stuff so I can see more of it?

At first, when I looked at them, I felt very nervous and uneasy inside, like what I was doing was wrong, but it didn't take me long to get addicted to it. It began to consume me to the point where I was not thinking of anything else—my family, or work, or sleep. I started to think and feel lower of myself.

During breaks at work, we would go to someone's car, and some-one would pull out a magazine, and we would laugh about it and carry on. The guys that were deeply involved in it were not satisfied with just looking. They would talk about all the girls they had slept with and they didn't seem to care about anything else in life. That was all their conversations were about, the magazines, films, and sex.

Late one afternoon, as I was working, I heard some of my co-workers start whistling and calling out rude sexual remarks. I looked up to see what the commotion was, and there was my younger sister just getting out from her car, looking for me. I overheard someone say, "I'd like to get a piece of that!" I turned angrily and said, "Shut up! That's my little sister!"

I was so disgusted. I left the job, just before quitting time, and drove around for a while by myself. I just kept thinking about how hurt my sister looked, to be treated so horridly when her intentions had been so innocent.

The next day, when I went back to the job, and the guys passed around the magazines, I got up and moved. At first it took a lot of strength, but as I did it more and more, it became easier. When con-versations started that were crude and distasteful, I would walk away and go someplace else. I didn't think it was amusing anymore. I realized they were talking about somebody's sister.

● GET REAL

As we close this chapter, let me just share a couple of final thoughts. I once was talking to a girl named Larissa about sharpening the saw, and she gave me an earful. "Get real, Sean. Who has time? I'm at school all day, I have activities after school, and I study all night. I need to get good grades to get into college. What am I supposed to do, go to bed early and then fail my math test tomorrow?"

Let me just say this. There's a time for everything. A time to be balanced and a time to be imbalanced. There are times when you'll need to go without much sleep and push your body to its limit, for a day, a week, even a season. And there will be times when eating junk food out of the vending machine is your only alternative to starving. This is real life. But there are also times for renewal.

If you go too hard for too long, you won't think as clearly, you'll get cranky, and you'll start losing perspective. You may think you don't have time to exercise, build friendships, or get inspired in be-tween trying to get good grades or to make varsity sports. In reality, you don't have time *not* to. The downtime you spend sharpening your saw will pay you back immediately, 'cause when you resume your normal routine, you'll cut faster, naturally.

**You Can
Do It** (Y)ou're probably already doing a lot of saw-sharpening without even knowing it. If you're working hard at school, you're sharpening your mind. If you're into athletics or fitness, you're caring for your body. If you're developing friendships or being a good son/daughter/grandson/granddaughter/sibling, you're nourishing your heart. If you're spending quality time alone, you're bettering your relationship with yourself. Often you can sharpen the saw in more than one area at once. Melanie once told me how, for her, horseback riding did this. The physical nature of riding exercised her body. Thinking deeply while riding exercised her mind. And being in nature nurtured her soul. I then asked her, "What about relationships? How does riding develop your heart?" She said, "I get closer to my horse." Well, I guess sometimes horses can be people, too.

Sharpening the saw won't just happen to you. Since it's a Quadrant 2 activity (important but not urgent), you have to be proactive and happen to it. The best thing to do is to take out time each day to sharpen the saw, even if it's only for fifteen or thirty minutes. Some teens set apart a specific time each day—early in the morning, after school, or late at night—to be alone, to think, or to exercise. Others like to do it on the weekends. There's no one right way—find what works for you.

Abraham Lincoln was once asked, "What would you do if you had eight hours to cut down a tree?" He replied, "I'd spend the first four hours sharpening my saw."

★ ★ ★

COMING ATTRACTIONS

You'll like the next chapter because it's real short. You might as well just finish the book right now!

Body

1. Eat breakfast.

2. Start a work-out program and do it faithfully for 30 days. Walk, dance, swim, bike, skateboard, lift weights, etc. Choose something you really enjoy.

3. Give up a bad habit for a week. Go without alcohol, soda pop, fried foods, chocolate, or whatever else may be hurting your body. A week later, see how you feel.

Mind

4. Read blogs that have educational value.

5. Checkout online newspapers. Pay special attention to the headline stories and the opinions page.

6. Take your next date to a museum or to an ethnic restaurant you've never been to before. Expand your horizons.

Heart

7. Go on a one-on-one outing with a family member like your mom or your brother. Catch a ball game, go shopping, or catch a movie for old times' sake.

8. Begin today to build your humor collection. Bookmark the funniest memes or videos you know, or start your own collection of great jokes. In no time, you'll have something to go to when you're feeling stressed.

Soul

9. Watch the sunset tonight or get up early to watch the sunrise.

10. If you haven't already done it, start keeping a journal today.

11. Take time each day to meditate, reflect upon your life, or pray. Do what works for you.

Keep Hope
Alive!

KID, YOU'LL MOVE MOUNTAINS

Several years ago the Reverend Jesse Jackson spoke at the Democratic National Convention. He delivered a powerful message that set the convention on fire. He used only three words: "Keep hope alive. Keep hope alive! **KEEP HOPE ALIVE!**"

The audience shouted these same words over and over and over for what seemed forever, and swelled with applause. You could feel the sincerity in his voice. He inspired everyone. He created hope.

That's why I wrote this book . . . *to give you hope!* Hope that you can change, kick an addiction, improve an important relationship. Hope that you can find answers to your problems and reach your fullest potential. So what if your family life stinks, you're failing school, and the only good relationship you have is with the games on your phone (and lately it hasn't been getting many texts). *Keep hope alive!*

If, after reading this book, you feel overwhelmed and don't have a clue where to start, I'd suggest doing this: Thumb through each chapter quickly for the key ideas, or ask yourself, "Which habit am I having the most difficult time living?" Then choose

> So be sure when you step
> Step with care and great tact
> And remember that life's
> A Great Balancing Act.
>
> And will you succeed?
> Yes! You will, indeed!
> (98 and ¾ percent guaranteed)
> Kid, you'll move mountains.
>
> DR. SEUSS
> FROM *OH, THE PLACES YOU'LL GO*

KEEP HOPE ALIVE

just two or three things to work on (don't get overzealous and choose twenty). Write them down and put them in a place where you will see them often. Then let them inspire you each day.

You'll be amazed at the results a few small changes can bring. Gradually, you'll become more confident, you'll feel happier, you'll get high "naturally," your goals will become realities, your relationships will improve, and you'll feel at peace. It all begins with a single step.

If there was a habit or idea that really hit home, such as Be Proactive or the Relationship Bank Account, the best way to internalize it is to teach it to someone else while it's still fresh in your mind. Walk them through it using your own examples and words. Who knows, maybe you'll get them fired up and they'll want to work with you.

If you ever find yourself sliding or falling short, *don't get discouraged*. Remember the flight of an airplane. When an airplane takes off it has a flight plan. However, during the course of the flight, wind, rain, turbulence, air traffic, human error, and other factors keep knocking the plane off course. In fact, a plane is off course about 90 percent of the time. The key is that the pilots keep making small course corrections by reading their instruments and talking to the control tower. As a result, a plane reaches its destination.

If you keep getting knocked off your flight plan and feel as though you're off course 90 percent of the time . . . so what? If you just keep coming back to your plan, keep making small adjustments, and keep hope alive, you'll eventually reach your destination.

Well, this is the end of the book. Thank you for journeying with me, and congrats on finishing. I just want you to know that I truly believe in your future. You are destined for great things. Always remember, you were born with everything you need to succeed. You don't have to look anywhere else. The power and light is already in you!

Before signing off, I'd like to leave you with a favorite quote of mine, by Bob Moawad, which sums it all up. I wish you all the best. Sayonara.

You can't make footprints in the sands of time by sitting on your butt.
And who wants to leave buttprints in the sands of time?

BOOK STUDY GUIDE

I hope you've enjoyed reading *The 7 Habits of Highly Effective Teens.* If you're ready to do some deeper thinking about the topics we covered, here are some questions you can ponder on your own or in a group setting. If you are leading a book study discussion, you might find the Facilitator Guide at www.theleaderinmeonline.org to be a helpful resource.

- ## PART I: THE SETUP

Get in the Habit
1. How do your habits either make you or break you?
2. Why is it important to master the Private Victory before mastering the Public Victory?

Paradigms and Principles
1. What is a Paradigm Shift?
2. What makes friends an unstable center?
3. Why does not centering your life on a boyfriend or girlfriend strengthen the relationship?
4. What makes a principle-centered life stable?

- ## PART II: THE PRIVATE VICTORY

The Personal Bank Account
1. What does it mean to change from the inside out?
2. What would be an example of a deposit into your Personal Bank Account?
3. Why does focusing outward rather than inward help a person feel more positive?

Habit 1: Be Proactive
1. How can the language you choose affect your actions and moods?
2. How does "victimitis" hold a person back?
3. If you were to be a change agent in your family, what would start doing? Stop doing?
4. Which of the four human endowments (self-awareness, conscience, imagination, willpower) is your strongest area? Your weakest area?

Habit 2: Begin with the End in Mind

1. What similarities are there between a Personal Mission Statement and the roots of a tree?
2. What are the first three words that come to mind when you think about your Personal Mission Statement?
3. Why is a written goal more powerful?

Habit 3: Put First Things First

1. If you spent more time in Quadrant 2, what more would you be able to accomplish?
2. How can planning provide freedom?
3. What does "It's not the mountain we conquer, but ourselves" mean?
4. Why is belonging so important?

• PART III: THE PUBLIC VICTORY

The Relationship Bank Account

1. Why is interdependence a more mature level than independence?
2. Why is success with self so important to succeed with others?
3. Why are little things considered to be big things in relationships?
4. Consider three of your closest relationships. How well do you listen in each?

Habit 4: Think Win-Win

1. How would you describe Habit 4—Think Win-Win—in your own words?
2. Why is the Private Victory a prerequisite to thinking Win-Win?
3. How can competitions and comparisons affect the ability to Think Win-Win? When is "no deal" sometimes the best solution?

Habit 5: Seek First to Understand, Then to Be Understood

1. Why do you think the deepest need of the human heart is to be understood?
2. Which of the poor listening skills do you have the most difficulty with and what can you do to improve it?
3. What do you think would be a deposit in a Relationship Bank Account you have with a parent or guardian?
4. Why are "I" messages received more positively than "you" messages?

Habit 6: Synergize

1. How is synergy different than compromise or cooperation?
2. In what ways does celebrating diversity differ from tolerating diversity?
3. Which of the three roadblocks to synergy (ignorance, cliques, or prejudice) do you struggle with the most?
4. Are you a plodder, a follower, an innovator, a harmonizer, or a show-off?

● PART IV: RENEWAL

Habit 7: Sharpen the Saw

1. In which of the four dimensions do you need to spend more time?
2. Why is balance important?
3. If you stopped a current addiction, what would you do with the extra money?
4. Where do you find inspiration?

Keep Hope Alive!

1. Why is hope so critical in moving forward in life?
2. What are your unique strengths and talents?
3. What will you do to make your life extraordinary?

Thank Yous

They say that writing a book is like eating an elephant. For some reason the two years I spent writing this book felt more like eating an entire herd of elephants. Luckily, I didn't have to eat them all by myself. There were many others who contributed in many ways to make this book possible. I would like to thank each of them:

Thank you, Annie Oswald, for being the ultimate project leader and for your tirelessness, leadership, and initiative. Without a doubt, you were the key to making this book what it is.

Thank you, Trevor Walker, for your can-do attitude and for helping me get this book off the ground in the beginning.

Thank you, Jeanette Sommer, for your unusual level of dedication to this project and for somehow always finding that impossible story.

Thank you, Pia Jensen, for contributing as a core team member for over two years and for your outstanding stories.

Thank you, Greg Link, for being a brilliant deal maker and a good friend, and for leading the PR and marketing efforts.

Thank you, Catherine Sagers, my sister, for your great work on the "baby steps" and for contributing in many other ways. XOXO

Thank you, Cynthia Haller, my oldest sister and the "mother hen," for your superb editorial assistance, stories, and ideas. XOXO

Thank you, Mark Pett, for being the creative mind behind the majority of the illustrations in the book and for contributing several illustrations.

Thank you, Eric Olson (the book's primary illustrator) and Ray Kuik (the book's art director) of Raeber Graphics, Inc., for your creative genius and for fulfilling my vision of making this book a visual feast. All I can say about you guys is "Wow!"

Thank you, Debra Lund, Janeen Bullock, and team, for your proactive efforts in collecting all those lovely endorsements.

Thank you, Tony Contos and team at Joliet Township High School in Illinois, for serving as our primary test site. (Tony, your constant encouragement kept me afloat.) In particular, thanks to Sandy Contos, Flora Betts, Barbara Pasteris, Gloria Martinez, Lina Brisbin, Susan Graham, John Randich, Lynn Vaughn, Jennifer Adams, Marie Blunk, Cathe Ghilain, Marvin Reed, Bonnie Badurski, Judy Bruno, Richard Dobbs, Pat Sullivan, Shawna Kocielko, Reasie McCullough, Nichole Nelson, Michael Stubler, Nichol Douglas, Joseph Facchina, Kaatrina Voss, Joy Denewellis, Jordan McLaughlin, Allison Yanchick, Stephen Davis, Chris Adams, Neal Brockett, and Marisha Pasteris.

Thank you, Rita Elliot and the other staff members and students of the North Carolina Legislator's School, for your insights and interviews. Specifically, thanks to Kia Hardy, Natarsha Sanders, Crystal Hall, Tarrick Cox, Adam Sosne, Heather Sheehan, Tara McCormick, and Terrence Dove.

Thank you, Kay Jensen and the Sanpete Child Abuse Prevention Team, for so courageously sharing your stories.

Thanks to the Heritage School administration, faculty, and students.

Thank you, Cindi Hanson and the Timpview High School Executive Tech class, for allowing me to teach you the 7 Habits. In particular, thanks to Kristi Borland, Spencer Clegg, Kelli Klein, Jennie Feitz, Brittney Howard, Tiffany Smith, Becky Tanner, Kaylyn Ellis, Rachel Litster, Melissa Gourley, T.J. Riskas, Willie Morrell, Brandon Kraus, Stephan Heilnor, Monica Moore, and Amanda Valgardson.

Thank you, students of Utah Valley High Schools, for your important participation in numerous focus groups. In particular, thanks to Ariel Amata, Brett Atkinson, Amy Baird, David Beck, Sandy Blumenstock, Megan Bury, Brittany Cameron, Laura Casper, Estee Christensen, Ryan Clark, Carla Domingues, Ryan Edwards, Jeff Gamette, Katie Hall, Liz Jacob, Jeff Jacobs, Jeremy Johnson, Joshua Kautz, Arian Lewis, Lee Lewis, Marco Lopez, Aaron Lund, Harlin Mitchell, Kristi Myrick, Chris Nibley, Whitney Noziska, Dianne Orcutt, Leisy Oswald, Jordan Peterson, Geoff Reynolds, Jasmine Schwerdt, Josie Smith, Heather Sommer, Jeremy Sommer, Steve Strong, Mark Sullivan, Larissa Taylor, Callie Trane, Kelli Maureen Wells, Kristi Woodworth, and Lacey Yates.

Thanks to the many speakers, authors, and youth leaders who assisted in one way or another, namely Brettne Shootman, Mona Gayle Timko, James E.H. Collins, Brenton G. Yorgason, James J. Lynch, Matt Clyde, Dan Johnson, Deborah Mangum, Pat O'Brien, Jason Dorsey, Matt Townsend, Vanessa Moore, Dr. Cheryl Gholar, and John Bytheway and Premier School Agenda and team.

A special thanks to all those who contributed interviews and stories, including Jackie Gago, Sara Duquette, Andy Fries, Arthur Williams, Christopher Williams, Tiffany Tuck, Dave Boyer, Julie Anderson, Liz Sharp, Renon Hulet, Dawn Meeves, Chris Lenderman, Jacob Sommer, Kara Sommer, Sarah Clements, Jeff Clements, Katie Sharp, Brian Ellis, Donald Childs, Heidi Childs, Patricia Myrick, Naurice Moffett, Sydney Hulse, Mari Nishibu, Andrew Wright, Jen Call, Lena Ringheim Jensen, Bryan Hinschberger, Spencer Brooks, Shannon Lynch, Allison Moses, Erin White, Bryce Thatcher, Dermell Reed, Elizabeth Jacob, Tawni Olson, Ryan Edwards, Ryan Casper, Hilda Lopez, Taron Milne, Scott Wilcox, Mark C. Mcpherson, Igor Skender, Heather Hoehne, Stacy Greer, Daniel Ross, Melissa Hannig, Colleen Peterson, Joe Jeagany, Tiffany Stoker Madsen, Lorilee Richardson, Stephanie Bushey, Robert Clack, Adkins Jones, Todd Lucas, Andrea McNear, Mary Beth Sylvester, Dr. Cheryl Gholar, and Vanessa Moore.

And finally, thank you to the hundreds of others who contributed in different ways.

INFO CENTRAL

You or a friend or loved one may be in a situation and feel hopeless or confused about what to do. There are many people and organizations out there who want to help. Please call or visit the websites listed below. If you don't get the kind of help you want or need with the first call or visit, please try again. Remember: Keep hope alive!

Substance Abuse

If you suspect that you may be drinking too much and you don't know what to do or you are worried about a family member or friend who drinks too much, call Alcoholics Anonymous or visit the website
(www.alcoholics-anonymous.org.uk)
0845 769 7555

If you or a friend are using illegal drugs or abusing any drug, visit the Narcotics Anonymous website for information and help
www.ukna.org

You may also want to visit the following websites for information:
Cocaine Anonymous
www.cauk.org.uk

Drugscope
www.drugscope.org.uk

Eating Disorders

If you suspect that you or one of your friends may have anorexia, bulimia, or an overeating disorder and you want to get help, call Beat Eating Disorders (Beat) or visit their website at
www.-b-eat.co.uk
0845 634 7650

Physical and Mental Health

If you or a friend are considering suicide, PLEASE call the Samaritans
(www.samaritans.org.uk) They are available 24 hours a day
08457 90 90 90

ChildLine also operates a free, 24 hour helpline for children or young people. Counsellors are trained to help with bullying, child abuse, domestic violence, eating disorders, pregnancy, STDs and suicide
0800 1111

If you or your friends are concerned about contracting or having a venereal disease or contracting AIDS, call The HIV support centre
(www.thehivsupportcentre.org.uk)
0800 137 437

The National Aids Trust can also provide information
www.nat.org.uk

If you need to know where to go to get help on abortion, contraception, pregnancy or sexually transmitted diseases then contact the FPA (*www.fpa.org.uk*)

Another website aimed at young people looking for information or advice on having sex is
www.help4me.info

Grief and Loss

If you or a friend are struggling with a tragedy or the loss of a loved one or acquaintance and don't know how to cope, call or visit:
Cruse Bereavement care
www.cruse.org.uk
0844 477 9400

Teen Pregnancy

If you are pregnant or worried about becoming pregnant and need more information about your options, call or visit: Straight Talking
www.straighttalking.org
020 8546 4665

Abuse

If you are in a dating relationship with an abusive person, call or visit:
Refuge
www.refuge.org.uk
0808 2000 247

If you or a friend, male or female, are a victim of rape, incest, or any form of sexual abuse, call or visit: Rape Crisis England & Wales
0808 802 9999

If you or a friend or any family member is being abused at home, please call or visit: Respect
www.respect.uk.net
0808 801 03

If you or a friend is being bullied, visit:
Beat Bullying
www.beatbullying.org

If you or a friend is being cyberbullied, visit: CyberSmile
www.cybersmile.org
0808 783 1113

NSPCC Child Protection Helpline
www.nspcc.org.uk
0808 800 5000

Gang Prevention

Go online to find out more
www.safenetwork.org.uk

Education

If you are considering further education then visit the following website for information on higher education in the UK
www.ucas.com
0844 477 9400

If you want to learn how to handle money wisely or to save for your future, visit:
http://mymoney.gov

Volunteering

If you and your friends are interested in making a difference and learning leadership skills at the same time, visit: Vinspired
www.vinspired.com

General Youth Support Services

If you're homeless and need somewhere to stay, food to eat, and crisis care, visit: Centrepoint
www.centrepoint.org

If you think you may have a problem with on-line gaming addiction, call or visit: Step by Step
www.stepbystep.org

GREAT BOOKS FOR TEENS

Classics

Anne of Green Gables
Lucy Maud Montgomery

A Tree Grows in Brooklyn
Betty Smith

*Adventures of
Huckleberry Finn*

*The Adventures of
Tom Sawyer*
Mark Twain

Bless Me, Ultima
Rudolfo Anaya

The Book Thief
Markus Zusak

The Chronicles of Narnia
C. S. Lewis

Cry, the Beloved Country
Alan Paton

Ender's Game
Orson Scott Card

Fahrenheit 451
Ray Bradbury

The Fault in our Stars
John Green

The Giver
Lois Lowry

The Goose Girl
Shannon Hale

Hatchet
Gary Paulsen

Harry Potter series
J. K. Rowling

Holes
Louis Sachar

*I Heard the Owl Call
My Name*
Margaret Craven

Lord of the Flies
William Golding

The Lord of the Rings
and *The Hobbit*
J. R. R. Tolkien

To Kill a Mockingbird
Harper Lee

Night
Elie Wiesel

Of Mice and Men
John Steinbeck

The Old Man and the Sea
Ernest Hemingway

The Once and Future King
T. H. White

O Pioneers
Willa Cather

The Other Wes Moore
Wes Moore

The Outsiders
S. E. Hinton

*Parrot in the Oven:
Mi Vida*
Victor Martinez

The Princess Bride
William Goldman

*Red Scarf Girl: A Memoir of
the Cultural Revolution*
Ji-Li Jiang

Speak
Laurie Halse Anderson

*The Watsons Go to
Birmingham—1963*
Christopher Paul Curtis

Where the Sidewalk Ends
Shel Silverstein

Self-Help

*The 6 Most Important
Decisions You'll Ever Make*
Sean Covey

The Book of Virtues
William J. Bennett

*Chew On This: Everything
You Don't Want to Know
About Fast Food*
Eric Schlosser and
Charles Wilson

*Chicken Soup for the Teenage
Soul on Tough Stuff: Stories
of Tough Times and Lessons
Learned*
Jack Canfield, Mark Victor
Hansen, and Kimberly
Kirkberger

*The Fiske Guide to Getting
Into the Right College*
Edward Fiske and Bruce
Hammond

*The Grieving Teen: A Guide for
Teenagers and Their Friends*
Helen Fitzgerald

*How Could You Do That?!:
The Abdication of Character,
Courage, and Conscience*
Dr. Laura Schlessinger

*Making College Count: A
Real World Look at How to
Succeed in and After College*
Patrick S. O'Brien

*The Measure of Our Success:
A Letter to My Children and
Yours*
Marian Wright Edelman

*My Orange Duffel Bag: A
Journey to Radical Change*
Sam Bracken

*Rich Dad, Poor Dad for
Teens: The Secrets About
Money—That You Didn't
Learn in School*
Robert Kiyasaki

The Secret to Teen Power
Paul Harrington

*The Shyness and Social
Anxiety Workbook for Teens:
CBT and ACT Skills to Help
Build Social Confidence*
Jennifer Shannon and
Doug Shannon

*Beneath the Mask:
Understanding Adopted Teens*
Debbie Riley and John E.
Meeks

Wreck This Journal
Keri Smith

*YOU: The Owner's Manual
for Teens: A Guide to a
Healthy Body and Happy Life*
Michael Roizen and
Mehmet Oz

*Your Pregnancy & Newborn
Journey: A Guide for
Pregnant Teens*
Jeanne Warren Lindsay and
Jean Brunelli PHN

BIBLIOGRAPHY

PARADIGMS AND PRINCIPLES

Greyling, Dan P. "The Way the Cookie Crumbles." Reprinted with permission from the July 1980 *Reader's Digest*. Copyright © 1980 by The Reader's Digest Association, Inc.

MacPeek, Walter. *Resourceful Scouts in Action*. Nashville: Abingdon Press, 1969.

THE PERSONAL BANK ACCOUNT

Barton, Bruce. *The Man Nobody Knows*. New York: Collier Books, 1925.

MAN IN THE MIRROR. Words and Music by Glen Ballard and Siedah Garrett. © Copyright 1987 Music Corporation of America, Aerostation Corporation and Yellowbrick Road Music. All rights for Aerostation Corporation Controlled and Administered by MCA Music Publishing, A Division of Universal Studios, Inc. International Copyright Secured. All Rights Reserved.

HABIT I

Lemley, Brad. "The Man Who Won't Be Defeated." New York: *Parade*. Reprinted with permission from *Parade*. Copyright © 1989.

Nelson, Portia. "Autobiography in Five Short Chapters." From *There's a Hole in My Sidewalk*. Copyright © 1993 by Portia Nelson. Hillsboro, Oregon: Beyond Words Publishing, Inc., 1–800–284–9673.

HABIT 3

Nelson, Portia. *There's a Hole in My Sidewalk*. Copyright © 1993 by Portia Nelson. Hillsboro, Oregon: Beyond Words Publishing, Inc., 1-800-284-9673.

HABIT 4

Lusseyran, Jacques. *And There Was Light*. Edinburgh: Parabola Books, 1985. Reprinted with permission.

HABIT 6

Armstrong, Thomas. *7 Kinds of Smart*. New York: Plume, 1993.

Rodgers, Richard, and Oscar Hammerstein II. "You've Got to Be Carefully Taught." Copyright © 1949 by Richard Rodgers and Oscar Hammerstein II. Copyright Renewed. WILLIAMSON MUSIC owner of publication and allied rights throughout the world. International Copyright Secured. Reprinted by Permission. All Rights Reserved.

Sanders, Bill. *Goalposts: Devotions for Girls.* Grand Rapids, Mich.: Fleming Revel, a division of Baker Book House, 1995.

HABIT 7

Litchfield, Allen, contributor. From the Especially for Youth recording *Sharing the Light in the Wilderness.* Salt Lake City: Deseret Book, 1993.

Anderson, Walter. *Read with Me.* Boston: Houghton Mifflin Co., 1990.

INDEX

FRANKLINCOVEY OFFICES WORLDWIDE

FranklinCovey Angola
Integrated Solutions Angola,
SA
Rua Joaquim Rodrigues da
Graça # 151
Bairro Azul. Luanda -
Angola, C.P. 6185,
ANGOLA
Tel: +244 227 210 108 / +244
227 210 109 (Office Phone)
msuega@franklincovey.co.ao

FranklinCovey Argentina
LFCA S.A.
Cerrito 774, Piso 11
Ciudad de Buenos Aires, CP
Argentina C1010AAP
Tel: +54 11 4372 5820
Fax: +54 11 4372 5648
info@franklincovey.com.ar
www.franklincovey.com.ar

FranklinCovey Pty Ltd
Australia
Level 1, 139 Coronation Drive
Milton, QLD 4064
Australia
Tel: +61 (7) 3318 9700
info@franklincovey.com.au

FranklinCovey Austria
Leadership Institut GmbH
Kaasgrabengasse 52/1/10
A-1190 Wien
Tel: +43 1 320 16 22
Fax: +43 1 320 16 23
info@franklincovey.at
www.franklincovey.at

FranklinCovey Belgium
Airport Plaza
Da Vincilaan 19
1831 Diegem/Brussels
Belgium
Tel: +32 2 719 02 15
jolanda@franklincovey.be

FranklinCovey Botswana
Event Ventures (Pty) Ltd
Private Bag 262
Gaborone
Botswana
Tel: +267 318 4706
adam@eventventures.co.bw

FranklinCovey Bermuda
Effective Leadership
Bermuda
4 Dunscombe Rd.
Warwick, Wk08 Bermuda
Tel: +441 236 0383
Fax: +441 236 0383
franklincoveybda@logic.bm

FranklinCovey Brasil
Rua Florida 1568
Brooklin - São Paulo – SP
CEP 04565-001
Brazil
Tel: +55 11 5105 4400
Fax: +55 11 5506 6965
info@franklincovey.com.br
www.franklincovey.com.br

FranklinCovey Central
Eastern Europe
FC PL Sp z o o
Ul. Wlodarzewska 33
02-384 Warszawa
Poland
Tel: +48 22 824 11 28
Fax: +48 22 824 11 29
office@franklincovey.pl
www.franklincovey.pl

FranklinCovey Colombia
FranklinCovey Organization
Services (Colombia & Peru)
Av. Carrera 45 (autopista
norte costado oriental)
103–34 oficina 202
Edificio Logic 2
Bogotá
Colombia
Tel: +57 1 610 2657
amesa@franklincovey.com.co

FranklinCovey Czech and
Slovacs
Ohradni 1424/2b
140 00 Praha 4
Czeska Republika
Tel: +420 261 099 341
Fax: +420 261 099 343
info@franklincovey.cz
www.franklincovey.cz

FranklinCovey Denmark
FranklinCovey Nordic
Approach
Langebrogade 5
1411 København K
Denmark
Tel: +45 7022 6612
kin@franklincovey.dk

FranklinCovey Dominican
Republic
Human C x A
Ave. Abraham Lincoln esq.
Mejía Ricart
Torre Piantini, Suite 904
Piantini, Santo Domingo,
D.N.
REPUBLICA DOMINICANA
Tel: +1 (809) 922-8677
ney.diaz@franklincoveydr.com

FranklinCovey Ecuador
Covey Leadership Center
Ecuador
Finlandia 192 y Suecia
Edif. Escandinavia
Loft Of. 5D
Ecuador
Tel: +593 02 333 120
mfcorral@franklincoveyecuador.
com

FranklinCovey Egypt
Leadership Training Center
Villa 7, 1st Touristic District
P.O. Box 27
Mena Garden City
Postal Code 12582
City of 6 October
Egypt
Tel: +20 2 38 37 17 21/23/29
eman.yassin@
franklincoveyegypt.com

FranklinCovey Germany
Leadership Institut GmbH
Bavariafilmplatz 3
D-82031 Grünwald bei
München
Tel: +49 89 45 21 48 0
Fax: +49 89 45 21 48 48
info@franklincovey.de
www.franklincovey.de

FranklinCovey Gibraltar
24/10 Crutchetts Ramp
Gibraltar
Tel: +350 58008143
info@pro-tivity.com

FranklinCovey Middle East
Qiyada Consultants
PO Box 53703
Dubai, UAE
Tel: +971 4 33 222 44
Fax: +971 4 33 222 82
info@franklincoveyme.com
www.franklincoveyme.com

FranklinCovey Hellas
DMS / FranklinCovey Hellas
Group
SA 36
P.S. Stathmou Str.
546 27 Thessaloniki
Greece
Tel: +30 (231) 02 73 979
antoniadis@franklincovey.gr

FranklinCovey Hong Kong
Right Management
Suite 1401
Dorset House
Taikoo Place
979 King's Road
Quarry Bay
Hong Kong
Tel: +852 2290 0168
vicky.hui@right.com

FranklinCovey Hungary
FCCoL Hungary
Management Consulting and
Training Ltd.
1124 Budapest
Némctvölgyi út 64
Hungary
Tel: +36 1 202 0448
brigitta.bessenyei@
franklincovey.hu

FranklinCovey India &
South Asia
JIL Tower A
Institutional Area
Ground Floor
Plot No. 78
Sector 18
Gurgaon 122 001
India
Tel: +91 124 4782222
lavleen@franklincovey.co.in

FranklinCovey Indonesia
P.T. Dunamis Intermaster
Jl. Bendungan Jatiluhur 56
Pusat, Jakarta 12440
Indonesia
Tel: +62 21 572 0761
Fax: +62 21 572 0762
info@dunamis.co.id
www.dunamis.co.id

FranklinCovey Israel
Momentum Training Ltd
9 Rehov Haomanut
Poleg Park
Natanya
Building A1 Entrance
East Iris, Second Floor
Israel
Tel: +97 (2) 986 56226
roni@momentum.org.il

FranklinCovey Italy
Centro Direzionale
Milanofiori
Strada 1 Palazzo F3
20090 Assago
Milano
Italy
Tel. +39 02 80 6721
chiara.barbieri@cegos.it

FranklinCovey Japan
Seito-kaikan, 7F, 5-7, Sanban-
cho
Tokyo, Chiyoda-ku 102-0075
Japan
Tel: +81 3 3237 7711
training@franklincovey.co.jp

FranklinCovey Kenya
Raiser Resource Group
Ground Floor
Jumuia Place
Lenana Rd.
Nairobi
Kenya
Tel: +254 (0) 20 271 2164/5/7
ian.ngethe@raiser.co.ke

FranklinCovey Lebanon
Starmanship & Associates
Badaro Street, Beirut,
Lebanon
Tel: +961 1 393494
Fax: +961 1 486451
starman@cyberia.net.lb
www.starmanship.com

FranklinCovey Luxembourg
13 rue de Folschette
L-8613 Pratz
Luxembourg
Tel: +352 (266) 244 60
sebastian.eberwein@
franklincovey.lu

**FranklinCovey Malaysia &
Brunei**
Leadership Resources
(Malaysia) Sdn. Bhd.
D4-1-8
Solaris Dutamas 1
Jalan Dutamas 1 50480
Kuala Lumpur
Malaysia
Tel: +6 03 62055550
sitham@leadershipresources.my

FranklinCovey Malta
Achieve Business Consulting
and Training
Know Now Ltd
44/7, Dingli Circus,
Sliema
SLM1912
Malta
Tel: +356 3550 0345
j.naudi@franklincovey.com.mt

**FranklinCovey Maroc
(Morocco, Libya & Tunisia)**
Zenith Millenium I
Etage 5, Bureau 511 –
Lotissement Attaoufik
Sidi Maarouf
20190
Casablanca
Morocco
Tel: +212 5 22 789 833/832
*meriem@franklincoveymaroc.
com*

FranklinCovey Mauritius
Seven H Ltd
105 Avenue Roches Brunes
Beau Bassin
Mauritius
Tel: +(230) 454-8743
cyrilckl@intnet.mu

**FranklinCovey Mexico/CAC/
Chile**
Leadership Technologies, Inc.
Edificio Alfaro – 1er piso
Bella Vista
Avenida Federico Boyd
Ciudad de Panama,
Panama
Tel: +507 264 8899
jmiralles@franklincoveyla.com

FranklinCovey Mozambique
FranklinCovey Brasil, Ltda
Rua Flórida 1568 - Brooklin
São Paulo - SP
Brazil 04565-001
Tel: +267 318 4706
jarrais@franklincovey.com.br

FranklinCovey Namibia
Chase & Associates CC
Unit no. 4 no. 6 Luther Street
Windhoek
Namibia
Tel: +264 61 255 492
afras@chase.com.na

FranklinCovey Netherlands
F&UB. V.
Daam Fockemalaan 10
3818 KG Amersfoort
The Netherlands
Tel: +31 (33) 45 30 627
j.kuipers@franklincovey.nl

FranklinCovey Nigeria
ReStraL Ltd
12th Floor, St. Nicholas
House
Catholic Mission Street
Lagos
Nigeria
Tel: +234 1 264 5885
Fax: +234 1 2635090
enquiries@restral.com
www.franklincoveynig.com

FranklinCovey Philippines
Center for Leadership &
Change, Inc.
4/F Ateneo Professional
Schools
130 HV Dela Costa St.
Salcedo Village, Makati City
Philippines
Tel: +632 817 2726
*elaine.rodriquez@
franklincoveyphilippines.com
www.franklincovey.ph*

FranklinCovey Portugal
Avenida 25 de Abril
Edificio Grei No 184
Piso 1
2750-511 Cascais
Portugal
Tel: +351 214 820 258
*maria.pantaleao@franklincovey.
com.pt*

FranklinCovey Puerto Rico
Urb. Eleanor Roosevelt
501 Calle Alfredo Carbonell
Hato Rey, PR 00918
Puerto Rico
Tel: +787 977 4065
iarroyo@franklincoveypr.com

**FranklinCovey Reunion
Island**
J2L
ZAC Les Celestins
12 Rue des Cypris
97 434 La Saline Les Bains
Reunion Island
Tel: + 262 (0) 692 320162
julien.lescs@j2l.re

FranklinCovey Russia
Management Training
International Ltd (MTI)
5 Kosmonavta Volkova Street
Building 1
125229
Moscow
Russia
Tel: +7495 9981 0272
a.oleynik@franklincovey.ru

**FranklinCovey Singapore &
China**
Right Management Singapore
Pte Ltd
10 Hoe Chiang Road
#21–06 Keppel Towers
Singapore 089315
Tel: +65 6532 4100
zulinah.mooksan@right.com

FranklinCovey South Africa
5 Bauhinia Street
Unit 32 Cambridge Office
Park
Highveld Techno Park
Centurion 0157
South Africa
Tel: +27 12 940 0658
marlinie@franklincoveysa.co.za

FranklinCovey South Korea
Korea Leadership Center
312–4 Gijwa-ri
Bogae-Myun
Anseong City 456-871
South Korea
Tel: +82 (2) 2106 4000
shkim@eklc.co.kr

FranklinCovey Spain
TEA-CEGOS FranklinCovey
C/ Fray Bernardino de
Sahagún, 24, 28036 Madrid
Spain
Tel: +34-912 705 000
Fax: +34-912 705 001
franklincovey@tea-cegos.es
www.tea-cegos-franklincovey.
com

FranklinCovey Switzerland
Leadership Institut GmbH
Bogenstrasse 7
CH-9001 St. Gallen
Switzerland
Tel: +41 71 277 19 33
Fax: +41 71 277 19 64
info@franklincovey.ch
www.franklincovey.ch

FranklinCovey Tanzania
NFT CONSULT
(TANZANIA) LTD
Plot 304 Ring Street
Mikocheni Area
P.O.Box 13395
Dar-es Salam
Tanzania
Tel: +255 22(2)773 237 588
badru.ntege@nftconsult.com

FranklinCovey Thailand
PacRim Leadership Center
Co. Ltd
59/387-389 Moo 4
Ramkhamhaeng Road
Sapansoong, Bangkok 10240
Thailand
Tel: +662 728 0200
Fax: +62 728 0210
plc@pacrimgroup.com
www.pacrimgroup.com

**FranklinCovey Trinidad &
Tobago**
Leadership Consulting Group
Ltd.
4–6 Chancery Lane
San Fernando
Trinidad & Tobago
Tel: +1 (868) 652 6805
curtis.manchoon@lcg.co.tt

FranklinCovey Turkey
FranklinCovey / ProVista
Management Consulting Ltd
Polcenter
Büyükdere Cad. Eczac Ali
Kaya Sk.
No.4 Kat.-2
34394 Levent
Istanbul
Turkey
Tel: +90 212 705 62 30
suresh.gunaratnam@
franklincovey.
com.tr

FranklinCovey Uganda
CEMM Group
20 Dewington Rise
(Madhvani Building)
Kampala
Uganda
Tel: +256 7124 25617
egbusonfe@cemmgroup.com

FranklinCovey UK & Ireland
Grimsbury Manor,
Grimsbury Green,
Banbury
Oxfordshire OX16 3JQ
UK
Tel: +44 (0)1295 274 100
info@franklincovey.co.uk
www.franklincovey.co.uk

FranklinCovey Zambia
Mac Recruitment Ltd
Private Bag E835
Post Net No 84
386 Independence Avenue
Lusaka, 10101
Zambia
Tel: +260-211-266247
mubanga@mac.co.zm